THE HOLISTIC MANIFESTO

Centre-Left Policies for the Twenty-First Century

E. P. ANTHONY

ISBN: 978-1-4834-5509-9 (sc)
ISBN: 978-1-4834-5508-2 (e)

Library of Congress Control Number: 2016912216

Because of the dynamic nature of the Internet, any web addresses or links contained in this book may have changed since publication and may no longer be valid. The views expressed in this work are solely those of the author and do not necessarily reflect the views of the publisher, and the publisher hereby disclaims any responsibility for them.

Any people depicted in stock imagery provided by Thinkstock are models, and such images are being used for illustrative purposes only. Certain stock imagery © Thinkstock.

Lulu Publishing Services rev. date: 12/29/2016

In memory of Dad
Who wouldn't have agreed with half of this

Acknowledgements

Lisa, mum and the kids for their patience.
Si Collier and Tita Conchy for the inspiration.
Editing and proofreading by proofreadingservices.com.
Cover by ilk agency

Contents

1. Introduction

1.01. Introduction

The last few years have been marked by the publication of several important books about the political economy, inequality, and the social breakdown of the developed countries of the West. These books have been huge in their scope, questioning the form of capitalism and the structure of society in the twenty-first century. The solutions to these problems will not be the usual technocratic tweaks to the economic consensus, which have been the norm since the general acceptance of the Reagan-Thatcher revolution of the 1980s.

Thomas Piketty's *Capital in the Twenty-first Century* offers a historical and data-driven perspective of inequality, which he argues was moderated for much of the twentieth century but is very likely to return with great force, if it has not done so already. *Plutocrats*, by Chrystia Freeland, is a study of the main beneficiaries of this new inequality, the richest 0.1 percent of society, and Michael Lewis documents the rise of the financial sector and the associated fall in ethical standards in a series of books starting with the seminal *Liar's Poker*.

In *What Money Can't Buy*, author Michael J. Handel notes that the free market has entered most aspects of modern life, intruding into places where it maybe should not and sometimes crowding out superior moral considerations. Oliver James, in *Affluenza* and *The Selfish Capitalist*, argues that the pervasive influence of money, and modern lifestyles more generally, is not good for us as individuals or a society, and in *The Spirit Level*, Wilkinson and Pickett gather the statistical evidence for this.

Meanwhile, superior analysis and discussion of these phenomena have moved from the traditional media of TV and newspapers into the blogosphere, especially in the economic field. Paul Krugman, Brad DeLong, and Simon Wren-Lewis provide excellent commentary on these and other issues. The discussion of economics, inequality, and society in most mainstream media is currently woefully shallow, trivial, or downright false.

Usually we would expect the political beneficiaries of discontent about inequality and living standards to be the parties of the centre left. However, in many Western democracies the centre left has been in long-term decline in terms of membership and share of the vote.[1] This process actually accelerated after the financial crisis of 2007–08, a bizarre response by the voting public to the taxpayers' bailout of the financial sector, which was the biggest transfer of wealth from poor to rich in recent history. Thomas Frank's *What's the Matter with Kansas* and *Pity the Billionaire* offer some of the reasons for this apparent dichotomy from a US perspective.

If we are to create policies to reduce inequality or to mitigate its effects, and to carry popular support while doing so, we must understand these phenomena, and we must understand how we arrived at this point in the first place. In

---

[1] Ian Holland and Sarah Miskin, Interpreting Election Results in Western Democracies, Politics and Public Administration Group, Parliament of Australia, 27 August 2002.

section 2, Causes of Inequality, we examine the forces which have widened inequality.

In section 3 we ask, 'Why is Inequality a Problem?' This may to many seem self-evident, but weighing up the various arguments lets us formulate responses that target the more destructive consequences of inequality. We can also examine how inequality is tackled in different developed countries, how it was addressed historically, and with what level of success. We do this in section 4, 'Existing Solutions for Inequality'.

Nothing up to this point is particularly new to students of the field. The purpose of the early sections is to make accessible the important bodies of work that have emerged recently. To do this we summarise the arguments with the minimum possible economics, philosophy, and statistics. We try to cover most of the economics and statistics in the next few chapters.

In section 5, 'The Holistic Manifesto', we study policy solutions to inequality. This is where we hope to add value. We draw on the findings of the previous sections and on the experiences of the major developed economies. The focus is the United Kingdom and the other Anglo-Saxon economies, but we also examine the major developed economies of East Asia and continental Europe. Using this background, we can construct consistent, efficient, and realistic policy solutions that will stand the test of time and we hope can carry popular support.

This should be a contrast to the current policy solutions offered by parties of the centre left, which seem to be a mix of retro-populist policies or centre-right solutions with a dash of social conscience. There appears to be no consistent economic or philosophical framework through which these issues are viewed, and so it should be of no surprise if many voters turn to parties of the far right that offer simplistic excuses for their plight or to the radical but backwards-looking philosophy of the extreme left. Or, most depressingly, don't bother to engage in politics or society at all.[2]

---

[2] Thomas G. Clark, The decline in political participation and the rise of the non-traditional parties, Another Angry Voice, September 27, 2014. http://anotherangryvoice.blogspot.sg/2014/09/decline-political-participation.html

1.02. Terms and Phrases

The following words and phrases are used frequently in this book. They can have different interpretations, so we need to clarify the way they are used.

Capital

We use this word in the broadest sense to mean assets, both physical and financial, that can be used to generate income. Property, land, bonds and shares, bank deposits, and cash are included, but 'human' capital is not.

Labour

This, again, is a broad term that represents workers who exchange their services for a wage or salary. There is a grey area here where self-employed people are concerned. In the modern economy, many of these are lone-traders who sell their services to companies for fees and, in this sense, are effectively labour providers.

Equity

We will use this in the narrow sense of stocks or shares in companies.

Utility

This is a term describing the benefit or use a consumer gets from a good or service.

Rentiers

This is an economic term for people or companies that engage in rent-seeking behaviour. Rent seeking, in this sense, is the taking of value from others without making any contribution to productivity, and often actually reducing productivity. Put simply, it is grabbing a bigger share of the pie without making the pie any bigger. Bribe-taking officials awarding big contracts to favoured companies are a good example—the official gets money he or she has done nothing to earn, and if the contract goes to the less efficient firm, the economy is worse off.

Median and Mean

These are both forms of averages. In a sample, the median is the middle number if you line up all the numbers from smallest to largest. The mean is what most people call the average, the sum of the entire sample divided by the number of items in the sample. These are crucial terms in the inequality debate, as can be shown with a simple example. Imagine the following are annual incomes, in thousands, in two economies of nine people.

Economy 1: 30 40 40 50 **50** 50 60 60 70
Economy 2: 10 10 10 10 **10** 10 10 10 370

It should be obvious which the more unequal economy is. Economy 1 has a narrow spread of incomes, while Economy 2 has most people earning a low income and one person earning a fortune. However, the sum of these terms is the same,

450,000, so both of these economies are the same size—not just that: the means of both samples are the same at 50,000. The median, in bold type, is the only statistic that gives a sense of the disparity in incomes here. The median in Economy 1 is 50,000 but 10,000 in Economy 2. This shows that a big gap between the median and mean, such as in Economy 2, can be a good indicator of inequality and that the median can be a better guide to the economic health of the majority in an economy.

The Normal Distribution

Most standard observable human traits are known to be distributed on a normal distribution, sometimes called a bell-curve due to its shape. Heights, body fat, and IQ are typical examples. Using IQ as an example, in a typical population there are a small percentage, 2.1 percent, of geniuses and people with mental retardation with IQs above 130 and below 70, with most of the population closer to the average of 100. The population is symmetrical around the average, so half of the population have an IQ above 100 and half below.

Network Effects

A network effect occurs when a good or service becomes more valuable as more people use it. Each new user that joins creates a positive externality for the existing users. The traditional example is a telephone network. More recently social networks exhibit this effect, where the more people that join a network, the more others want to join.

The number of unique connections in a network of a number of users n can be expressed mathematically as $n(n-1)/2$. As the number of users increases, the number of connections increases exponentially. Industries with large network effects, for example, transportation, communications, and some software applications, can be predisposed to monopoly, as it is inefficient from the user's perspective to have several small networks.

VAT and GST

VAT (value-added tax) and GST (goods and services tax) are used interchangeably even though there are technical differences between the two taxes.

1.03. Economics 101

The following economists and economic theories appear frequently in this book. Here is a brief background on them.

1.03.1. Adam Smith and Classical Economics

> **'He is in this, as in many other cases, led by an invisible hand to promote an end which was no part of his intention. Nor is it always the worse for the society that it was not part of it. By pursuing his own interest he frequently promotes that of the society more effectually than when he really intends to promote it'.**
> —Adam Smith, *The Wealth of Nations*

Adam Smith is an eighteenth-century Scottish economist, much beloved of right wing think tanks. He is famous for his description of how the 'invisible hand' of the market leads economic agents, acting in their own self-interest, to outcomes that are both fair and efficient. This idea would later be formalised in the theory of perfect competition and Pareto optimality. Classical economics assumes all prices in an economy (goods, wages, interest rates, etc.) are flexible.

Although Adam Smith is often cited as the patron saint of laissez-faire (letting things be) economics, he did support a role for government, funded by taxation, in providing infrastructure, regulating finance, and breaking up private companies with excessive market power. He also advocated taxing economic rents. These views would lead to his exclusion from many parties of the right today.

1.03.2. Alfred Marshall and Neoclassical Economics

Neoclassical economics can be seen as the beginning of the transformation of economics into a science, with the introduction of rational consumers, firms that try to maximise utility and profits, equilibrium supply and demand curves, and the introduction of mathematics.

Alfred Marshall was Keynes' tutor at Cambridge. One of his main contributions is the development of the standard supply and demand graph, with output on the x-axis and price on the y-axis. The supply curve slopes from bottom left to upper right, signifying that at higher prices more of a good will be supplied. The demand curve slopes from bottom right to upper left, showing that at higher prices less of a good will be demanded. Where the curves intersect we have the equilibrium output and price where the market 'clears'.

1.03.3. J. M. Keynes and Keynesian Economics

'The outstanding faults of the economic society in which we live are its failure to provide for full employment and its arbitrary and inequitable distribution of wealth and incomes'.

—J. M. Keynes[3]

---

[3] John Maynard Keynes, The General Theory of Employment, Interest, and Money (publication place: CreateSpace Independent Publishing Platform, 2013), ch.24.

Keynes rose to fame when he criticised the Versailles settlement after World War I in his book *The Economic Consequences of the Peace*. In it, he claims that the reparations asked of Germany would be impossible to repay and would lay the ground for future conflict in Europe.

Originally a Neoclassical economist, Keynes began to question the theory during the depression of the 1930s, believing existing theory could not explain the persistent unemployment of that decade. Although seen these days, especially in America, as an advocate of big government, Keynes was a Liberal, in the British-centrist sense, who believed capitalism needed saving from itself.

Among Keynes main insights were: [4]

Price Stickiness

Workers in recessions may resist pay cuts, and indeed some employers may be loath to cut wages due to its effect on morale. Thus, wages do not fall low or fast enough to make it profitable for firms to hire unemployed workers, leading to persistent unemployment.

Inadequate Aggregate Demand

Entrepreneurs and investors, being mentally scarred by a severe recession, are risk averse. Instead of seeking profitable investments, they put money into safe assets such as government bonds. This can be seen currently in the record low

[4] Robert Skidelsky, John Maynard Keynes, 1883–1946: Economist, Philosopher, Statesman (New York: Penguin Books, 2005).

yields of European government bonds. There is 'excess' saving, and overall demand in the economy for real goods and services is too low to reduce the unemployment of labour and equipment.

Multiple Equilibria as a Justification for Government Action

Keynes believed that where there is insufficient demand, an economy could find itself at equilibrium at a suboptimal level. The government, by boosting monetary and fiscal policy, can increase demand to a superior full-employment equilibrium.

The Liquidity Trap

In severe recessions, the interest rate cannot fall far enough to clear the market, as it is difficult to push the interest rate below zero. This is known as the liquidity trap, and once this point has been reached, the onus is 100 percent on fiscal policy to restore full employment. We examine this in further detail when we look at the financial crisis of 2008, and the policy of austerity that followed soon after, in chapter 2.13.

1.03.4. Milton Friedman and Monetarist Economics

In 1947, Professor Friedrich Hayek convened a meeting of economists and philosophers in the Swiss resort of Mont Pèlerin. The purpose of the meeting was to form a society to counter the collectivist policies that were popular following World War II and to promote personal freedom and liberty as well as free market economics. Geoffrey Howe, Margaret Thatcher's first finance minister, was later a member.[5]

The American economist Milton Friedman was president of the society from 1970 to 1972. He argued that Keynesian demand management was at best ineffective and at worst destructive. Using fiscal policy to boost demand would, in the long term, lead to inflation and higher interest rates, which would offset the fiscal stimulus.[6] In a glance back to classical economics, monetarists believed markets left to their own devices would clear efficiently and that the depression of the 1930s was caused by overly tight monetary policy from the US Federal Reserve. The role of economic policy should be to keep the supply of money steady and to make the economy more efficient through supply-side policies. The theory is based on the quantity theory of money equation developed by Irving Fisher:

$$MV=PQ,$$

where

$P =$ price level,
$Q =$ output in the economy,
$M =$ stock of money in the economy, and
$V =$ velocity of money (how many times money flows through the system in a period).

---

[5] Wikipedia, https://en.wikipedia.org/wiki/Mont_Pelerin_Society#Participants, modified on 9 March 2016

[6] Jeff Madrick, Age of Greed: The Triumph of Finance and the Decline of America, 1970 to the Present, ch.2., (New York: Knopf Doubleday Publishing Group, 2011).

The equation itself is not controversial, as it simply states that the nominal level of output, **PQ**, is equal to the amount of money, **MV**, needed to pay for it. What is controversial is that monetarists rearrange the formula as

P=MV/Q

They then claim that **V** is stable in the long term, yielding the result that prices, **P**, are positively correlated to the amount of money, **M**. Therefore, the government should stabilise the money supply **M**, in order to stabilise prices **P**, and thus inflation. In practice, the velocity of money, **V**, has proven to be anything but stable. We examine the implementation, implications, and success of monetarism in chapter 2.11.

1.03.5. Rational Expectations Theory and the Efficient Markets Hypothesis

Rational expectations economics and the efficient markets hypothesis are classical economics on steroids. All agents in the economy are assumed to act rationally now and in forming expectations for the future.

In macroeconomics, rational expectations models imply that most government action is ineffective, as consumers, in response to increased government spending, will increase their savings to offset future expected taxes. Similarly, monetary policy will be offset by expectations of future inflation and interest rates. The theory, in its purest form, should be discredited mostly through its inability to explain economic booms and slumps. However, the Chicago school of economists still push the theory in the face of much counter evidence, and weaker forms of rational expectations are now incorporated in other economic theories.

The theory had its biggest influence on, and did the most damage in, finance. If rational expectations are applied to the trading of financial assets, the prices of those assets should reflect all available information. The prices of financial assets should exhibit a 'random walk', and no one should be able to systematically beat the market. This is the efficient markets hypothesis (EMH). We look at the effect of this theory on the 2008 market crash in chapter 2.12.

1.03.6. Hyman Minsky and Heterodox Economics

> **'It is necessary to have an economic theory which makes great depressions one of the possible states in which our type of capitalist economy can find itself'.**
>
> —Hyman Minsky

Heterodox economics literally means nonmainstream economics. In that sense, Keynes was a heterodox economist, with his views on sticky prices and multiple equilibria. US economist Hyman Minsky was influenced by Keynes and by Irving Fisher, though he drew very different lessons from his work than the monetarists did. Minsky emphasised the importance of credit and debt in modern economies and stressed how financial markets were inherently unstable, being driven by cycles of overconfidence and despair, which led to booms and depressions in the real economy. He advocated strong regulation of the financial sector, noting how frequent economic crises had been prior to the banking reforms of the 1930s.

Of the few economists to have warned about the 2008 financial crisis, many were heterodox economists and followers of Minsky. One of them, Steve Keen, points out that much of the mathematics at the heart of neoclassical economics, the theory of perfect competition, and the EMH is badly flawed.[7] He believes that economies, being complex, time-dependent systems, require nonlinear solutions, as found in the physical sciences, something mathematician Benoit Mandelbrot also explored in his book *The Misbehaviour of Markets*.[8]

---

[7] Steve Keen, Debunking Economics: The Naked Emperor Dethroned? (London: Zed Book, 2011).
[8] Benoit Mandelbrot and Richard L. Hudson, The Misbehaviour of Markets: A Fractal View of Financial Turbulence (New York: Basic Books, 2007).

2. Causes of Inequality

2.01. Why Did Inequality Begin to Increase Rapidly from 1980?

> 'And, you know, there is no such thing as society. There are individual men and women, and there are families'.
>
> —Margaret Thatcher

A major factor contributing to increased inequality over the last thirty years was the Reagan-Thatcher revolution, which started in the Anglo-Saxon economies in the 1980s before spilling over to much of the rest of the developed world. Many separate policies, taken in isolation, would have increased inequality, but together these formed part of a coherent philosophical whole that transformed the political and social landscape.

The philosophy emphasised the primacy of the individual and individual responsibility above society as a whole and placed the goal of economic efficiency above equitable outcomes. It saw collective action as a restriction on the freedom of the individual. Heavily influenced by Milton Friedman and the economic theory of monetarism, it saw Keynesian deficit spending as useless, if not outright harmful. The size of the state was to be shrunk and taxes lowered, a large state sector being described by Hayek as 'the road to serfdom' in his book of the same name.

Policy changes seemed to run in parallel on both sides of the Atlantic. Capital controls and subsidies were swiftly eliminated. Lowering inflation by controlling the money supply was prioritised over full employment, leading to very high interest rates, deep recessions, and levels of unemployment unseen since the 1930s. Landmark battles against trade unions were fought and won, against the air traffic controllers in the United States and the coal miners in the United Kingdom. Top rates of tax were cut throughout the decade in the name of incentives, while welfare payments to the poor were cut for the same reason. Large utilities were privatised to improve economic efficiency, and the finance industry was deregulated.

These policies unleashed or amplified other powerful and long-term forces, increasing inequality, as shown in Figure 1. Ending capital controls and tariffs on imported goods sowed the seeds of increased globalisation. Deregulation of finance allowed corporations and rich individuals to seek superior investment returns around the globe. Trade union legislation diminished the bargaining power of workers, allowing companies to pursue shareholder value maximisation without opposition. Privatisation and deregulation created the environment for large corporations to generate huge profits, through monopoly rents or oligopolistic practices. We examine the policies and their effect on inequality in later chapters in this section. First, however, we use Piketty's *Capital in the Twenty-First Century* to look at the history of inequality, and we examine his *r>g* formula that captures statistically the forces driving inequality.

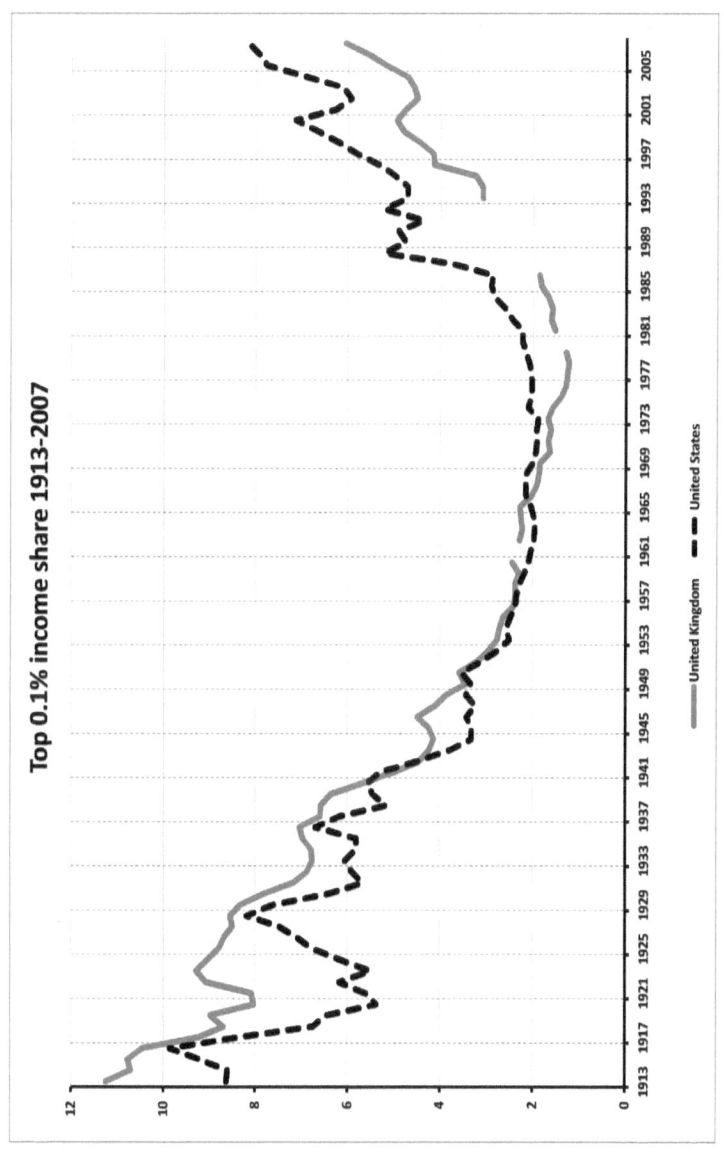

Figure 1 Top 0.1 percent income share 1913–2007

E. P. Anthony, 2016. Data: The World Wealth and Income Database.

2.02. Piketty and Pareto

2.02.1. Thomas Piketty, *Capital in the Twenty-First Century*[9]

In *Capital in the Twenty-First Century*, Thomas Piketty shows that if the return on capital in an economy, *r*, is higher than the rate of growth, *g*, inequality will increase until it approaches an equilibrium level. This is because the total income generated from investments of existing wealth will outstrip the total income generated from growth. The greater *r* is than *g*, the greater the equilibrium level of inequality will be. The formula *r>g* has become synonymous with Piketty.

He then goes on to argue that, as far back as good data is available, *r* has been higher than *g* and that a high level of inequality has been the historical norm. In his opinion, the twentieth century—with two world wars destroying vast fortunes, high levels of inflation eroding the value of capital, and heavily redistributive policies—was an anomaly that came to an end in the late 1970s. Since then we have been reverting to historical levels of inequality and *r* is again much greater than *g*.

According to Piketty, growth has been decreasing recently in developed economies due to aging populations and falling levels of productivity. Growth in the long term is simply a function of the number of workers and their productivity. Increased inequality itself may also slow the rate of growth of an economy, creating a negative feedback loop.

---

[9] Thomas Piketty, Capital in the Twenty-First Century, trans. Arthur Goldhammer (Cambridge, Mass.: The Belknap Press of Harvard University Press, 2014).

Return on capital, *r*, is high, at least for the very wealthy, due to lower taxes on capital and sophisticated wealth planning. Additionally, globalisation and the free movement of capital have given the superwealthy access to increased investment opportunities that are not available to most. The move towards share price maximisation, globalisation, and the rise of the corporation as a political force over the last thirty years also help to explain this phenomenon. We examine all these forces over the next few chapters.

2.02.2. Vilfredo Pareto

Vilfredo Pareto was a nineteenth-century Italian economist. He observed that in Italy, at that time, 80 percent of land was owned by the top 20 percent of the population. Then, considering this top part of the population, 80 percent of the land in this sample was owned by the top 20 percent of the top 20 percent, and so on. He observed this 80–20 rule in various measures of wealth and income in different countries. This became known as the Pareto principle. This is not to say the same 20 percent of families own 80 percent of wealth forever. There is movement in and out of the wealth tranches, as occasionally poorer citizens make good, while richer ones fall on hard times, but the 80–20 rule remains for the population as a whole.

Economic theory suggests that *r* will decline as wealth increases due to fewer good investment opportunities, and therefore any rise in inequality will be self-limiting. We can, and do, argue that the very wealthy often find superior opportunities for investment given their global reach and powerful connections. Additionally, are we as a society comfortable with the level of inequality we reach before r starts to decline?

Pareto's observations support Piketty's view that there are strong forces generating a high level of inequality. Nevertheless, Piketty and Pareto take very different lessons from this analysis. Piketty sees this distribution of outcomes as unjust and inefficient: we should attempt to raise g relative to r to create a different outcome from 80-20, such as we had during the mid to late twentieth century. Pareto, however, having seen this result across many different countries and industries, believed these outcomes were 'in the nature of man'. The 20 percent deserved their good fortune in his analysis, and the poor theirs, and the fight of the poorer 80 percent to enter the elite is what drove progress. Therefore, he believed, these outcomes were fair and efficient and the result of economic 'survival of the fittest'. Writing in the early twentieth century, Pareto's analysis, which seems to suggest genetic reasons for inequality, was seized upon by the extreme right to justify their social and economic policies, as some individuals and races could be seen as superior or inferior to others

We analyse the economic efficiency argument and the fairness or otherwise of the 80–20 outcome later. Yet it should be intuitively clear that policies that attempt to raise growth g, and to raise g relative to r, are desirable in reducing inequality. Even if the twentieth century was an anomaly, it is an anomaly we have to try to replicate.

2.03. Perfect Competition and Supply-Side Economics

2.03.1. Perfect Competition

The theory of perfect competition is the bedrock of modern free-market economic theory, and the political right uses the results it generates to justify the current economic system and its outcomes. Thus, it is important we understand the theory and its flaws. Perfect competition is a model of how a free-market economy should operate. [10] The results of the theory rest crucially on its assumptions, which we describe below. Examples of markets that demonstrate the theory are very thin on the ground, which would suggest most markets do not run in this way. The closest example that would be familiar to most people is a fresh-food street market with many people operating small stalls.

The main assumptions are as follows:

1. There is a large number a buyers and sellers in the market, none of whom are big enough to influence the price. The participants are price takers, having to trade at the price supply and demand the market dictates.
2. There are no economies of scale. Firms that grow bigger cannot reduce their cost per unit of output.
3. There is zero friction in the economy and no barriers to entry. Firms can enter and leave the market costlessly,

---

[10] Stuart Wall, Microeconomics, Economics Express (Harlow, England: Pearson, 2013) pp. 146-155

they can substitute machinery and labour costlessly, and there are zero transactions costs.

4. Participants in the market are rational and have complete information about the market.
5. There are no hidden costs or benefits.

Given these assumptions, if firms in the market are making large profits, competitors rush into the market, driving down the price until profits are eroded. Firms that try to sell goods at too high a price will be unable to sell any; firms that sell too low will lose money and leave the market. Workers that set wages too high will not be hired.

Without going into the technicalities of perfect competition, at equilibrium we get the following results:

1. Firms make 'normal' profits. This means the owners of the firms are compensated for their time, effort, and capital at the prevailing market rate. There is no opportunity cost, in the sense that the owners could use their time more profitably somewhere else, but there are also no excess profits over this level either.
2. Workers are paid their marginal cost. Firms will hire workers until the value of the output of the last worker equals what it costs to hire the person, and the profit on the last worker is zero. In other words, workers are paid what they are 'worth', the value of their production. This is one of the key results used by the political right, as under this theory people 'get what they deserve'. The owners of capital get a fair return, CEOs

'deserve' their huge salaries, and those at the bottom 'deserve' their meagre wages.

3. The outcome for the whole market is efficient in the sense that no one in the market can be made better off without making someone else worse off. This result, originally derived by Vilfredo Pareto, is known as Pareto efficiency. This result is also attractive to the political right, as resources are seen to be allocated and used most efficiently.

We can see why this theory is vital to proponents of free-market economics, as it is the only theory of capitalism that says resources in the economy are used most efficiently, no one can be made better off without making someone worse off, and everyone in the economy gets paid their economic worth. Note, however, that even if the theory holds, it says nothing about how equal or otherwise the outcomes are.

If the assumptions that are required for perfect competition are violated, we have an imperfect market, and the results deviate from those described above. Generally, the more the assumptions are violated, the more the results are not efficient or fair. In addition, if we see sectors of the economy with large firms making consistently large profits, this is an obvious sign that the market is not perfect. We look at these cases over the next few chapters, but first we examine how perfect competition helps to support the argument for trickle-down economics.

2.03.2. The Laffer Curve and Supply-Side Economics

'Voodoo economics'
—George H. W. Bush on trickle-down economics

Supply-side economics is a branch of classical economics that claims the best way to raise productivity and growth is to remove obstacles to investment and production. It has become synonymous with trickle-down economics. In the theory of perfect competition, any taxes, other than lump-sum taxes, result in an inefficient outcome. This result gives cover to those who wish to lower taxes on investors and business owners, as the more progressive a tax is, the more distortionary it is claimed to be. The theory, even if correct, says nothing about distribution, so it is a stretch to go from this result to claim that the benefits of the more efficient outcome necessarily 'trickle down' to the poorer members of society.

The economist Art Laffer, who was a member of Ronald Reagan's economic team, provided additional impetus to lower marginal tax rates. At a lunch in Washington, D.C., in 1974, Dick Cheney and Donald Rumsfeld joined Laffer (maybe you should judge a man by the company he keeps).[11] Laffer pointed out that tax revenue would be zero with taxes rates at 0 percent, obviously, and with taxes at 100 percent, because no one would bother to work. There must be a curve

---

[11] Haley Geffen, 'The Napkin Doodle That Launched the Supply-Side Revolution', Bloomberg Businessweek, December 4, 2014, http://www.bloomberg.com/news/articles/2014-12-04/laffer-curve-napkin-doodle-launched-supply-side-economics

of positive tax revenue between these points. Therefore, at some level of high tax rates, a government could cut tax rates and raise revenue, as people would work harder, invest more, and not engage in tax avoidance.

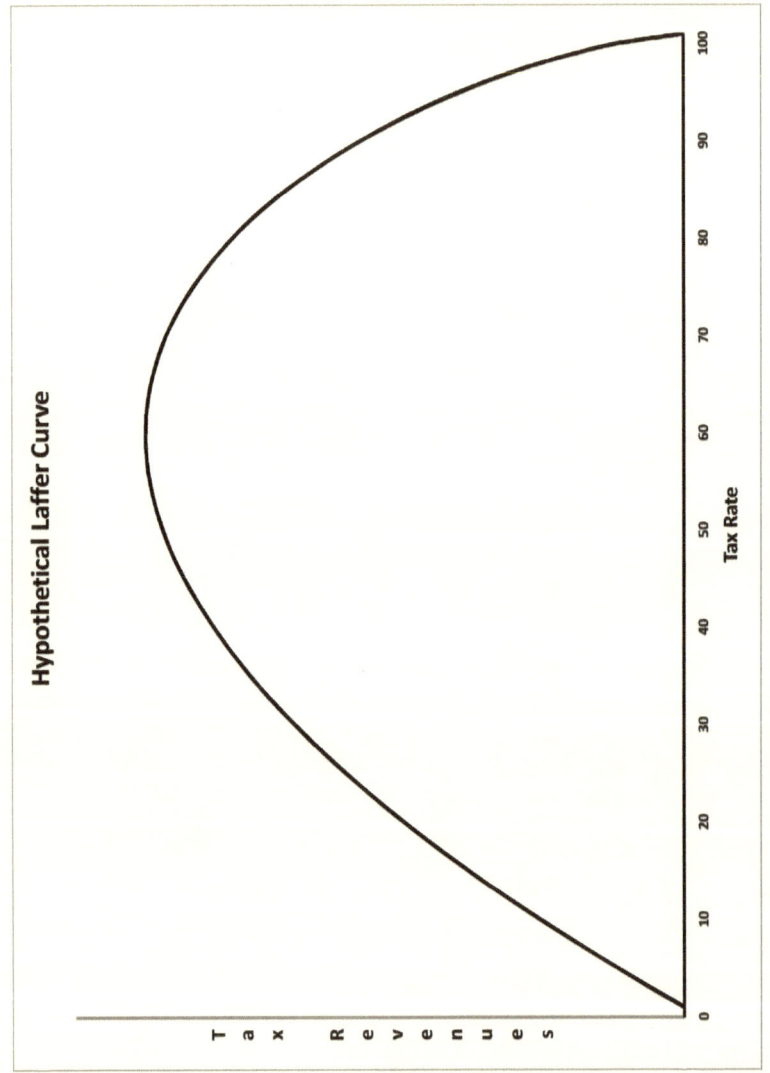

Figure 2 Hypothetical Laffer Curve
E. P. Anthony, 2016.

Note that the Laffer curve says nothing about where tax revenues are maximised, just that it is between 0 percent and 100 percent. Empirical studies of the 1980s estimated that tax revenues are maximised with marginal rates between 50 percent and 80 percent.[12] More recent studies, which attempt to allow for increased mobility of labour and capital, more aggressive tax planning, and long-term incentive effects—in other words the worst-case scenario—suggest that tax revenues are maximised with rates around 50 percent.[13] The recent French experiment with a 75 percent top marginal income tax rate was fairly unpopular and largely unsuccessful in raising revenue.[14]

So while the evidence suggests that cutting tax rates from the 70 percent to 90 percent levels that existed in the 1950s in many developed economies may have resulted in increased tax revenues, it does not support cuts below 40 percent. This is easy to demonstrate intuitively. A cut of average tax rates from 40 percent to 30 percent is a 25 percent cut in proportional terms. Taxable revenues, at the 30 percent rate of tax, would have to rise by 25 percent just to raise the same tax revenues as at the 40 percent rate of tax, a result which is implausible even in the long term (although this simple analysis

---

[12] Mathias Trabandt and Harald Uhlig, 'The Laffer Curve Revisited', Journal of Monetary Economics 58, no. 4 (May 2011): 305–27.

[13] Neil O'Brien, 'So what should the top rate of tax be? It all turns on the longterm effects of high taxes', The Telegraph, March 23rd, 2012, http://blogs.telegraph. co.uk/news/neilobrien1/100146421/so-what-should-the-top-rate-of-tax-be-it-all-turns-on-the-long-term-effects-of-high-taxes/

[14] Anne Penketh, 'France Forced to Drop 75 Percent Supertax after Meagre Returns', The Guardian, 31 December 2014, http://www.theguardian.com/world/2014/dec/31/france-drops-75percent-supertax.

is less clear in complex tax systems with many different marginal tax bands).

However, the synthesis of these two theories, perfect competition and Laffer curves, drove marginal tax rates on income and capital in the 1980s to 40 percent or below in many developed countries. This meant that, on average, revenues from these taxes fell, and this revenue gap had to be recovered from somewhere else. This was mostly achieved through broadening the base of these taxes (taxing more items than previously), increasing more regressive sales taxes, or by cutting government expenditure. Meanwhile, implicit marginal tax rates on the poorest can now be as high as 80 percent because of how welfare benefits are withdrawn as they earn more.[15] Clearly, this redistribution of tax and spending has been one of the main drivers of increased inequality.

When the conditions for perfect competition are not met, we are said to have market failure. This is a technical term, as most markets are not perfect but function perfectly well. In the next few chapters, we look at the more extreme cases where markets have clearly failed, especially those that can exacerbate inequality.

[15] Greg Mankiw, 'The Poverty Trap', Novemeber 11, 2009, http://gregmankiw. blogspot.sg/2009/11/poverty-trap.html

2.04. Monopolies and Privatisation

Two key assumptions of perfect competition that are frequently violated are the assumptions of no economies of scale and zero barriers to entry. In reality, many firms find that as they grow their cost per unit of output falls, so we end up with many industries where there are a few large firms dominating the market.[16] Where one or two firms dominate, we have a monopoly market. A problem in these kinds of markets is that the firms have the market power to influence prices. It can be in their interest to restrict supply and thereby raise prices to maximise profits. This scenario is clearly bad for inequality. Prices are higher than they should be, harming consumers, while the owners of the firms make excess profits. Output is lower than it should be, potentially meaning employment is lower than it could be.[17] *Forbes* ranked Carlos Slim as the world's richest man from 2010 to 2013. Slim owns half of Telmex, a Mexican telecom firm that controls 80 percent of the Mexican landline market, and in return, Mexicans pay some of the highest line-usage fees in the world.[18]

In a market of perfect competition, competitors would rush into such a market, reducing prices and profits. However, in monopoly markets there are barriers to entry that prevent this from happening. One of the barriers can be the economies of scale themselves—the established large firms have built up

[16] Keen, 'Debunking Economics', ch.5.

[17] Wall, Microeconomics., pp.155-162

[18] Dara Kerr, 'Telecom monopoly overcharging Mexicans billions', CNET, January 31, 2012, http://www.cnet.com/news/telecom-monopoly-overcharging-mexicans-billions/

insurmountable cost advantages over any new entrant. Where the economies are very large, we have what is called a natural monopoly. This is often the case where there are large costs in setting up a network. Other barriers could be in the form of patents or government regulation granting monopoly status. Indeed, patents are coming increasingly under the spotlight as a source of monopoly power, especially in the technology sector.

Responses to monopoly have evolved over time. Initially private monopolies in energy, transport, and utilities were tolerated. Nevertheless, many of these private monopolies were both abusing their pricing power and inefficient, as they operated locally and did not take advantage of economies of scale. In the United States, Teddy Roosevelt was elected on a policy platform of aggressive antitrust (monopoly) legislation. In the United Kingdom, a mix of regulation, central organisation in the form of coordinating boards for utilities, and subsidies for transport were used on a case-by-case basis.

During World War II, governments took control of many industries for the war effort. In the United States, most of these were returned to private ownership after the war, but in the United Kingdom, industries that were seen to have monopoly rents or large economies of scale remained in public ownership until the 1980s, when Mrs Thatcher's government started a wave of privatisations that were then copied widely in the developed world. There are several arguments for privatisation. It is argued that there is an 'agency' problem in that the management of nationalised industries are answerable to civil servants and politicians, not to customers and shareholders. Privatising these companies and introducing the profit motive could make them more efficient and more customer focused. Companies can then use profits to invest back into the industry. In nationalised firms, setting a lower price equal to marginal cost, while maximising public welfare means the firm operates at a loss, requiring tax revenues for investment. In tough economic times, these investments are often cut, leading to severe underinvestment and thereby poor performance by the industry. Another argument is that trade unions in nationalised industries seem to act more aggressively than in private firms, maybe because they know they can exert pressure on politicians more easily than on private shareholders.[19]

There are also strong arguments against privatisation. By selling off a profitable industry, the government and taxpayer may be giving up future revenue streams, implying taxes in the future will be higher or government spending lower. Using the proceeds of privatisation to pay debt can be seen as an accounting trick.[20] Debt is reduced now, but future cash flows are given up in return. There are strongly regressive redistributive forces in privatisations, as assets and future revenue streams, which are theoretically owned by all taxpayers, are transferred to shareholders. Even with a very public offering of shares, many are eventually sold by small investors and end up concentrated in a few hands. If the industry is sold too cheaply, or if prices are raised aggressively post-privatisation,

[19] Tim Leunig, 'The right to strike is an important one, but the public and private sectors should be treated equally', LSE, November 30th, 2011. http://blogs.lse.ac.uk/politicsandpolicy/public-private-sector-strike-equality/
[20] Simon Wren-Lewis, 'Privatisation and Government Debt', Mainly Macro, 5 June 2014, http://mainlymacro.blogspot.sg/2014/06/privatisation-and-government-debt.html.

the result is even more regressive. Additionally, once an industry is privatised, employment tends to fall, as the private firm attempts to make efficiency savings to boost profits.

Massimo Florio, in *The Great Divestiture*, examines the UK privatisations of the late twentieth century.[21] He finds that the efficiency gains of privatisation varied from industry to industry but that the redistributive outcome was strongly regressive. From an efficiency perspective, the most successful privatisations were naturally those where real competition entered the market, prices fell, and service improved, such as in telecoms, electricity, and air transport. In other industries, powerful regulators still set price caps for the industry, mimicking the effect of competition, and in water and rail transport, prices have increased steeply.

The question in these industries is, are the efficiency gains worth the increase in inequality? This should be studied on a case-by-case basis but too often is simply judged from an ideological perspective of private provision good, government bad, or vice versa.[22] Politically, the electorate seem to have a more nuanced view. Where there are clear efficiency gains they will accept the regressive outcomes, but where prices have risen, service is poor, and competition is absent, they will listen to calls for renationalisation.

---

[21] Massimo Florio, The Great Divestiture: Evaluating the Welfare Impact of the British Privatizations, 1979–1997 (Cambridge, Mass.: MIT Press, 2004).

[22] Simon Wren-Lewis. 'The State, Corporations, and Markets'. Mainly Macro, 26 May 2014, http://mainlymacro.blogspot.sg/2014/05/the-state-corporations-and-markets.html.

2.05. Oligopolies and Corporate Power

Perfect competition and monopoly are two ends of the spectrum of industrial organisation. Most industries fall between these two extremes and are analysed by the economic models of monopolistic competition and oligopoly. Of more interest to us in studying inequality is oligopoly. Oligopoly is a market structure where three to five large firms dominate an industry. Sheth and Sisodia, in *The Rule of Three*, use empirical data, economics, and game theory to argue that most industries end up being dominated by three large firms, with possibly some small niche players on the margins.[23]

If oligopoly is the natural and dominant market system, it is important to study its effect on inequality. There are many different types of oligopoly, and this a complex topic where economics and game theory overlap.[24] Jean Tirole won the 2015 Nobel Prize for his analysis of these markets and how they must be treated on a case-by-case basis. We examine the abuses of oligopoly power that give rise to the most inefficient or unequal outcomes.

An obvious way for oligopolistic firms to gain an advantage is to collude—they can set prices jointly to maximise profits. If this collusion goes unchecked, we end up with the same negative results as in a monopoly: higher prices and lower output. Other pricing policies involve setting prices for certain products below cost for a short time. In penetration pricing, firms set a low price to gain market share and drive out

---

[23] Jagdish Sheth and Rajendra Sisodia, The Rule of Three: Surviving and Thriving in Competitive Markets (New York: Free Press, 2002).
[24] Wall, Microeconomics.

competition, and later either raise prices or cut costs to make a profit. In loss-leader pricing, retailers sell some goods below cost to attract customers, making back the costs on the other products the customer buys.

At first glance, the consumer would seem to have the potential to gain from these policies of under-pricing. However, the firm in both cases is taking advantage of giving the customer incomplete information about future prices, or the prices of other goods, to make profits elsewhere. There is also the effect on smaller competitors to consider. The large firms are using their size to sell at a loss, which smaller firms cannot afford to do. This either acts as a barrier to entry or drives the smaller firms out of business. Consider the effect a large supermarket loss leading on bread has on the local bakery. These forms of pricing, along with the use of loyalty discounts and other special deals, have led some to claim that supermarkets are running a 'confusopoly' of opaque pricing.[25]

'Half of the turnover of an independent local retailer goes back into the local community, while just 5 percent of the turnover of a supermarket does'.

—Local Works, 'Save Our Communities form Large Supermarkets'[26]

---

[25] Rebecca Smithers, 'UK Supermarkets Dupe Shoppers out of Hundreds of Millions, says Which?' *The Guardian*, 21 April 2015, http://www.theguardian.com/business/2015/apr/21/uk-supermarkets-dupe-shoppers-out-of-hundreds-of-millions-says-which.

[26] Local Works, 'Save Our Communities from Large Supermarkets', Local Works, n.d., http://localworks.org/pages/supermarkets.

Many large firms use advertising, branding, and pricing to take advantage of consumers' imperfect information and irrationality. One of the assumptions of perfect competition is that firms, workers, and consumers are rational. Nobel Prize winner Daniel Kahneman, in *Thinking, Fast and Slow*, provides evidence of psychological biases that cause people to make economically irrational choices.[27] This affects many fields of consumer choice that we come across in this book. Large firms have become very sophisticated in playing on these biases, through pricing and advertising, and later we examine the negative effects of this interaction of inequality and advertising.

Large corporations are the biggest gainers from globalisation. They can move production and even profits abroad to take advantage of friendlier regimes and can take advantage of the huge economies of scale in having a global labour market to choose from and a global market for their goods. We look at this in more detail in chapter 2.07 on globalisation. The modern oligopolies are very powerful institutions politically due to their influence on employment, taxation, and consumer choice in countries where they operate. They have come to wield this power more overtly since the 1980s.[28] The most obvious way is in direct contributions to political parties, or candidates, where they are clearly trying to buy influence. The Citizens United ruling in the United States, allowing unlimited contributions from companies and individuals, has opened the floodgates in this respect.

More subtly, firms in an industry often combine to form

---

[27] Daniel Kahneman, Thinking, Fast and Slow (London: Penguin Books, 2012).
[28] Andrew Prokop, '40 Charts that Explain Money in Politics'. Vox. 30 July 2014. http://www.vox.com/2014/7/30/5949581/money-in-politics-charts-explain.

an industry pressure group to lobby politicians for favourable policy outcomes, either directly or by quietly funding think tanks that churn out favourable policy prescriptions. Generally, these policies have favoured the owners and executives of companies at the expense of employees, consumers, and the environment. In *Merchants of Doubt*, Naomi Oreskes and Erik Conway describe how climate change denial in the media and academia is funded mostly by the large energy companies, who are using the playbook developed by the cigarette companies in the 1950s.[29] First, any negative effect is denied, then it is claimed the science is unclear, and personal attacks are launched on opposing scientists, and then it is said changes will harm consumers. Large companies also use their considerable advertising spend to lean on media organisations to bury unfavourable stories. In 2015, Peter Oborne resigned as chief political commentator of the *Daily Telegraph*, accusing the paper of burying a story on HSBC and its Swiss subsidiary's tax evasion scandal after pressure from the advertising department.[30]

Another example of the influence of large corporations is regulatory capture, where the regulator who is supposed to be monitoring an industry is influenced directly with the possibility of future employment or indirectly by constant contact with senior executives in the industry (which is known as cognitive capture.). Tax loopholes are created or left in place, existing

[29] Naomi Oreskes and Erik M. Conway, Merchants of Doubt: How a Handful of Scientists Obscured the Truth on Issues from Tobacco Smoke to Global Warming (New York: Bloomsbury Publishing, 2010).
[30] Peter Oborne, 'Why I Have Resigned from the Telegraph', Open Democracy UK, 17 February 2015, https://www.opendemocracy.net/ourkingdom/peter-oborne/why-i-have-resigned-from-telegraph.

tax law is loosely enforced, and banking regulation is watered down by pressuring or assimilating regulators.

Clearly, the modern multinational firm has come to be a large driver of inequality in the developed world by influencing policy to the benefit of its executives and shareholders, often at the expense of taxpayers, employees, and the environment. Not all large firms act in this way, but on balance, the combination of corporate power, technology, and globalisation has increased inequality in developed economies, as we see in the next few chapters.

2.06. Technological Change

The term 'Luddite' has been somewhat corrupted to mean someone who is a Neanderthal, technologically backwards. The original Luddites were actually skilled textile workers who destroyed the automated looms that were displacing them. In what is a familiar theme from the period before trade union legalisation, the authorities brutally put them down and imprisoned or executed the leaders.

It is received wisdom that technological progress benefits society and that even workers suffer only temporarily before they retrain and move up the value chain into the new industries. Keynes in his 1930 paper 'Economic Possibilities for our Grandchildren', foresaw a time when the economic gains of technological progress meant the main problem for society would be how to spend its leisure time.[31] There are three main problems with this theory.

Firstly, it can take the labour force generations to benefit from the change in technology. During the Industrial Revolution, wages were stagnant for many decades.[32] Secondly, there is no automatic economic process that means new technology benefits the majority. Technological progress may increase overall wealth, but if the gains accrue only to a few, the majority can be worse off. Economists call one type of technological change capital-biased technology, which implies the

---

[31] John Maynard Keynes, Essays in Persuasion (New York: Classic House Books, 2009).

[32] James Bessen, 'How Technology Has Affected Wages for the Last 200 Years', Harvard Business Review, April 29, 2015. https://hbr.org/2015/04/how-technology-has-affected-wages-for-the-last-200-years

benefits accrue to the owners of capital. Lastly, what if there is no value chain for the displaced workers to move up into? This has been a constant worry of economists over the years, as workers moved from agriculture to manufacturing and, recently, into the service sector. Human ingenuity and educational advancement have overcome these challenges to raise living standards for everyone. What if we have reached the limit of this process?

J. E. Meade examines the potential effects of capital-biased technology in a 1964 book, *Efficiency, Equality, and the Ownership of Property*, that still reads well today.[33] A capital-intensive industry may result in high levels of output per worker, as the new technology aids productivity, but can also lead to a low marginal product of labour, where adding an extra worker does not raise output by much. For example, in the digital distribution industries today, movies, music, and books can be delivered for almost no extra cost to the distributor. Most of the gains in these kinds of industries accrue to the owners of the firms, and Meade points out that as capital is not evenly distributed, this means the gains will accrue to a few individuals. Keynes's dream about a leisure class assumed that the gains from technological progress would be split fairly evenly. Additionally, employment in these industries need not be large. Many workers will be unable to find employment in these industries, and the wage rate at which this surplus labour can be fully employed in more labour-intensive industries could fall to very low levels. As Meade puts it in *Efficiency, Equality, and the Ownership of Property*:

---

[33] James E. Meade, Efficiency, Equality and the Ownership of Property (London: Routledge/Taylor & Francis, 2012).

There would be a limited number of exceedingly wealthy property owners; the proportion of the working population required to man the extremely profitable automated industries would be small; wage rates would thus be depressed; there would have to be a large expansion of the production of the labour-intensive goods and services which were in high demand by the few multi-multi-multi-millionaires; we would be back in a superworld of butlers, footmen, kitchen maids, and other hangers-on.

He calls this twenty-first century version of Downton Abbey a 'hideous prospect'.

There is strong debate about whether we have been witnessing capital-biased technological change for the last few decades. On the one hand, labour's share of national income has been declining, as wages have lagged productivity gains, which is what we would expect from capital-biased technology. On the other hand, overall productivity gains have been small and interest rates are low, which should not be the case in a technology boom, as entrepreneurs should be fighting to raise funds to invest in these new profitable opportunities. One explanation for this is that the new technology industries are exploiting market power and claiming economic rents.[34] This could explain investors being willing to invest huge sums into start-up tech companies with large operating losses, as

[34] Paul Krugman, 'Technology or Monopoly Power?' *The New York Times*, 9 December 2012, http://krugman.blogs.nytimes.com/2012/12/09/technology-or-monopoly-power/.

they build scale via huge network effects, which they then monetise later.

The last fifteen years have seen a divergence in the wages of educated and unskilled workers, possibly because of routine manufacturing jobs being automated by companies that require skilled technicians. Recently, however, many nonmanual routine tasks have started to be automated, such as legal document research, simple call-centre operations, and medical diagnosis. The key to automation is whether the task is routine and rule following, rather than manual, or not. This suggests that there will soon be downward wage and employment pressure on middle-class professions, such as medicine, law, and accounting.[35]

Looking further into the future, a McKinsey report highlights breakthrough technologies that will disrupt economies over the next ten years.[36] The ones they say will have the greatest effect on employment and inequality are advanced robotics and 3-D printing, which will make further inroads into manufacturing jobs, as well as automation of knowledge work and self-driving vehicles. McKinsey says consumers will be big winners from these changes, but will this offset the disruption to employment? If these advances do favour capital, Moore's Law, which states that technology advances at an exponential

[35] Erik Brynjolfsson and Andrew McAfee, Race Against the Machine: How the Digital Revolution Is Accelerating Innovation, Driving Productivity, and Irreversibly Transforming Employment and the Economy (Lexington: Digital Frontier Press, 2011).

[36] James Manyika, Michael Chui, Jacques Buguin, Richard Dobbs, Peter Bisson, and Alex Marrs, Disruptive Technologies: Advances that Will Transform Life, Business, and the Global Economy (Washington: McKinsey Global Institute, 2013).

pace, will mean that inequality has the potential to widen even more rapidly, especially when coupled with globalisation. Meade's 'hideous outcome' starts to look more likely.

Andrew Smithers, writing in the *Financial Times*, has a more optimistic outlook.[37] He notes that technological change has not seriously eroded labour's share of national income in France, Germany, and Japan, and suggests that the fall in labour income in the United Kingdom and United States can be attributed to management remuneration. This gives us some hope, as it suggests that changes to corporate governance can offset the changes from technology and have a meaningful effect on inequality.

---

[37] Andrew Smithers, 'Has Labour Lost Out to Capital?' *Financial Times*, 1 April 2015, http://blogs.ft.com/andrew-smithers/2015/04/has-labour-lost-out-to-capital/.

2.07. Globalisation

At the heart of globalisation is the free movement of capital, goods, and labour. These have far-reaching effects, some positive and some negative, on economies, employees, the environment, and inequality. The free movement of goods and capital is self-evidently good for owners of capital. They can invest in opportunities outside of their country of domicile to increase returns. Corporations can move production and offices to parts of the world with cheaper workers or with fewer workplace and environmental regulations. There is downward pressure on wages in the countries from where capital is withdrawn, while wages rise in the countries that attract investment. There is a similar race to the bottom in environmental protection—capital will generally move to countries with weaker regulation. Free movement of labour suggests that workers in poorer parts of the world will move to the richer parts with more or better paying jobs. In the short term, wages fall in the country the workers move to, but the workers that move there are better off.

On balance, it would seem that globalisation benefits capital and workers in poorer countries, while employees in developed countries and the environment are worse off. Inequality in developed countries rises, while inequality globally falls, as there are a greater number of workers in poorer countries that benefit. An empirical study by Milanovic and Lakner in 2014 backs this theory.[38] Figure 3 shows incomes for the poorest

---

[38] Cristoph Lakner and Branko Milanovic, Global Income Distribution: From the Fall of the Berlin Wall to the Great Recession (Washington: The World Bank, 2013).

70 percent globally have increased from 1988 to 2008. This is mostly the new middle class in India, China, and the rest of Asia. However, the hollow segment between 70 percent and 90 percent represents the stagnating income of less skilled workers in the developed world.

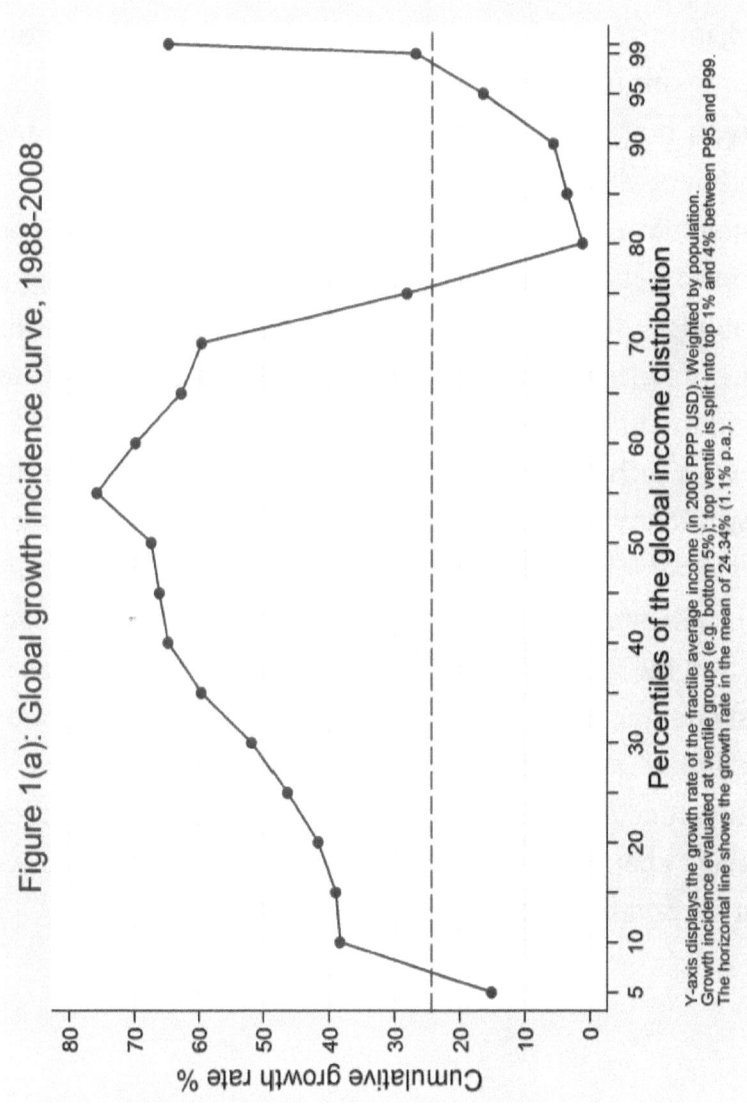

Figure 1(a): Global growth incidence curve, 1988–2008

Y-axis displays the growth rate of the fractile average income (in 2005 PPP USD). Weighted by population.
Growth incidence evaluated at ventile groups (e.g. bottom 5%); top ventile is split into top 1% and 4% between P95 and P99.
The horizontal line shows the growth rate in the mean of 24.34% (1.1% p.a.).

Figure 3 Change in global income deciles 1988–2008
Source: Milanovic and Lakner, 'Global Income Distribution'

Two other positive effects must be noted. Moving production around the world to lower cost centres lowers the prices of goods and services. As employees are also consumers, they benefit from lower prices in goods and services. Second, immigration into wealthier countries by workers from poorer regions has been shown to increase growth in the host country in the long term. Immigrants tend to be young and entrepreneurial. They add to the tax base and improve the demographics of the host country, which could be an important consideration in developed countries with rapidly aging populations.[39] Nevertheless, these longer-term and broader benefits are often not felt by the lower-skilled workers in the host country who are displaced, and we must consider this.

As with technological change, globalisation is a powerful force with complex results. It is unlikely it could be reversed easily even if we wished to do so. What we can try to do instead is mitigate the inequality generated in developed economies and the global environmental impact. As we discuss in the last chapter, globalisation and technological change need not lead to greater inequality in the developed world. That is more of a function of how multinational corporations choose to manage change and distribute the financial gains, and we look at corporate policy next.

---

[39] James Pomeroy, 'An Age-Old Question: Massive Demographic Changes Help Emerging Markets—But Will Cut Global Growth', HSBC, 30 November 2015, http://www.gbm.hsbc.com/insights/growth/an-age-old-question.

2.08. Shareholder Value Maximisation

2.08.1. Limited Liability and Joint Stock Companies

When talking about inequality, the focus is often on the role of the state in the form of government spending and taxation, and solutions tend to stem from that analysis. Corporate governance can seem a very dry and insignificant topic by comparison. People don't tend to go on protest marches with placards calling for greater employee representation on the board. However, this area is an important cause of inequality and therefore demands closer study.

Limited liability companies began to emerge in the United Kingdom in the seventeenth century following government acts that established joint stock companies (JSC) and the principle of general limited liability. A JSC is a company that has a large and changing ownership through shareholders, whose funds can be pooled to create the large amount of capital required by modern companies. JSC status was initially granted to railways and public utilities that required vast amounts of capital. Due to the constantly changing ownership of these companies, the role of management is separated from ownership, and because of this split, the shareholders require limited liability in the event of impropriety or the insolvency of that company, as they do not have day-to-day management oversight. This is essentially the modern legal form of the company we find ourselves with today.

The standard theory behind JSCs is that they encourage entrepreneurship by allowing shareholders, who will not be actively involved in the running of the company, to fund the growth of large companies without fear of being wiped out, and thus foster growth and innovation in an economy. These ideas at the time were not uncontroversial, and in marked contrast with today, those of a more conservative persuasion opposed the JSC. Some disliked limited liability due to the moral hazard of separating risk taking from consequences. Shareholders have unlimited upside in terms of profits, but can lose, at most, only their initial investment. As in an insurance market, the fear is that the limited downside encourages more reckless behaviour. *The Times* at the time derided JSCs as 'a means of making money in idleness'. The economist Adam Smith believed the separation of ownership from management was inefficient, and he did not see the shareholders as owners in the traditional sense. He believed JSC status should be granted only where the capital needs and risks were large and where there was a clear public benefit.

More recently, Paddy Ireland, in *Limited Liability, Shareholder Rights, and the Problem of Corporate Irresponsibility*, argues that JSCs are 'a political construct developed to accommodate and protect the rentier investor'.[40] He believes they were not a natural consequence of the needs of industry, which could fund most capital expenditures from profits, but were developed to meet the needs of finance, which had exhausted good investment opportunities by the mid-seventeenth century. These investors began to buy shares in JSCs, but with unlimited liability, and were frequently wiped out, eliciting little sympathy at the time. However, as these investors began

---

[40] Paddy W. Ireland, 'Limited Liability, Shareholder Rights, and the Problem of Corporate Irresponsibility', Cambridge Journal of Economics 34, no. 5 (2010): 837–56.

to fund the expansion of the railways and other public utilities, they became politically more powerful, and the law was amended to give shareholders limited liability.

Shareholders now had no liability, and as day-to-day management of companies was in the hands of the board and senior employees, they had no responsibilities other than the election of directors to the board. As JSCs became bigger, ownership of companies became even more detached from management, as the board passed a lot of the responsibility for daily operations to the senior employees (executives) of the firm. Many boards and executives saw their duties as looking after the interests of all the stakeholders of a company—the shareholders, creditors, employees, suppliers, and customers.

2.08.2. Shareholder Value Maximisation

When US equity markets stagnated in the early to middle 1970s, the separation of management and ownership was seen by some as the problem, echoing Adam Smith from years before. Referencing the theories of perfect competition and Pareto optimality, Milton Friedman argued that the sole purpose of business is to maximise profits, and given that under the efficient markets hypothesis the current share price is the present value of expected future profits, the aim should be to maximise the current share price. This theory became known as shareholder value maximisation (SVM). The way to achieve this was believed to be by aligning the interests of the executives with those of shareholders, and the most obvious way to do this was to link executive pay to the share price. After the lows in the mid-1970s, US equity markets went on an almost uninterrupted march to the upside for the next twenty-five years. This would suggest that SVM was successful, but we have no way of knowing the counterfactual condition. When we dig deeper into the data, it seems that SVM may not have been so successful in boosting equity returns in the long term, and even if SVM did achieve its main aim, it had some nasty side effects.

James Montier examines this in his white paper, *The World's Dumbest Idea.*[41] He shows that equity returns were actually slightly higher in the era before SVM came into being. Next, comparing companies that signed up to SVM to those that took a broader and longer view, he finds those devoted to SVM performed worse. He uses IBM and Johnson & Johnson as examples of the former and the latter. Looking for where this possible underperformance has come from, an obvious candidate is that during the SVM era, executive pay has gone through the roof, mostly through the granting of stock and stock options.[42] Options on stocks give executives 'all of the upside and none of the downside of stock ownership', and this is on top of the zero liability of regular stocks. Executives are heavily incentivised to maximise the short-term price of the stock, especially now that the average CEO tenure has halved to six years. Ironically, the supposed alignment of executives with shareholders under SVM theory has resulted in

[41] James Montier, 'The World's Dumbest Idea', GMO, December 2014, https://www.gmo.com/docs/default-source/research-and-commentary/strategies/asset-allocation/the-world's-dumbest-idea.pdf.

[42] Chris Dillow, 'The Bosses' Pay Con-Trick', Stumbling and Mumbling, 28 October 2011, http://stumblingandmumbling.typepad.com/stumbling_and_mumbling/2011/10/the-bosses-pay-con-trick.html.

rent-seeking behaviour from executives and worse long-term performance of the company.

> **'In 1980, the average U.S. CEO made forty-two times as much as the average worker. By 2012, that ratio had skyrocketed to 380'.**
> —Chrystia Freeland, *Plutocrats: The New Golden Age*[43]

According to Montier, giving executives incentives to boost the short-term share price of a company has three adverse effects on the broader economy. Firstly, it reduces business investment. This may seem counterintuitive, as the executives should want to increase risk taking to increase the share price. However, given many business investments are uncertain or have a long life-cycle, executives do not want to take risks on projects that may fail or not bear fruit for many years, by which time they may be gone. Instead, they focus on sure things to boost the share price in the short term, such as cost cutting and share buybacks, where the company uses profits to buy back its own shares, thereby boosting the price. Executives may nevertheless want to take business risks that generate revenues in the short term, with the risks or costs coming due long after they have left. This latter strategy is especially noticeable in finance. Secondly, as the stock market is 80 percent owned by the richest 10 percent, this boosting of share prices increases inequality.

Lastly, the other side of SVM is that workers, and other stakeholders, are squeezed to generate profits for the

---

[43] Chrystia Freeland, Plutocrats: The Rise of the New Global Super-Rich and the Fall of Everyone Else (New York: Penguin Books, 2012), ch.1.

executives and shareholders. If you add globalisation into the mix, with the board and executives no longer looking out for the interests of other stakeholders in the firm, it is no surprise that firms will happily move jobs and supply chains offshore to lower-cost economies, adding further downwards pressure to worker compensation in their domestic market. So, we can see that limited liability companies and shareholder value maximisation have actually been one of the main drivers of inequality over the last thirty years. If we want to tackle ine-quality, we have to reform this sector of the economy.

2.09. Externalities—Pollution and Playing Fields

An externality is an economic term for a cost or benefit from an action that has an effect on a third party.[44] In the absence of any corrective action, the agent making the economic decision will not take into account the external cost or benefit, and the optimal level of output and price in the market is different from the optimal level for society as a whole. This is an example of market failure, as society's well-being is not maximised. The classic example of a negative externality is pollution. A polluting factory will maximise profit at a lower level of price and higher level of output than the social optimum because the population outside of the factory pays the cost of pollution.

The traditional solutions to negative externalities are regulation or taxation. A regulation could limit the amount of pollution the firm can produce, with fines or imprisonment as deterrents. Alternatively, a tax could be imposed and set equal to the external cost of the pollution, thus forcing the factory to 'internalise' the cost and set output to the social optimum. Both methods should lead to higher prices, harming consumers, and lower output adversely affecting business owners and workers, while the benefit flows to the local population, which gains from the lower pollution and any tax revenue. The push for deregulation of the last thirty years can be seen, in some cases, as a transfer of costs from businesses to society as a whole.

---

[44] Wall, Microeconomics, pp.246-260.

What is actually going on in the background of problems of externalities is an argument about the assignment of rights, known as the Coase theorem. In the example above, the government, on behalf of society, decides that the factory does not have the right to impose pollution on the local population. While this may seem logical and sensible to most people, it could be argued that the liberty of the factory owner is being restricted. In less clear-cut cases, the conflict between liberty and costs can be contested and political influence and power may become the deciding factors in who is assigned the rights. The debate over fracking permits can be seen as such a case.

This is well-established economic theory, and regulations and taxes have reduced traditional forms of pollution. However, the world currently faces the mother of all negative externalities in the form of climate change. It is a particularly difficult externality to tackle politically, because the negative effects of climate change are geographically diverse and diffuse, and the largest effects will be well into the future. Meanwhile, the costs of addressing climate change fall on business owners, workers, and consumers now. For the sceptical, Chapter 12 of *The Signal and the Noise* by Nate Silver is an excellent even-handed summary of the debate about climate change and its long term effects.[45]

'What we are now doing to the world, by degrading the land surfaces, by polluting the waters and by adding greenhouse gases to the air at an unprecedented rate—all this is

---

[45] Nate Silver, 'The Signal and the Noise: Why So Many Predictions Fail-but Some Don't .' Penguin Publishing Group, . (2012-09-27), Kindle Edition.

**new in the experience of the earth. It is man-
kind and his activities that are changing the
environment of our planet in damaging and
dangerous ways'.**

—Margaret Thatcher in a speech to the
United Nations on 8 November 1989

If we look at the standard climate models, the major economic effects of climate change are that:[46]

1. Extreme weather events such as heatwaves, droughts, floods, and fires will have direct effects.
2. The extreme weather will adversely affect agriculture, fishing, and water supplies, implying rising prices for food and water.
3. Warm weather diseases such as malaria and dengue fever will spread to new areas of the world.
4. Sea-level rises will make many urban centres unliveable.
5. Millions will be displaced worldwide, leading to huge levels of migration and, potentially, global conflicts over resources.

The last effect is potentially the greatest ignored threat. Dhaka, the capital of Bangladesh, is growing by five hundred thousand people a year, many of them refugees from flooding in the south. Thomas Friedman, in the Showtime series *Years of Living Dangerously*, reports on how recent unrest in Egypt and Syria had severe drought, food shortages, and population

[46] Christopher B. Field and Vicente R. Barros, eds., Climate Change 2014: Impacts, Adaptation, and Vulnerability (New York, NY: Cambridge University Press, 2014-)

displacement as catalysts.[47] Many of the areas of the world most vulnerable to climate change are places whose people and governments are poorly placed to deal with them, mostly high population centres in Asia and Africa, so the scale of any migration crisis is unimaginable.

Climate change can be seen to have a huge negative effect on economic output and inequality. The effects will hit the poorest hardest. The well-off will be able to relocate to higher and more temperate areas of the globe to avoid sea-level rises and extreme weather. Meanwhile, it is the poor who will suffer most from disruptions and price rises in food and water, and the rise in disease and migration.

The underappreciation of positive externalities can also have a significant influence on inequality and economic output. Education is a classic example of a good or service that has positive externalities. A well-educated population positively affects economic output and also health, crime, and other social problems in addition to the positive benefit in higher wages for the educated individual. Left to the private market, however, many parents would not be able to afford to educate their children to a good level. Another example is medical research into rare diseases and conditions, which the private sector may find unprofitable.

There are two main policy options to correct market failures of positive externalities. The government can subsidise the good or service by the value of the externality. This will increase output of that good or service and lower its price to the socially optimal level. The alternative is for the government

---

[47] Years of Living Dangerously, season 1, Showtime Networks, 2014, (USA: Showtime), TV.

to provide the good or service directly, as it does with education. As with negative externalities, one of the problems with many of these policy solutions is that the cost is borne now, while the benefits are in the future and often spread, almost imperceptibly, among the population. When governments are trying to reduce the size of the state, as in the 1980s, or attempting to implement austerity, as now, it can seem easy to cut costs on programmes whose benefits are not measured immediately in the national accounts. Consider the long-term costs in the adverse health outcomes of selling off sports fields from schools, or the educational effect of closing libraries, or the long-term social consequences of the removal of assistance to new parents.

These policies of underestimating and underreporting positive externalities has, and will, lead to increases in inequality, as the removal of subsidies for government provision of these goods and services mean the poor can longer afford them. Society overall will be poorer as a result. Externalities must be measured in the national accounts if we are to stop so-called savings in the form of reduced provision of important services and the wilful indifference to climate change. These 'savings' are in reality an accounting trick, frontloading the gains and ignoring the future costs associated.

2.10. Trade Union Legislation and Labour Markets

Trade unions came to prominence during the Industrial Revolution in Great Britain, when workers moved from the countryside to work in the new industries of metals, mining, transport, and textiles. Previously, collective bargaining on the part of workers had been outlawed, and the authorities had brutally put down several labour disputes at the behest of factory or mine owners. The unions campaigned not only for higher wages but also for improved working conditions, as the rate of workplace accidents was very high, hours and conditions were terrible, and female and child labour were often employed. Many workers were paid in company scrip, currency which could only be used at company stores, a practice that amazingly can still be seen today. In 2008, the Mexican Supreme Court ordered Wal-Mart to stop paying their workers in store vouchers.[48]

Monopoly purchasing power is known as monopsony. Prior to the formation of unions, many employers had a monopoly position in the hiring of labour, as big industrial towns often had only one large employer. In monopsony, the employer uses their wage-setting power to set wages and employment lower than in a competitive market. This clearly has serious implications for increased inequality. What the trade unions did through collective bargaining was to create a monopoly supply of labour to counter the monopsony power of the employer.

---

[48] Jurist. 'Mexico Supreme Court Orders Wal-Mart to Stop Paying Workers in Store Vouchers', Jurist, 5 September 2008, http://jurist.org/paperchase/2008/09/mexico-supreme-court-orders-wal-mart-to.php.

They could then try to negotiate wages and employment back up to competitive levels or even beyond. The overall outcome, where you have a competing monopsony employer and a monopoly labour force, is unclear and depends on the relative bargaining strengths but is probably a better outcome for workers and inequality than would exist otherwise.

By the 1970s, employer power had diminished and trade union power had increased via legislation and increased union membership[49] and it could be argued that unions now had monopoly power to set wages and employment levels higher than would exist otherwise, potentially making firms unprofitable. There was an increase in industrial disputes, especially in the public sector and vital services. In the United Kingdom, this came to a head in the Winter of Discontent in 1978, which many commentators believe cost the Labour Government the general election of 1979, which was won by Margaret Thatcher's Conservative Party. The backlash against unions translated into antiunion legislation enacted by the Thatcher and Reagan administrations of the 1980s. Unions were an anathema to the ideology of these administrations, who favoured the individual over the collective and believed the unions were strangling economic efficiency and entrepreneurial endeavour. Privatisation and contracting out of government services moved employment from the public sector, which was heavily unionised, to the private sector, which was not. All these policies led to a fall in the power and the membership of trade unions in the Anglo-Saxon economies.

---

[49] Tejvan Pettinger, 'Trade Union Membership in the United Kingdom, 1892–2007', Economics Help, April 19, 2013. http://www.economicshelp.org/wp-content/uploads/blog-uploads/2012/11/union-membership-1900-2007-500x329.png

The shift in power from unions to employers also meant that the share of rewards shifted from employees to management and shareholders, a major factor in the increase in inequality over this period. Indeed, a 2015 IMF study indicates that economies that saw the greatest drop in union membership saw the greatest rise in inequality.[50]

Whether we have returned to a situation where employers can exploit a monopsony position is a difficult and controversial question. Most towns and cities no longer have a single employer, and workers are more mobile than they used to be. In a few circumstances, however, it seems employers can take advantage of a strong position. When we have high unemployment, employers can hire people at low wages, especially low-skilled workers. In remote and rural areas, where competing jobs are out of commuting range, some employers may be the sole option for workers.[51] We can see evidence of this in the historically low wages for agricultural workers. In many two-income households, the second worker often has to fit work in around household chores and childcare. The person has to take any job that will accommodate his or her hours, often in return for low levels of pay. The increase in part-time and contract work has been a major structural change in most developed economies over the last thirty years. Even in high-skilled sectors employers can collude via noncompete

[50] Florence Jaumotte and Carolina Osorio Buitron, 'Power from the People', IMF, Finance & Development 52 (March 2015), http://www.imf.org/external/pubs/ft/fandd/2015/03/jaumotte.htm.

[51] Daniel O'Keefe, 'Down on the farm: agricultural workers receive lower wages than other workers', Chicago Policy Review, February 13, 2015. http://chicagopolicyreview.org/2015/02/13/down-on-the-farm-agricultural-workers-receive-lower-wages-than-other-workers/

agreements. In 2015, Apple, Google, Intel, and Adobe agreed a settlement after colluding to not compete for each other's engineers and scientists.[52]

Outside of the labour markets, another part of the economy has seen an increase in monopsony power over the last thirty years: the relationship between large retailers and their suppliers. The retailer uses its bargaining power to force down the prices suppliers can charge. The orders from the retailers are so large that a small supplier could struggle to find buyers elsewhere for its output. This dynamic can be seen clearly in the relationship between the food conglomerates and supermarkets and farmers in the United Kingdom and the United States. As in the labour market, this is a redistribution of wealth from smaller, poorer producers to larger corporations and their shareholders and management.

[52] Lance Whitney, 'Apple, Google, Others Settle Anti-Poaching Lawsuit for $415 million', CNET, 3 September 2015, http://www.cnet.com/news/apple-google-others-settle-anti-poaching-lawsuit-for-415-million/.

2.11. Monetarism and Unemployment

After the depression of the 1930s and the successful use of central planning and management of the economy during World War II in the United Kingdom and the United States, Keynesian demand management became the accepted model of economic management. During economic downturns, the government used fiscal and monetary policy to boost demand and thereby stabilise incomes and employment. This method worked successfully until the 1970s, when a combination of shocks created economic turmoil in the developed economies. In 1971, the United States broke the link between the US dollar and gold, ending the Bretton-Woods monetary system that had been in place since the end of World War II. In 1973, the oil-producer cartel OPEC cut oil production in response to the Yom Kippur War, sending oil prices up 400 percent. Additionally, the 1970s were a period of increased industrial turmoil and strikes by trade unions. These were all large negative supply shocks, especially to Western economies that were mostly oil importers, which triggered falling output and rising inflation.

When governments responded by cutting interest rates, this had a greater effect on inflation, driving it higher than output and leading to stagflation. Although, in retrospect, the response by developed economies could be seen as a policy error, misreading a supply shock for a demand one, Keynesian demand management fell out of favour. The theory of monetarism, which had predicted the adverse outcomes of the 1970s, was ready to take its place. In 1979, Margaret Thatcher became Prime Minister of the United Kingdom, and Jimmy

Carter appointed Paul Volcker as chairman of the Federal Reserve, which controls US monetary policy. Although monetarism was abandoned in the United Kingdom by 1984, and although Volker was never actually a monetarist, the emphasis on using monetary policy to keep prices stable and letting output adjust became the accepted form of economic stabilisation policy. It also chimed with the political orthodoxy of the time, as the onus fell on supply-side policies and individual endeavour to increase growth and wealth.

> **'Rising unemployment and the recession have been the price that we have had to pay to get inflation down. That price is well worth paying'.**
>
> —Norman Lamont, former UK Chancellor, 1991

While people can, and will, argue about optimal economic policy, it is apparent that focussing on restraining prices, raising interest rates, and reducing government spending increased unemployment during the early 1980s. This increased inequality during that period, as many manufacturing workers were moved onto welfare benefits, but it also had a long-term effect through what is known as hysteresis, whereby current conditions lead to a future suboptimal outcome. In the industrial centres worst affected by the recessions of the early 1980s, the spectre of long-term persistent unemployment unseen since the 1930s reappeared. When this occurs, workers in these areas find that their skills atrophy, and they struggle to become re-employed, leading to a life on welfare benefits. Prices in the area, including wages, can take a long time to adjust and fall to a point where employers wish to re-enter the area. Workers who do find a new job often take a large pay cut in doing so. Support industries and service industries in the area also suffer from falling demand from the former industrial workers. As is discussed later, this can lead to all manner of social problems and to a vicious cycle of poverty and increasing inequality over the long term.

Another criticism that has been levelled at using monetary policy exclusively as the tool of inflation targeting and demand management is that cutting interest rates in response to falling demand or economic shocks, such as during the 1987–2003 period, creates speculative bubbles in assets such as housing and financial instruments, and that this contributed to the 2007–08 Great Financial Crisis (GFC).[53][54] Indeed, financial traders coined the phrase 'the Greenspan Put' to describe the belief that Alan Greenspan, chairman of the Federal Reserve, would always cut interest rates to bail out financial markets. We look at the GFC in more detail in the next chapter.

---

[53] Steve Randy Waldman, 'Bernanke on Monetary Policy and Inequality', Interfluidity, 2 June 2015, http://www.interfluidity.com/v2/5918.html.

[54] Simon Wren-Lewis, 'The Last 7 Years are an Argument against Inflation Targeting', Mainly Macro, 22 October 2015, http://mainlymacro.blogspot.sg/2015/10/the-last-7-years-are-argument-against.html.

2.12. Deregulation, Finance, and the Great Financial Crisis

2.12.1. Deregulation

As touched upon previously, regulation can be a way to deal with market failure and the assignment of rights. The externality of pollution is often dealt with through regulation, either limiting the amount or banning it altogether, as with CFCs. Another frequent use of regulation is to correct the market failure of asymmetric information, where a buyer or a seller of a good or service knows more than the opposing party does. For example, the food industry may be forced by regulations to put ingredients, country of origin, and nutritional information on labels. The food companies have this information while consumers do not, and the state can decide that consumers have the right to know exactly what they are eating. Food labelling is a good example of the arguments for and against regulations. The food industry argues that these regulations increase their cost of doing business, which ends up costing producers and consumers money. Advocates for labelling argue that better-informed consumers can make better judgements, especially with regards to nutrition, and there are large benefits to society in this.

Most of the arguments follow this pattern. Impose too many regulations and you can add costs to business and increase prices to consumers; impose too complex regulations and the larger and smarter firms can find loopholes to exploit them. Heavily regulated economies have been linked with increased corruption, as large firms capture regulators financially or intellectually.[55] Too few regulations, however, and customers can be taken advantage of, smaller producers can be disadvantaged, and workers and the environment can suffer.

2.12.2. The Finance Industry

One of the most heavily regulated industries is finance and banking. There are good reasons for this. Firstly, there can be large information asymmetries. Financial products can be complex and difficult to understand even for sophisticated purchasers. Secondly, there are huge externalities in finance. A well-functioning finance sector can direct capital efficiently and give a safe, reasonable return to lenders. An over-regulated financial sector can slow growth in an economy and foster corruption, with lending dictated by politicians and regulators to favoured firms and industries. The Great Financial Crisis (GFC) showed that an underregulated financial sector could take excessive risks and engage in fraud, eventually leading to a credit bubble, a crash, and a depression. Lastly, because the financial sector is so important, it receives implicit subsidies from the state in the form of insurance and cheap funding. Customer deposits are explicitly insured by the state up to a certain level, and there is implicit assurance from the state, in which many financial institutions believe, that when push comes to shove, the state will not allow them to fail. This encourages them to take on more risk than they would otherwise. Additionally, retail banks can borrow from the central bank at rates of

---

[55] George R.G. Clarke, 'Does over-regulation lead to corruption?', Texas A&M International University, 2014. http://www.aabri.com/LV2014Manuscripts/LV14025.pdf

interest lower than those available to other sectors of the economy. The idea is to help the retail arms of banks foster growth through lending to consumers and businesses and to smooth over temporary funding gaps. Prior to 2008, many banks used the cheap funding from their retail divisions to fund their risk-taking activities in the investment-banking arm.

The most famous financial crisis in history was the Wall Street Crash of 1929, although there were many before in the late nineteenth century.[56] In a script that may seem familiar, a cocktail of high private debt and leverage, over exuberance, and product mis-selling and fraud by financial institutions caused a global economic collapse leading to company failures, bank runs, deflation, and mass unemployment. Some of the lessons learnt from this crisis meant that, in 2008, large fiscal and monetary stimuli prevented disaster on the scale of the 1930s. In the 1930s, while the macroeconomic response may have been too small, the regulatory response was stronger. The centrepiece was the Glass-Steagall Act of 1933, named after the sponsors of the bill in the US Senate and Congress. This act separated the risk-taking parts of banks from the everyday retail activities of taking deposits and making loans and mortgages.

> **'The most important financial innovation that I have seen the past twenty years is the automatic teller machine'.**
>
> —Paul Volcker, former chairman of
> the Federal Reserve, 2009

---

[56] Madrick, Age of Greed p.12

The success of the act can be seen in the relative financial stability of US and global financial markets for fifty years after its implementation. From the 1970s onwards, however, the legislation was watered down and slowly repealed by acts of Congress in the name of efficiency, innovation, and growth.[57] The budgets of regulators were cut, and their salaries stagnated, meaning that many financial regulators were regulating people earning vastly more than they did. Rules, especially financial ones, are only as good as the people policing them. Perhaps not surprisingly, this deregulation coincided with an increase in the number of financial crises from the 1980s onward. The notable crises were the 1987 stock market crash, the 1994 Mexican peso crisis, the 1997 Asian financial crisis, the 2000 dot-com bust, the 2007 housing crash, and the financial crash of 2008.

2.12.3. The Great Financial Crisis of 2008

At the heart of the 2008 crisis was excessive leverage by global financial institutions, especially in the 'shadow' banking sector, and housing bubbles in many major economies, especially the United States, United Kingdom, Ireland, and Spain. Many mortgages from the United States were securitised (turned into bonds) and sold globally, which meant the crash, when it came, spread to major European financial institutions.[58] Numerous global financial institutions were borrowing day to day to fund long-term lending, and when the crash came

[57] Madrick, Age of Greed, ch.14

[58] Michael Lewis, The Big Short: Inside the Doomsday Machine (New York: W.W. Norton, 2011).

and funds dried up, the asset-liability mismatch caused them to fail. Northern Rock in the United Kingdom and Lehman Brothers in the United States were both borrowing huge sums overnight to lend long term and went bankrupt. Many other financial institutions were bailed out by governments and, thereby, taxpayers.

One of the disturbing features of the bailout of the banks is that after shareholders were wiped out, bondholder creditors to the banks, the next in line on the capital structure to take a hit, were in many cases protected 100 percent by governments at the expense of taxpayers, perhaps demonstrating the extent of capture of regulators and lawmakers by the large financial institutions.[59] This was basically a transfer from taxpayers to the bondholders and employees of these banks, possibly the biggest transfer of wealth from poor to rich in modern economic history. Government action in bailing out the banks and in implementing large fiscal stimuli to prevent the slowdown becoming a depression meant that numerous governments went heavily into deficit. After the crisis passed, many governments implemented austerity to tackle their budget deficits. In this way, it can be seen that taxpayers were being made to pay twice for the profligacy of the banks.

---

[59] Andrew Ross Sorkin, Too Big to Fail: The Inside Story of How Wall Street and Washington Fought to Save the Financial System—and Themselves (New York: Penguin Books, 2010).

2.13. Austerity and Spending Cuts

The policy response to the GFC was straight out of the Keynesian playbook. Interest rates were slashed globally, and fiscal stimulus was enacted. This response almost certainly stopped the economic downturn being quite as devastating as the depression in the 1930s, at least in the short term. Interest rates quickly fell close to zero around the world, which meant that boosting spending was the only policy option left for maintaining demand in economies. However, in the years 2010–2011, the narrative that excessive government debt was a bigger risk than slow growth took hold, propagated by some of the same economists who had given us financial deregulation and supported by electoral victories for right-of-centre parties in the UK general election and US midterms. The major economies of the world turned quickly from stimulus to austerity. This narrative had three flawed theoretical pillars.

First, Rogoff and Reinhart published *This Time Is Different*, in which they claimed that at a ratio of 90 percent government debt to GDP economies start to suffer, slowing growth.[60] There were several criticisms of the theory, not least of which was their spreadsheet data had errors in it. Once corrected, 90 percent ceased to be such a significant Rubicon. Their theory also said nothing about causation. Countries suffering from slower growth tend to have larger debts, so it is not clear that the debt causes the slow growth rather than the other way around.

Next, it was argued that austerity could increase growth by restoring confidence in the business and investment

---

[60] Carmen M. Reinhart and Kenneth Rogoff, This Time Is Different: Eight Centuries of Financial Folly (Princeton: Princeton University Press, 2009).

community. Yet the quoted examples of successful austerity were in very different circumstances to the situation in 2010. Many of the successful austerity policies of the past had been accompanied by offsetting interest rate cuts or by export-led growth to a faster growing global economy, policies that were clearly not possible in 2010 with interest rates at zero and a depressed world economy. For example, Canada, in the mid-1990s, was able to offset a fiscal contraction with lower interest rates and exports to a booming United States.

Keynes made the point that, when the world economy was last in such a predicament in the 1930s, austerity can be self-defeating.[61] With interest rates at zero, if everyone tries to cut spending at once, demand falls, as one person's spending is another person's income. Thus, spending cuts would lead to a fall in growth, lower tax receipts, and little improvement in the budget situation of the country. This can be seen by comparing the experience of the United Kingdom and the United States after 2010. Both countries cut spending, but the United Kingdom did so more aggressively than the United States. The outcome was that the United States grew faster, and its deficit shrunk more than that of the United Kingdom. The United Kingdom quietly relaxed austerity in 2012 while pretending not to do so.[62][63]

[61] John Maynard Keynes, The Great Slump of 1930 (1930; Project Gutenberg, 2008). http://www.gutenberg.ca/ebooks/keynes-slump/keynes-slump-00-h.html

[62] Brad DeLong, 'Optimal Control, Fiscal Austerity, and Monetary Policy', The Washington Center for Equitable Growth, May 7, 2015. http://equitablegrowth.org/optimal-control-fiscal-austerity-monetary-policy/

[63] Ben Chu, 'Do the Latest GDP Revisions Vindicate Osborne's Austerity?' The Independent, 30 September 2015, http://www.independent.co.uk/.

The other source of pressure to reduce government debt came in 2011 from the crisis in the Eurozone. The collapse in growth from the GFC hit the previously high-growth countries of southern Europe and Ireland particularly hard—their budget deficits ballooned, mostly because of falling tax revenues and from having to bail out their banks that were damaged by collapsing housing markets. Lenders feared these countries could default and pushed up the cost of servicing these countries' debt to unsustainable levels until July 2012, when Mario Draghi, the head of the European Central Bank (ECB) said, 'The ECB is ready to do whatever it takes to preserve the euro'. Investors took this to mean that the ECB would stand behind the credit of the high debt countries, confidence returned, and the interest rates on Irish, Spanish, and Italian bonds fell.[64]

The exception was Greece. In Greece, not only did the GFC widen the deficit, the Papandreou Government, elected in October 2009, revealed that the previous government had been incorrectly reporting its accounts and that the deficit was much larger than previously reported. This was a very different situation from that in the other high deficit countries, and investors doubted that the rest of the Eurozone would support a regime that had cooked the books. Greece's interest rates on their bonds remained high, and they required emergency loans from the IMF and Eurozone, with strict conditions attached, to finance day-to-day activities.

For countries experiencing high budget deficits, Greece was held up as a salutary lesson of the perils of continuing to

[64] Tejvan Pettinger, 'EU Bond Yields 2010–2014', Economics Help, 20 March 2014, http://www.economicshelp.org/blog/3371/economics/eu-bond-yields-and-debt/

run budget deficits, and political pressure was brought to bear in the United Kingdom, United States, and other developed economies to reduce deficits lest the interest rate at which the government could borrow exploded, as in Greece. The supposed pressure of higher interest rates was noticeable by its absence. Indeed, the wrong lesson was taken from the Eurozone crisis, which is that what is key in how much a government can borrow in a depressed global economy before the financial markets take fright, is control over one's own currency. As soon as the ECB stated it would do 'whatever it takes' to preserve the euro, the borrowing costs of all Eurozone countries fell to low levels. Greece's rates did not fall because it was clear the ECB and Eurozone countries would not support their borrowing. The United Kingdom, United States, and other governments who have control over their own central banks and currencies were never at risk of a Greece situation. Japan has gross government debt of over 200 percent of GDP and is, at the time of writing, borrowing at negative interest rates when issuing ten-year maturity bonds.

However, the Rogoff-Reinhart theory and the Eurozone crisis was used by politicians and economists, some of whom should, and maybe did, know better, to call for large sudden reductions in government deficits. Not only that, but the call was for most of the reductions to come in the form of cuts to government spending. When France raised taxes to reduce their deficit, European Union commissioner Olli Rehn criticised them, saying they would 'destroy growth and handicap the creation of jobs'. This suggests that the 'crisis' of government deficits was a political device used by politicians and economists of the right to implement policies they favoured ideologically. Indeed, many of the cuts in spending were made to welfare budgets and public investment. This not only increases inequality—this is exactly the opposite of what authorities should do when interest rates are at zero and the global economy is depressed.

Why is it important to refute the need for the austerity that was implemented in much of the developed world from 2010 onwards? First, because it is bad economics, and there is little enough understanding of economics amongst the voting public as it is. Next, because austerity is used to justify a political agenda of spending cuts as outlined above. Questions about spending and taxes should be debated on their merits, and austerity should not be implemented because the public have been falsely told the country may 'become Greece' by City economists who are little more than public relations officers with an agenda to push.[65] Lastly, and most importantly, we must make sure that the correct policies, especially fiscal stimulus, are available for the next crisis. If these tools have been unfairly denigrated during the recent crisis, they may not be politically feasible options for the next crash, and a repeat of the depression of the 1930s and the associated political upheavals become more likely.

---

[65] Simon Wren-Lewis, 'The Austerity Con', London Review of Books 37 (4): 9–11.

2.14. Tax Avoidance, Tax Evasion, and Hidden Regressive Taxes

Tax avoidance is the legal, or semilegal, minimisation of taxes by individuals or companies, whereas tax evasion is the illegal underreporting of taxable income. Both clearly lead to lower government revenues than would otherwise be the case. Measuring the scale of these tax shortfalls is self-evidently difficult, especially in a historical context. Tax Research UK estimates that the scale of tax evasion is large and has been increasing in recent years. [66] The charges brought by the United States against Swiss-based banks for aiding evasion suggest the figures for the United States are also significant. This somewhat contradicts one element of Art Laffer's theory, that the lowering of tax rates over the last thirty years would reduce tax evasion. It seems that if you give plutocrats an inch, they will take a mile.

2.14.1. Tax Avoidance

Tax avoidance has many forms, but usually has the characteristic that taxable income is moved across jurisdictions, time, or classification to minimise tax.[67] When the United Kingdom raised the top rate of tax to 50 percent in 2009, many companies and individuals used a tactic called forestalling to bring

---

[66] Richard Murphy, 'The Tax Gap', Tax Research UK, September 2014, http://www.taxresearch.org.uk/Documents/PCSTaxGap2014Full.pdf.

[67] The Economist, 'Tax havens: The missing $20 trillion', Feb 16th 2013, http://www.economist.com/news/leaders/21571873-how-stop-companies-and-people-dodging-tax-delaware-well-grand-cayman-missing-20

forward income into the previous tax year to avoid paying the new top rate. Companies and individuals also attempt to have certain kinds of income reclassified to take advantage of lower rates or loopholes in tax law. It is usually better to take income in the form of capital gains, which are taxed at a lower rate, than employee earnings. In the United States, there has been controversy over the tax treatment of carried interest, used by private equity firms to minimise their taxes. Famously, billionaires Warren Buffett and Mitt Romney both revealed they paid an effective tax rate of less than 20 percent in 2011, far less than most average workers. President Obama proposed a Buffett Rule of a minimum effective tax rate on earnings over $1 million. High net-worth individuals have even taken to parking assets such as fine art and precious stones in free ports at airports such as Geneva and Singapore, which were originally intended as transit facilities. As these facilities are technically airside, that is, before customs and immigration, there are no taxes liable on goods stored there or bought and sold there. These facilities obviously attract the proceeds of illegal activities also.[68]

Transfer pricing is a grey area of corporate tax avoidance where subsidiaries of the same company buy and sell products or services at off-market prices to move profits to more favourable tax jurisdictions. A company in a low tax jurisdiction will 'buy' a product at an artificially low price from another subsidiary and then sell it at an inflated price to yet another subsidiary in a higher tax regime. Taxable income is thereby maximised in the middle, tax-friendly subsidiary and minimised in the source

---

[68] The Economist, 'Freeports: Überwarehouses for the ultrarich', Nov 23rd 2013, http://www.economist.com/news/briefing/21590353-ever-more-wealth-being-parked-fancy-storage-facilities-some-customers-they-are

and end countries. Amazon, Google, and Starbucks, aided by the large accountancy firms, were recently accused of engaging in this practice within the European Union, and Facebook is currently under investigation in the US. Transfer pricing is in the strictest sense illegal, yet it is very hard to prove and prosecute. The situation is not helped by the fact that, in an example of regulatory capture, there is often a revolving door in employment between the tax regulators and the tax departments of the large accounting firms. HMRC, the UK tax authority, was criticised for cutting soft deals with large corporations, notable examples being the waiving of £10 million late interest owed by Goldman Sachs and for not following up on a file of tax evaders at HSBC that it received in 2010.[69]

2.14.2. Tax Evasion

Tax evasion is thought to be the largest source of revenue shortfall, a combination of untaxed criminal activity, trading in the shadow economy, and evasion by companies and individuals. The National Fraud Authority estimates a loss of £14 billion due to evasion for 2011/12. Tax Justice UK estimates a much higher figure.[70] Perversely, the UK government, in the name of austerity, have cut the resources available to HMRC, treating the department as a cost centre in an epic failure of long-term cost-benefit analysis. This should be listed in the

[69] Tom Peck, "'Sweetheart' deal between HMRC and Goldman Sachs was struck to save Government embarrassment, court hears', Independent, 3 May 2013. http://www.independent.co.uk/news/uk/home-news/sweetheart-deal-between-hmrc-and-goldman-sachs-was-struck-to-save-government-embarrassment-court-8601007.html

[70] Murphy, 'The Tax Gap'

dictionary next to the phrase 'false economy'. Compare this with the attitude from the government and the popular media towards benefit fraud in the United Kingdom, which HMRC puts at £1.9 billion for the same year.[71]

2.14.3. Hidden Regressive Taxes

Lower tax rates on various forms of income, coupled with evasion and avoidance, means the gap in revenues has to be filled with other taxes, which are usually more regressive. Duties, so-called sin taxes on alcohol, tobacco, and petrol, and goods and services taxes tend to fall more heavily on the poor, who spend most of their income and tend to have less healthy lifestyles. Many countries now use public lotteries to fund certain charitable causes. While many see lotteries as laudable and good fun, it should be noted that these tend to be highly regressive, favoured as they are by the poor, while the rich tend to play less, recognising the very low payout ratios.[72]

> 'The pay-out ratio for lottery is typically 50 percent, compared to 74 percent in bingo, 81 percent in horseracing, 89 percent in slot

---

[71] Jake, 'Cost of Fraud (£billions) 2012-13', Ripped-Off Britons, 28 December 2013, http://www.blog.rippedoffbritons.com/2013/12/graphs-at-glance-how-government-goes.html#.Vt7mBtBftf6.

[72] Charles T. Clotfelter and Philip J. Cook, 'On the Economics of State Lotteries', Journal of Economic Perspectives 4, no. 4 (1990): 105–19.

machine, and 98 percent in blackjack played according to the basic rules'.

—Charles T. Clotfelter and Philip J. Cook, 'On the Economies of State Lotteries', 1990

In addition, cuts in transfers to local governments and certain government services have led to those agencies trying to make up the shortfall through the imposition of fees and fines, which are regressive in nature. Charges for parking at municipal buildings and hospitals and charges for the use of municipal parks and recreation centres are often greater than the cost of the service provision, and fines for traffic violations are out of all proportion to the economic cost or deterrence value[73]. Not only are these fees and fines regressive, they smack of unfairness and add to the grind of everyday life.

---

[73] Jill Insley, 'NHS Hospitals Generating Millions from Parking Charges, Finds Which?' *The Guardian*, 9 June 2010, http://www.theguardian.com/money/2010/jun/09/nhs-generating-millions-parking-charges.

3. Why is Inequality a Problem?

3.01. The Philosophical, Religious, and Moral Arguments against Inequality

3.01.1. The Utilitarian Argument

Utilitarians, such as J. S. Mill and Jeremy Bentham, argue for maximising the sum of social utility. This puts the needs of society ahead of those of the individual, so that policies that make some people worse off while making others better off are justified if the net effect is positive. If, as is widely thought, wealth has diminishing marginal returns, in that an extra dollar to a poor person increases that person's wellbeing a lot more than an extra dollar to a wealthy person increases the wellbeing of a wealthy person, the welfare of society can, and should, be increased in most circumstances by reducing inequality. Obviously, those who prioritise the rights of the individual will reject this argument, as will those who believe the loss of economic efficiency from redistribution outweigh the reduction in inequality.

3.01.2. The Rawlsian Argument

John Rawls argues that inequality can be justified if there is equality of opportunity for everybody, and that an action is justified if it makes everyone better off, even if that increases inequality. This could be a basis for arguing for the merits of trickle-down economics, where the rich can get relatively wealthier, so long as the poorer members of society benefit in some way and do not have their opportunities diminished.

3.01.3. The Eliminating Suffering Argument

One could argue that a society where there is extreme inequality but the poorest have comfortable lives is acceptable, even if the utilitarian and Rawlsian conditions are not met. We later examine whether relative inequality in itself is unhealthy for a society. However, where society is wealthy and yet so unequal that the poor are suffering, many would argue that society has a moral obligation to act, even if the wealthy are made worse off and the Rawlsian argument is not met. Of course, this could rest on the definition of suffering, but by many metrics (health, unemployment, nutrition, crime, etc.) the poor in a lot of the developed world are indeed suffering at this time.

3.01.4. The Meritocratic Argument

In theory, in a meritocracy, people attain and keep the wealth and power they deserve based upon their talents and effort. However, implicit in meritocracy is the notion that everybody has an equal chance to succeed. We shall see later that high levels of inequality lead to reduced opportunity for the children of the poor, through social harm in their early years and a lack of educational opportunity and resources, and the reverse is true for the wealthy. This implies intergenerational inequality should be minimised so the next generation start with a level playing field. Indeed, a complete meritocracy would have 100 percent inheritance taxes, no private education, and excellent public services for children. The current generation could enjoy the rewards of their talents, but they could not, in theory, pass them on to their children. Some would argue that this is not a meritocratic outcome, exposing the internal conflict at the heart of meritocracy. There is the further question of whether it is fair that outcomes are based, to some extent, on a genetic lottery, or whether we would want to live in such a stratified society.

3.01.5. Religious Arguments

Scripture can be sliced and diced to support most perspectives on most issues. Those who wish to take selective lines out of context can find a way to suggest that inequality is not an issue that need concern them. Look at the religious texts as a whole, however, and a common broad perspective on inequality is easy to ascertain. Most major religions forbid usury, or the charging of interest—God Himself says r should be zero! Many religions ask their followers to tithe or give a percentage of their income to the poor. The Torah even has laws for regular debt Jubilees (debt forgiveness) and wealth cancellation. In 2014 Pope Francis tweeted that 'Inequality is the root of social evil'.[74] For the religious, the imperative to reduce inequality is clear.

---

[74] Pope Francis, Twitter post, 28 April 2014, 4:Source: 28 a.m., https://twitter.com/pontifex/status/460697074585980928

3.02. Affluenza and The Spirit Level—Inequality is Bad for You

'We are intensely relaxed about people getting filthy rich'.

—Peter Mandelson, former UK trade

and industry secretary, 1998

In the previous chapter we asked, is relative inequality, in and of itself, harmful? While it is clear to most that a high degree of inequality, such that the poorest are suffering, is undesirable, how about the case where there is little absolute poverty but the rich are extremely wealthy?

Richard Wilkinson and Kate Pickett attempt to answer this question in their important book *The Spirit Level*.[75] They constructed an index of inequality for the major developed economies of the world using the ratio of incomes of the richest 20 percent to the poorest 20 percent and plotted the relationship to various indicators of societal distress, such as mental illness, crime, health, and educational attainment. They found strong evidence that more unequal societies are unhealthier, less educated, and more criminal, as shown in Figure 4.

Just as importantly, they found that these adverse outcomes do not apply only to the poor and middle-income groups—they found that even the richest suffer in more unequal societies. This result gives weight to policies designed to reduce inequality, even if the incomes of the richest are reduced, as the utility of all of society, including the wealthy, is increased. Comparing

---

[75] Richard G. Wilkinson and Kate Pickett, The Spirit Level: Why Equality Is Better for Everyone, (London: Penguin Books, 2010).

the societal indicators to the average income of the same countries, they found no strong relationship, ruling out the average wealth of a society as a contributing factor. Additionally, they tried several different measures of inequality and found the same results. To rule out cultural causes, they studied inequality across the different states in the United States and found the same link between inequality and social harm.

Health and social problems are worse in more unequal countries

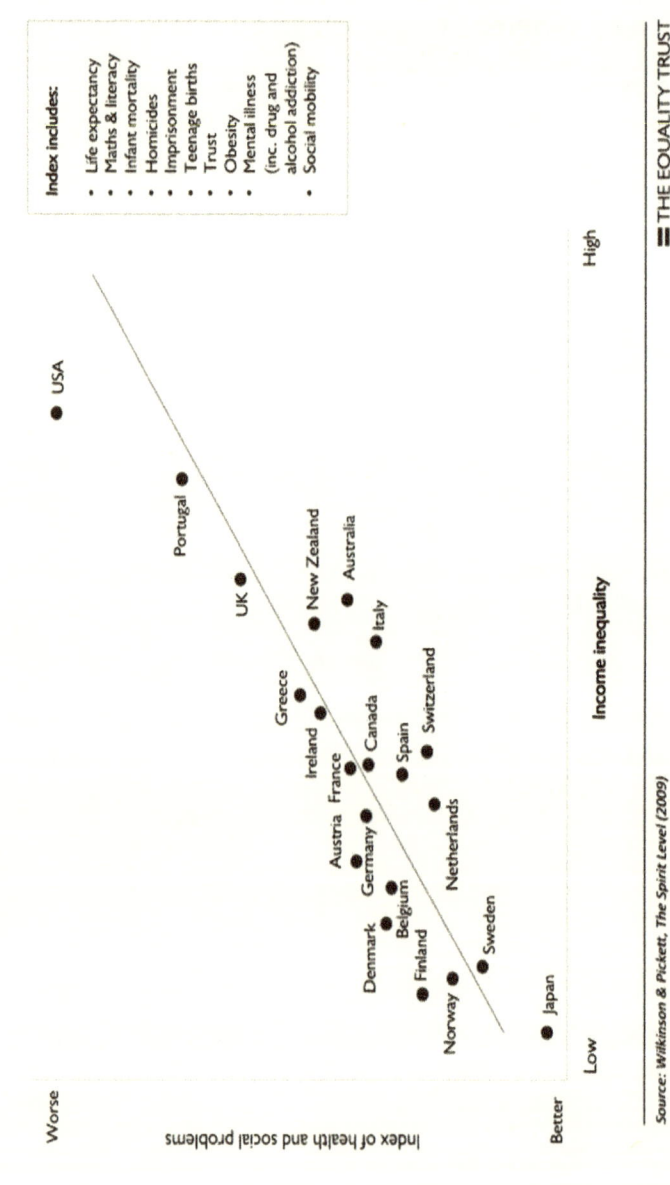

Index includes:
- Life expectancy
- Maths & literacy
- Infant mortality
- Homicides
- Imprisonment
- Teenage births
- Trust
- Obesity
- Mental illness (inc. drug and alcohol addiction)
- Social mobility

Source: Wilkinson & Pickett, The Spirit Level (2009)

Figure 4 Income inequality versus index of social ills

Source: Richard G. Wilkinson and Kate Pickett, The Spirit Level

☰ THE EQUALITY TRUST

What links inequality and these adverse outcomes? And why are the richest also affected? Wilkinson and Pickett point to the psychological effects of stress and status. For the poorest, there are the feelings of shame of diminished status in societies that measure worth in economic terms. Moreover, the poor are caught in a vicious cycle, where children are often raised in a stressful environment of poor diet and health as well as absent fathers, leading to inferior economic outcomes later in life.

> **'The Selfish Capitalist toxins that are most poisonous to well-being are the systematic encouragement of the ideas that material affluence is the key to fulfilment, that only the affluent are winners and that access to the top is open to anyone willing to work hard enough, regardless of their familial, ethnic or social class background—if you do not succeed, there is only one person to blame'.**
>
> —Oliver James, *The Selfish Capitalist:*
> *Origins of Affluenza*

Oliver James goes into the detail of these drivers of emotional distress in his books *Affluenza* and *The Selfish Capitalist: Origins of Affluenza*.[76] [77] He finds that early adverse childhood experiences are a main driver of emotional distress later in life.

---

[76] Oliver James, The Selfish Capitalist: Origins of Affluenza (London: Vermilion, 2008).

[77] Oliver James, Affluenza: How to Be Successful and Stay Sane (London: Vermilion, 2007).

Those from poorer backgrounds are more likely to be exposed at an early age to violence, drugs, alcohol abuse, and other stressors, which can even affect the development of the foetus in the womb.

What about the wealthiest in more unequal societies, why do they suffer also? James points to materialism and consumerism in those societies, reinforced by advertising, leading people to compare themselves unfavourably to those above them, all the way up the income scale. The top 10 percent look enviously at the top 1 percent, who in turn feel they are doing badly next to the top 0.1 percent. In societies where the dominant political and economic model says that you are worth what you earn and where wealth is heavily concentrated at the top, it is not surprising many people feel inadequate. They then turn to material possessions to assuage these feelings, thus perpetuating the vicious cycle. Indeed, the modern economic model relies on reinforcing these feelings of inadequacy to get consumers to purchase more and more.

Michael Sandel introduces another perspective in *What Money Can't Buy: The Moral Limits of Markets*.[78] He shows that free-market thinking and norms have entered many areas of life where they were previously absent, such as fast-track and VIP services for the wealthy in travel, healthcare, and banking, and the marketisation of sports and live entertainment, which have priced out the traditional fan base. This has two adverse effects. Firstly, in a more unequal world, putting a price on more and more goods and services exacerbates the effects of inequality. Secondly, economic considerations

---

[78] Michael J. Sandel, What Money Can't Buy: The Moral Limits of Markets (London: Penguin, 2013).

crowd out or corrupt superior moral concerns and motives of citizenship, altruism, and charity are degraded.

These studies and essays are crucial because they demonstrate that relative poverty, and not just absolute poverty, is harmful to society, and to all in society. There may be a trade-off between economic efficiency, in the free-market sense, and long-term social efficiency. Policies that reduce inequality at the expense of growth must now at least be considered.

'For the first time since the Great Depression, focusing on redistribution makes more sense than focussing on growth'.

—Lawrence Summers, former US Treasury secretary

3.03. Superstars and Social Mobility

Thomas Piketty showed that within a few generations in an unequal society, income from wealth begins to dominate income from work, but he also acknowledges that much of the wealth over the last thirty years has been from earned income, what he describes as the 'rise of the supermanager'. Huge fortunes have been made by senior executives in large companies and by financiers, as well as in the traditional superstar fields of arts and sports. In this chapter, we ask several questions: Is the current level of *wage* income inequality fair and justified? If not, why not, and what does that imply?

Remembering that most human traits are distributed based on a normal distribution, a simple analysis would suggest an equitable income distribution should follow a normal distribution. We know from Pareto and Piketty that this is not the case. What about the Paretian idea that high inequality is 'the natural order of things'? It has been argued recently that certain work skills are not distributed normally. Most of these arguments can be traced back to *The Best and the Rest* by O'Boyle Jr. and Aguinis, which is a study of sportsmen and politicians, hardly people with regular careers.[79] While this is a convenient cover for paying senior business executives large salaries, the idea that while most regular human traits are distributed normally, the ability to give PowerPoint presentations and chair meetings fall into the same category as athletic prowess seems fanciful. Looking at the opposite end of a Pareto distribution, the other implication of this theory is

[79] E. O'Boyle Jr and H. Aguinis, 'The Best and the Rest', Personnel Psychology 65, no. 1 (2012): 79–119.

that the vast majority of employees contribute relatively little. This should seem intuitively questionable, unless you have had a very rough day at work.

It seems more reasonable to assume something must be happening in the structure of the economy or labour market to generate these income disparities. Employers could and should be choosing employees from the right side of the ability distribution. This would generate a non-normal distribution of incomes. In professional sports with large resources and the use of 'Moneyball' statistical analysis this seems plausible.[80] However, the selection processes for hiring senior executives is random and unreliable, and the output of senior executives is difficult to measure. Empirically, executive pay can be explained mostly by the size of the corporation and the broad direction of the overall stock market, not some superstar ability—in other words, rent seeking.[81]

> **'We looked at tens of thousands of interviews, and everyone who had done the interviews and what they scored the candidate, and how that person ultimately performed in their job. We found zero relationship'.**
>
> —Laszlo Bock, senior vice president for people operations at Google

---

[80] Michael.Lewis, *Moneyball: The Art of Winning an Unfair Game,*. New York: W.W. Norton, 2004.

[81] Paul Gregg, Sarah Jewell, and Ian Tonks, 'Executive Pay and Performance in the UK', London School of Economics and Political Science, November 2010, http://www.lse.ac.uk/fmg/workingPapers/discussionPapers/DP657_2010_ExecutivePayandPerformanceintheUK.pdf.

The marginal product theory of economics suggests that workers are paid the value of their output, so those workers in lucrative and growing industries, such as technology, will be paid more than those in other industries. In perfectly competitive markets, workers in other industries would retrain, enter these better paying industries, and thereby equalise wages across industries. In reality, it is not costless, or sometimes even possible, for workers to change careers, or for employers to chop and change employees, and so wages in certain industries can remain elevated for some time. In addition, some workers may have unique, untrainable attributes needed in well-paid industries. This can be seen as a barrier to entry, and as good fortune. The skills needed for a well-paid technology job now may not have been well rewarded thirty years ago, and may not be well rewarded in thirty years' time. The Luddites found their previously highly prized skills no longer valued through no fault of their own.

Another explanation of skewed income distributions came in an essay by Sherwin Rosen, 'The Economics of Superstars'.[82] Written in the early 1980s, this paper sought to explain the outsized rewards to the very best performers in the field of entertainment and sports. In these markets, he describes two common elements: the size of the potential market is very large and market size and rewards are skewed towards the most talented. The drivers of these results were that, in these markets, adding scale did not add to production costs, and there is imperfect substitution between the sellers. Or as Rosen puts it: many average singers do not make a good one.

[82] Sherwen Rosen, 'The Economics of Superstars', The American Economic Review, Vol. 71, No. 5 (Dec., 1981), pp. 845-858, http://www.jstor.org/stable/1803469 .

Depending on how imperfectly substitutable the output is, the greater the skew of rewards. Alfred Marshall had made similar observations a hundred years earlier, but Rosen was the first to create a formal model of the process. With globalisation and digital technology, many new markets are now potentially huge, meaning not only can low-skilled jobs be farmed out, but the very talented also can generate large rewards.

We now have plausible explanations of how talent could be normally distributed but the rewards can be massively skewed to those perceived to be the top performers, and they stem from rent seeking, barriers to entry, and imperfect substitution between both labour and goods. These are market imperfections, suggesting that these markets are not efficient and that redistributive taxation could actually increase efficiency. Such winner-take-all markets do not seem fair either.

Social mobility data also points to unfair outcomes in incomes. In genetics, the offspring of two high-ability individuals, measured by IQ, for example, is likely to be of high ability but less able than the parents due to mean-reversion. Conversely, the offspring of two low-ability parents should, on average, have greater ability than the parents do. Therefore, genetics would suggest, even with the recent trend to assortative mating, where people marry within their income and educational demographic, there should be a reasonable amount of social mobility. Kids of talented, rich parents should, on average, underperform their parents, and the kids of poorer parents should outperform theirs. The data on social mobility does not bear this out but, in fact, points to the reverse.[83]

[83] Wilkinson and Pickett, The Spirit Level (2009), https://www.equalitytrust.org.uk/sites/default/files/files/SpiritLevel%20slides.pptx.

We touched on the vicious circle for the poorest in society in the chapter on *The Spirit Level*. Early childhood stressors and other factors such as absent fathers, poor schooling, and lack of positive peer influence can severely damage the life chances of the children of disadvantaged parents. Additionally, Owen Jones, in *Chavs*, touches upon the acceptable demonisation of the poor in modern society.[84] While minorities from poor backgrounds also suffer similar fates, antidiscrimination laws can protect them from outright abuse in the public sphere, whereas the white working class are apparently fair game. 'Chavs' in the United Kingdom and 'trailer trash' in the United States are seemingly acceptable yet abusive names for the white working class, who additionally feel abandoned by the political classes, even those who are supposed to be on their side. Throughout history, the tactic of nationalists and the extreme right has been to destroy empathy amongst the general public for certain groups by implying they are subhuman, and this tactic is now being used to remove sympathy for the poor and justify high levels of inequality.

This has several adverse effects. As with all prejudice, individuals from certain sections of society, or certain neighbourhoods, are not given an equal chance of success. A University of Chicago study demonstrated that job applicants with 'white' sounding names were 50 percent more likely to be called to interview than those with 'ethnic' sounding names.[85] It

---

[84] Owen Jones, Chavs: The Demonization of the Working Class (London: Verso, 2012).

[85] Marianne Bertrand and Sendhil Mullainathan, 'Are Emily and Greg More Employable Than Lakisha and Jamal?' American Economic Review 94, no. 4 (2004): 991–1013.

doesn't seem a stretch to imagine the same discrimination against people with 'lower' class names or from poorer white neighbourhoods.

The forces work in reverse at the top of society where the children of the rich have access to the best childcare, schools, and universities.[86] So-called investment in their children by the rich has been rising as a percentage of income for the last forty years.[87] They gain not only from better grades but also from increased self-confidence and life-skills, and from the ability to network within the establishment. The children of the rich can afford to take unpaid internships or to start careers on extremely low salaries while being supported by their parents, opportunities that many others cannot afford to take. Many creative industries have a business model where new hires are expected to start their careers working long hours for very little pay. Not only are these vicious and virtuous circles unjust, they can also be inefficient; we examine the inefficiency of inequality next.

---

[86] Owen Jones, The Establishment and How They Get Away with It (London: Penguin Books, 2015).

[87] The Economist, 'America's Elite: An Hereditary Meritocracy', The Economist, 24 January 2015, http://www.economist.com/news/briefing/21640316-children-rich-and-powerful-are-increasingly-well-suited-earning-wealth-and-power.

3.04. Inequality, Inefficiency, and Growth

In this chapter, we consider how, in theory, inequality could cause inefficiency and lower growth in an economy, and then see if the evidence backs the theory. We saw in the previous chapter that some aspects of inequality lead to a vicious circle for those at the bottom and a virtuous one for the fortunate, and this could lead to inefficiencies. One of the more obvious ways inequality could be inefficient is that potential at the bottom of society remains undeveloped, while at the top who you know is as important as what you know, meaning the children of the rich are given opportunities greater than their talents merit.

The life chances, educational opportunities, and social problems of poorer communities we touched on before. Additionally, in areas of high unemployment, there is the problem of hysteresis where workers' skills atrophy. There is untapped potential and lower productivity amongst these less skilled workers, leading to lower growth. Some of these workers will be unemployable or will drop out of the labour force, meaning that when the economy recovers, it hits full capacity at lower levels of growth than previously, and inflation becomes a problem. In an economist's language, the natural rate of unemployment is higher.

Some of the opposite problems apply at the top of the income distribution. The children of the rich have the best education, at the best schools, which often gains them entry to the elite universities and grants them superior networking possibilities later in life. This could result in some being placed in senior roles above their true, innate abilities. This form of inefficiency is subjective and difficult to measure, but it is difficult to believe a meritocratic society would have so many children from elite educational institutions monopolising the top jobs, as they do in the United Kingdom, illustrated in the study *Elite Britain* by the Social Mobility and Child Poverty Commission.[88]

A larger problem is that with concentration of wealth comes concentration of power, as wealthy individuals or large corporations can use their money to influence politicians and regulators to mould policy to their benefit.[89] This results in monopolistic and oligopolistic practices going unchallenged and tax loopholes remaining open. As discussed earlier, monopolistic practices are suboptimal from an efficiency perspective, and tax avoidance leads to reduced government revenues and investment in public services and infrastructure.

A more prosaic effect of inequality is on consumer spending via the propensity to spend of the rich and the poor. The poor spend most of their income; some spend even more and go into debt. If increasing inequality cuts their income, they are forced to cut back on spending. At the other end of the scale, the very wealthy save and invest a large percentage of their income, so, as their wealth grows, only a small part of that is spent. This implies that increased inequality depresses consumer demand in an economy, meaning companies struggle to sell their products domestically.[90] Companies that have

[88] Social Mobility and Child Poverty Commission, Elitist Britain? (London: Social Mobility and Child Poverty Commission, 2014).

[89] Prokop,. '40 Charts that Explain Money in Politics'

[90] Atif Mian and Amir Sufi, 'Who Spends Extra Cash?', House of Debt, April13, 2014. http://houseofdebt.org/2014/04/13/who-spends-extra-cash.html

access to global markets can attempt to compensate by selling goods abroad, but smaller, domestic-based companies are likely to suffer.

If the economy and inequality are both growing, the rate of growth must exceed the rate of increase of inequality otherwise incomes at the bottom will stagnate or even decrease. That is why over the last thirty years the real incomes of the poorest in society have only grown during periods of high growth. If growth is to be subpar for the next few years, as forecast, and if inequality continues to increase, the real incomes of the poor are set to decrease further.

What does the empirical evidence show about the effect of inequality on efficiency? We can use the growth of GDP as a proxy for efficiency, although it is a very flawed measure, as we see later. The OECD, in a 2014 report, *Focus on Inequality and Growth*, refutes the theory of trickle-down economics and argues that inequality has hampered growth in the major developed economies. In the United Kingdom, for example, it estimates that inequality has shaved 20 percent off GDP over the last thirty years. The organisation reports that the inequality of the bottom 40 percent has especially negative effects on growth.[91]

However, Paul Krugman, hardly an apologist for the 1 percent, finds the data is more equivocal, with an unclear relationship between inequality and growth across developed

---

[91] Organisation for Economic Co-Operation and Development Directorate for Employment, Labour, and Social Affairs, Focus on Inequality and Growth ([Paris?]: OECD, 2014).

economies.[92] While the results of his analysis reject the argument that reducing inequality will kill incentives and growth, neither is there clear evidence that inequality depresses growth. There are possibly at least two explanations why increased inequality may not reduce growth, at least in the short term. Firstly, globalisation and technology can help companies avoid the negative effects of inequality in their domestic markets. An unskilled and unmotivated domestic workforce is not a problem if low-skill work can be automated or outsourced to cheaper overseas labour markets. Low domestic demand for a company's products can be more than compensated for by overseas demand and by offering credit to consumers.

Indeed, increased indebtedness is part of the second explanation for sustained growth in unequal societies, which is that several temporary factors have masked the symptoms of inequality for the last thirty years. Robert Reich, in the film documentary *Inequality for All*, shows how increased female participation in the workforce, increased hours worked, and more indebtedness have allowed families to maintain their consumption in the face of increased inequality.[93] We cannot rely on these factors for much longer, and in the next section we look at why we should worry even more about inequality going forward.

[92] Paul Krugman, 'Inequality and Economic Performance', lecture presented at Columbia University, New York, NY, December 2014, https://webspace.princeton.edu/users/pkrugman/PK_Columbia.pdf.

[93] Inequality for All, directed by Jacob Kornbluth (San Francisco: 72 Productions, 2013).

3.05. If You Tolerate This Your Children Will Be Next

As discussed in the last chapter, increased inequality has been masked by various coping mechanisms on the part of workers and families. While increased female participation and increased working hours are not bad in of themselves, the reality is that many are working longer hours for lower or unchanged per-hour real wages and that many women have to take low-paid part-time work while juggling family commitments. Dual income partners working longer hours have less time to spend with children and each other, so family life suffers. Going into debt is the other method of maintaining living standards. The very poor rely on credit cards and payday lending at usurious levels of interest, while the middle class have come to rely on releasing equity from ever increasing house prices. High household debt is stressful at the level of the family and destabilising at the level of the economy, as demonstrated by the crash of 2008. The crash had housing bubbles in the United States, United Kingdom, Ireland, Spain, and Portugal, funded and leveraged by the financial sector, at its core.

The problem for the future is that these coping mechanisms have probably reached their natural limit. Workers in the English-speaking developed economies already work long hours, it would be unwise for them to take on any more debt, and a large percentage of women are already in work. Indeed, during the last recession male unemployment in the United States was higher than that for females by the widest gap in history.[94] Higher house prices may give the illusion of wealth, but many parents are finding their children priced out of the housing market. Meanwhile, the large forces driving inequality are likely to continue. Although there are signs that the pace of globalisation may be slowing, the reach of technology into the labour market probably will increase. The McKinsey report on technological disruption we looked at in chapter 2.06 lists twelve potentially disruptive technologies. Advanced robotics and 3-D printing could replace many skilled manufacturing workers, and self-driving vehicles could clearly come to dominate the transport sector.

For many, the most frightening recent development is the automation of knowledge work. Jobs in law, accounting, medicine, and other industries that were seen as secure and well paid are beginning to be automated, as computers become more powerful and software more advanced. This also begins to bring into question the policy of expanding higher education as a cure-all for inequality. A paper by Henry Siu and Nir Jaimovich shows that the key distinction between jobs will soon be not whether they are cognitive or manual but whether they are routine or not.[95] Routine manual jobs such as car assembly and warehouse storage were the first to be automated. More recently, cognitive jobs such as bookkeeping, legal document searching, and filing have been automated. Needless to say, employment and pay in these sectors have

[94] Ayşegül Sahin, Joseph Song, and Bart Hobijn, 'The Unemployment Gender Gap during the 2007 Recession', Current Issues in Economics and Finance 16, no. 2 (2010).

[95] Nir Jaimovich and Henry E. Siu, 'The Trend is the Cycle: Job Polarization and Jobless Recoveries', NBER Working Paper No. 18334 (Cambridge, Mass.: National Bureau of Economic Research, August 2012, revised March 2014).

fallen, especially after the last recession. In addition, a plethora of businesses that aim to supply labour and services on demand is springing up. The taxi service application, Uber, is the poster child for these types of businesses. While these services are convenient for consumers and for workers who wish to work flexible hours, they disrupt traditional businesses and workers who rely on guaranteed regular work.

The probable result of these changes is that many jobs in the future are likely to become more irregular, less secure, and less well paid relative to today, even for careers previously considered blue chip. This suggests inequality, unchecked, will continue to increase, with a smaller and smaller elite grabbing the spoils from a larger insecure lower and middle class. Given the huge investment the rich make in their children and the current underinvestment in public services and education for the majority, this suggests social mobility will decrease. The exception to this is likely to be the children of middle-class families falling down the income scale. Even if you are doing reasonably well, it is increasingly likely that your children will not.

A 2014 NASA study has an even more apocalyptic vision. The HANDY model highlights the risk of a total collapse of civilisation caused by increasing inequality and climate change. Looking at past collapses of civilisation, the study shows the common factors were stretched resources, such as water, energy, and food, combined with the stratification of society into 'elites' who consume an outsized share of these resources and the 'masses' who struggle to get by.[96] If this seems far-

---

[96] Safa Motesharrei, Jorge Rivas, and Eugenia Kalnay, 'Human and Nature Dynamics (HANDY): Modelling Inequality and Use of Resources in the Collapse or Sustainability of Societies', Ecological Economics 101, no. 4 (2014): 90–102.

fetched, Thomas Friedman, in the documentary *Years of Living Dangerously*, investigates how the recent conflicts in Syria and Yemen had droughts and subsequent migration into cities as their catalysts for sectarian conflict, and in 2014 the Pentagon declared that climate change was an immediate threat to national security.[97][98]

[97] Years of Living Dangerously, season 1.
[98] US Department of Defense, 'Climate Change Adaptation Roadmap', US Department of Defense, 2014, http://tn.gov/assets/entities/health/attachments/CCA_Report_Pentagon_Climate_Change.pdf.

4. Existing Solutions for Inequality

4.01. Traditional Socialism and the Third Way

4.01.1. Traditional Socialism

An obvious, but flawed approach to the increased inequality is to reverse the policies of the last thirty years. Let's examine the implications of reversing some of these policies to see why this is unlikely to succeed.

In *Power from the People*, the IMF argues that inequality has increased the most in economies where trade union power and membership has fallen the most.[99] An obvious solution would be to restore trade union powers. There are several problems with this approach. Firstly, it may not be politically popular, with good reason. While the trade union movement secured many valuable improvements in wages and working conditions for workers in the early twentieth century, in the 1960s and 1970s they were perceived to be abusing their powers, with strikes becoming increasingly commonplace. In addition, at the time, unions were often bastions of discrimination, although now they do much good work in fighting for equal treatment of workers. Secondly, unions in Southern Europe are still seen to favour 'insiders' over the rest of the community and the economy as a whole. Unions in Italy and Spain prioritise wages and conditions for currently

---

[99] Jaumotte and Buitron, Power from the People.

employed members, making employers wary of or unable to hire new employees. This lack of labour market flexibility is seen in the obscene levels of youth unemployment in those countries. This strategy of setting prices (wages) too high and output (employment) too low is classic monopoly behaviour. There is no guarantee that restoring trade union power would not lead to this result again.

Another obvious reversal would be to renationalise many major industries. Again, we face a problem of political viability. Nationalised industries often had a poor reputation, especially where customer service and quality of product were concerned. The British Leyland Austin Allegro is sometimes described as one of the worst cars of all time.[100] There is an argument for nationalising some natural monopolies that have been privatised, as we discuss in an earlier chapter. These should be considered on a case-by-case basis, but the default position should be that the case for nationalisation should be compelling, economically and politically. To renationalise an industry and then do a poor job running it would be costly to public finances and lend itself to the narrative that government is the problem, not the solution. This would spill over into many other policy areas. We return to this subject in more detail in the next section.

Making tax rates more progressive is another common solution that is suggested. It has been pointed out, correctly, that periods of strong growth for middle-class incomes in the 1950s and 1960s occurred with top marginal tax rates of 90 percent or so. There are a couple of key differences

---

[100] Richard Porter, Crap Cars (London: BBC Books, ©2004) p.120

between then and now, however. Firstly, the idea of shared sacrifice after the world wars could be used to justify these tax rates politically. Justifying tax rates of 50 percent or above today would be difficult, as the state taking more than half of anyone's income is a very strong value statement. While we can argue about whether certain high incomes are justified, taking half of someone's income implies that it is not, and this seems unfair to many, even those on low incomes. Secondly, high-income workers and capital were a lot less mobile sixty years ago. Raising marginal tax rates too high would lead to a flight of talent and capital, although the scale of this is often overstated in both the level of flight and of 'talent'. We saw earlier that the 75 percent top rate of income tax recently introduced in France was a failure politically and economically.

4.01.2. The Third Way

The 1990s saw the implementation of policies in the United Kingdom and United States that were successful in terms of growth and alleviating some poverty at the bottom of society. In the third way, centre-left administrations accepted most of the reforms of the 1980s but sought to use tax revenues to increase public investment, and they used targeted means-tested tax credits to boost incomes at the bottom of the income scale, and minimum wages were increased or introduced. Although tax regimes were made more progressive at the margin, top tax rates were kept at fairly low levels. This meant that although growth was strong and incomes at the bottom increased, incomes at the top also increased, thus inequality did not decrease substantially, if at all.[101] While this is preferable to the situation in the 1980s that saw incomes at the bottom decrease, if we take the results of *The Spirit Level* at face value, growth that does not reduce inequality does not improve social outcomes. Moreover, at some point, the large underlying forces pushing inequality wider overwhelm the ability of the government to redistribute, or a recession reduces tax revenues. Tony Blair thought the upper limit of tax revenue had been reached in the United Kingdom in 2005.[102]

Another notable feature of the third way was the ends were more important than the means. 'What works' was what was important, both in policy and in winning elections. This was important because some on the left continued (and still continue) to push policy solutions that were well past their sell-by date, as we saw above, and to place ideological purity above electability. However, third-way policies such as welfare 'reform', which involved cutting benefits or making them harder to claim, and public service reform, which often involved privatising or outsourcing certain functions, alienated many of the traditional voters from the parties of the left. These policies, although helping the majority of the working poor, left behind a small but significant number of people, mostly the unemployed in the industrial towns and cities that had suffered most in the 1980s. To these people, there seemed to be little difference between the mainstream parties of left and right.

In addition, the very wealthy and large corporations continued to amass vast fortunes, as the third way did not seek to

---

[101] Piketty, Capital in the Twenty-First Century, p.316

[102] Tony Blair, A Journey (London: Arrow, 2011), p.526.

limit incomes at the top. Aside from being distasteful to some, this wealth could be used to lobby and buy political influence. Regulators were often seen to be 'captured' by the industries they were supposed to be regulating. This was especially the case in finance, with damaging consequences. Many politicians and regulators left for lucrative jobs in the private sectors of the industries they had oversight over. This led to general disillusionment with government and the political class, especially in the aftermath of the financial crisis.

4.01.3. Loss of Traditional Working Class Base

As mentioned above, the third-way policies only went some way to repairing the damage inflicted on some communities in the 1980s. Many traditional supporters of parties of the left felt abandoned. Some felt abandoned economically, as improving economic conditions for most did not touch many of the unskilled and unemployed in towns and cities with persistent unemployment that had lost traditional manufacturing and mining industries. Many of these voters simply gave up on politics. The very poorest in society have the lowest propensity to vote.[103]

The third way, to foster growth and appeal to centrist voters, adopted many policies that were pro-business, especially in facilitating free trade and increased immigration. As discussed previously, while immigration has positive long-term effects on

---

[103] Alexandre Afonso, 'Voting Intentions by Household Income, British Election Study Wave 4', The London School of Economics and Political Science, n.d., http://blogs.lse.ac.uk/politicsandpolicy/to-explain-voting-intentions-income-is-more-important-for-the-conservatives-than-for-labour/.

growth, in the short term it can be very disruptive, especially for less skilled workers. They found themselves competing against cheaper foreign labour at home and abroad, meaning many lost their jobs or had stagnating wages. Meanwhile, the liberal wings of the parties of the left were fighting to implement socially liberal policies as regards gender, sexuality, and race. Regardless of the merits of these policies, they were alien to many traditional working-class voters, who were often socially conservative and religious. It also meant that any discussion of the negative effects of immigration was muted for fear of accusations of racism. Many of these workers, who felt their jobs and values under threat, also stopped voting or turned to nationalist parties of the far right—the United Kingdom Independence Party (UKIP) and the British National Party (BNP) in England and the Tea Party in the United States. The Scottish National Party (SNP) in Scotland combines nationalism with more traditional socialist policies, capturing both sets of disillusioned former voters of the left.[104]

> **'And each successive administration has said that somehow these communities are going to regenerate. And they have not. So it's not surprising then that they get bitter, and they cling to guns or religion'.**
>
> —Barack Obama, 2008

Thomas Frank, in *What's The Matter with Kansas*, explains how the right in the United States have hijacked the

---

[104] Clark, 'The decline in political participation'.

political debate to get the mostly poorer 'values' voters to vote against their economic interests.[105] The Tea Party faction of the Republican Party pushes conservative positions on abortion, religion, and social policy while also advocating a far-right economic agenda. Many of these voters believe that no party will make much of a difference to their economic lives, and so the crucial debate for them is over social policy. Frank describes how 'Astroturf' (fake grassroots) lobby groups, funded by rich individuals and corporations, create fake controversies, such as the nativity play being 'banned' in schools, as a cover for a corporatist economic agenda. We can see similar tactics and similar political organisations springing up in the United Kingdom (UKIP) and other developed countries.[106]

This trend of traditionally left voters splintering into different factions was brought into sharp relief after the 2008 financial crash. Disgusted by the bailouts of major financial institutions, people formed two new political movements in the United States that had very different diagnoses and remedies for the crash. The Occupy movement placed the blame on the large corporations whose lobbying and money had corrupted regulators and politicians. Their goal, as far as can be ascertained, was to break up the large financial institutions, see jail time for the responsible executives, and remove corporate money from politics. The Tea Party laid the blame at the feet of the politicians. A false narrative was created that

[105] Thomas Frank, What's the Matter with Kansas? How Conservatives Won the Heart of America (New York: Henry Holt and Co., 2007).

[106] Marcus Roberts, Revolt on the Left, (London: Fabian Society, October 2014). http://www.fabians.org.uk/wp-content/uploads/2014/10/RevoltOnTheLeft-Final4.pdf

government assistance for mortgages in poor neighbourhoods was the cause of the financial crisis and that the bailout and subsequent stimulus were unnecessary, a waste of taxpayer money, and represented a government takeover of business. The solution, from their perspective, was smaller and less intrusive government involvement in both the economic and social spheres.

It is clear that for parties of the centre left, creating policies that appeal to all these strands of former disaffected voters will be extremely challenging to say the least.

4.02. The Scandinavian and Stakeholder Economic Models

To tackle inequality we can study countries that have successfully done just that. We use two simple measures of inequality to achieve this. The Gini coefficient is a measure of income inequality across the entire population. It works on an index from 0 to 1: 0 is perfect equality, where everyone earns the same income; 1 is perfect inequality, where one person earns all the income in an economy. In reality, most results fall between 0.20 and 0.60, as perfect equality is hard to produce in practice and extreme levels of inequality usually lead to political or social upheaval. Another measure is the ratio of the average income of the richest 10 percent to the poorest 10 percent. This is interesting to us, as Piketty and others state the main driver of inequality is the income of the top 10 percent relative to the rest.

The black bars in Figure 5 show the Gini coefficient for major developed large economies before transfers (taxes and welfare payments). South Korea, Switzerland, and the Nordic countries have low pretransfer inequality. There may be social or institutional reasons for this, which we address below. What may be surprising is that before transfers, Finland, France, Germany, and Italy have inequality on a par with the United States when this survey was taken in the late 2000s. The Anglo-Saxon economies have moderate to high inequality at this stage. The white bars on the graph show the magnitude of the effect of transfers on the Gini numbers. The black pretransfer Gini bars reduced by the white transfer bars give us the grey post-transfer Gini bars. The graph is sorted from left to right, from the most equal to the least equal post-transfer countries.

What is notable here is that the European countries which demonstrated inequality before transfers, Finland, France, Germany, and Italy, use large transfers to reduce inequality. Switzerland and South Korea have low inequality pretransfer and so require smaller transfers. The Nordic countries add above-average levels of transfers to below-average pretransfer inequality to become the most equal economies by the Gini measure, and the Anglo-Saxon economies do the reverse.

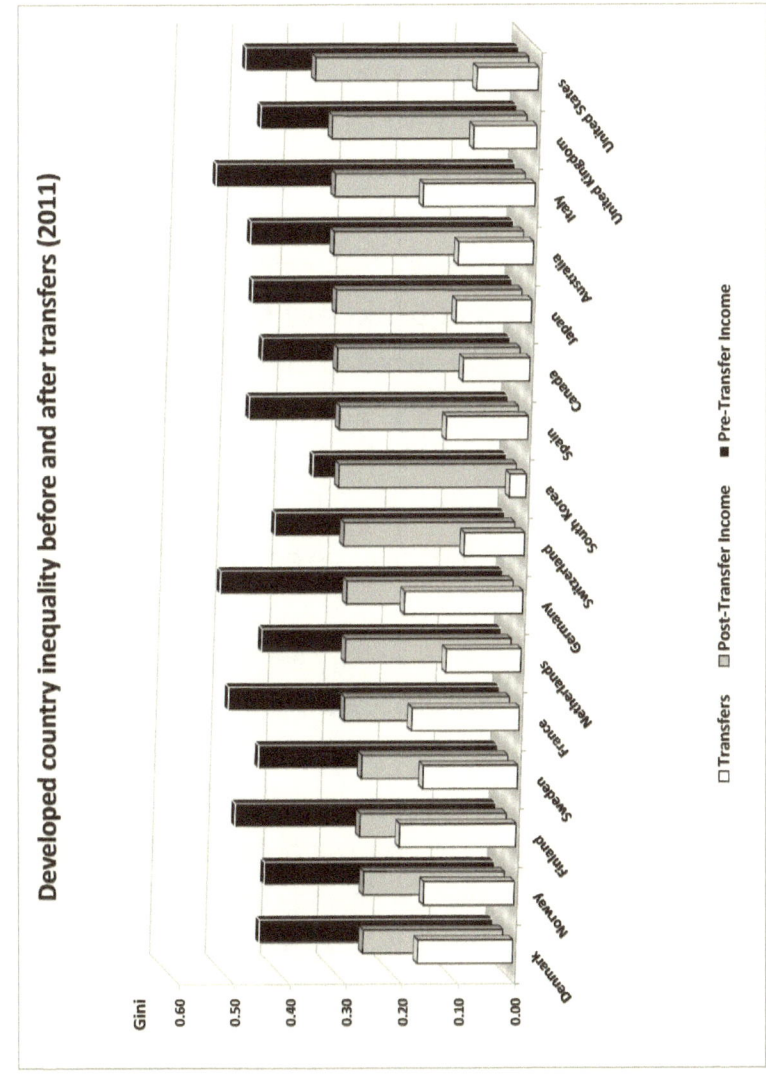

Figure 5 Developed country inequality before and after transfers (2011)
E. P. Anthony, 2016. Data: OECD, 2011.

117

Another measure of inequality is the ratio of top and bottom 10 percent of incomes. Here, the East Asian and Northern European economies stand out for their equality. We examine the reasons for this in the next section. Also notable in this analysis are Spain and Italy, which both show large levels of inequality between the very rich and very poor despite the high levels of transfers seen above.[107] This would imply either the wealthy are not paying a proportionate share of tax or that the poor are not benefitting greatly from welfare payments. Knowing that both countries have high youth unemployment and entrenched, corrupt elites, this result is not particularly surprising. This may also explain the notable rise of antiestablishment parties in both countries. Greece exhibits a similar structure of inequality. So it seems in terms of inequality we have an Anglo-Saxon problem (and a southern European problem), although for all developed countries it is a concern. How do the more equal societies achieve their outcomes?

4.02.1. The Scandinavian Model

The Scandinavian economies are said to follow a Nordic model, although there are differences between them. They perform very well on most economic and social indicators and in terms of social mobility. While they all tend to have high levels of taxation and welfare payments, they operate on the capitalist principles of free markets and trade. In return for high taxation, citizens receive efficient public services, transparent

---

[107] United Nations, Human Development Report 2009: Overcoming Barriers (New York: United Nations, 2009), http://hdr.undp.org/sites/default/files/reports/269/hdr_2009_en_complete.pdf

government, and low levels of corruption. Some public services are open to the private sector to provide. Welfare payments and public services tend to be universal, not means tested, and a high level of social trust in these countries means there is less demonisation of the recipients of welfare. State support is not widely viewed as a collectivist burden but rather as enabling individual autonomy and allowing citizens to fulfil their potential.[108] This is a stark contrast to the Anglo-Saxon societies, where even a welfare payment as targeted and limited as food stamps is under attack in the United States.

In addition, the Nordic model has an element of cooperation between stakeholders in companies. This stakeholder approach to corporate governance is at the heart of the East Asian economies of Japan and South Korea and can go some way to explaining why they have less pretransfer inequality than other economies and why the gap between the very wealthy and the very poor is narrower also.

4.02.2. The Stakeholder Model of East Asia

In this model, outside shareholders have limited influence on the running of public companies. Instead, the company has strong formal and informal links with the government, major banks, and suppliers. The bank and suppliers frequently own shares in their partner corporation and vice versa, meaning they have a strong mutual interest in the success of the

---

[108] The Economist, 'Special Report: The Nordic Countries, February 2nd 2013', The Economist. http://www.economist.com/sites/default/files/20130202_nordic_countries.pdf.

relationship.[109] Until recently, employees at such companies were guaranteed 'jobs for life' in return for their loyalty, and there were informal agreements between competitors against poaching staff. Companies often maintain strong links with the towns and communities in which they operate. Government policy in East Asian economies tends to favour producers over consumers and equity over 'efficiency'. The government in Japan has to some extent acted as 'employer of last resort', with large infrastructure projects keeping unemployment low.

It should be fairly obvious why such a model would lead to less inequality, as the interests of workers, suppliers, and the local community are uppermost in the minds of the executives running companies. The executives are not rewarded in shares or options as extensively as in the West, meaning they can make longer-term investment decisions than a CEO in the United States who is worried about his next quarterly numbers. The ratio of a CEO's pay to that of the median worker is only 67 in Japan compared to 354 in the United States, according to a study by US trade union AFL-CIO.[110]

Trying to replicate either of these economic models could be problematic for the developed English-speaking economies, as at least part of the success of these models is due to

[109] EWMI/PFS Program, 'Lectures on Corporate Governance - Three Models of Corporate Governance', December2005, http://www.emergingmarketsesg.net/esg/wp-content/uploads/2011/01/Three-Models-of-Corporate-Governance-January-2009.pdf
[110] AFL-CIO 'CEO-to-Worker Pay Ratios Around the World', April 1, 2013. http://www.aflcio.org/Corporate-Watch/Paywatch-Archive/CEO-Pay-and-You/CEO-to-Worker-Pay-Gap-in-the-United-States/Pay-Gaps-in-the-World#_ftn1

their cultural fit. However, given that we have seen that many developed economies have high pretransfer and post-transfer inequality, it makes sense to try to incorporate the more successful elements of both.

4.03. The Structure of Inequality

If we are to reduce inequality, we must understand its structure. Who are the 1 percent, how much wealth do they have, and how do they earn their money? How about the top 10 percent? Similarly, for the poorest, we must understand where they derive their income, and—given that they spend most, if not all, their income—what they spend it on. If we are to create policies to reduce inequality, we must make them politically saleable, and so we must study the income, wealth, and spending of the median household to ensure that any policies are attractive to this demographic. We examine each of these in turn.

Remember that income and wealth distributions seem to follow a power law structure. That implies that if the top 10 percent earn five times what the average of the 90 percent earn, the top 1 percent also earn five times what the next 9 percent earn. It follows that a lot of wealth is held by the top 1 percent and especially the top 0.1 percent. This sector of society earns its income mostly from investments in financial assets and property.[111] They also tend to be internationally mobile. Thus, high income-tax rates do not affect them much, as they tend to have relatively little salary income and can sometimes move domicile to avoid other forms of taxation. It is therefore difficult to tax this sector to reduce its wealth. There are solutions, but they are mostly long term, may seem

---

[111] Josh Zumbrun, 'How to Save Like the Rich and the Upper Middle Class (Hint: It's Not With Your House)', *The Wall Street Journal*, Dec 26, 2014. http://blogs.wsj.com/economics/2014/12/26/how-to-save-like-the-rich-and-the-upper-middle-class-hint-its-not-with-your-house/

marginal, and may not satisfy the bloodlust of the far left (What will?). Nevertheless, they are probably the best that can be achieved in the current political climate and will have a greater effect than may seem apparent at first glance.

First, we can look at the source of their income and see if the returns on financial assets are currently prioritised in the economic system over other forms of income. Next, we can examine tax systems to ensure there are no loopholes to exploit. The very rich often have dedicated wealth advisors helping them legally minimise their taxes. And of course outright tax evasion must be dealt with harshly, both for the individual and his or her advisors. More broadly, we can ask what the wealthiest want their fortunes for. They are not all stupid people, desperately craving another billion for the sake of it. Chrystia Freeland studies this demographic and their motivations in her book *Plutocrats*.[112] What becomes clear is that the vast fortunes are often a means to an end, the ends often being ego and power. If we can separate money from power in the corporate and political world, some of the motivation to accumulate vast fortunes will be removed. So possibly will some of the negative social effects of inequality. Once you allow for extreme poverty, what explains the negative effects of inequality at the bottom of society? Oliver James argues that it is often shame and feelings of inadequacy, and that the sense that the game is rigged in favour of the wealthy must contribute to this.

It has been suggested that society could appeal to the altruistic side of the plutocrats. For example, *Stakeholder Theory*

---

112 Freeland, Plutocrats.

by Freeman et al., in what could be described as an essay in bleeding-heart capitalism, seems to suggest that pointing out to CEOs and major shareholders that looking after all stakeholders improves long-term economic performance is sufficient to effect change.[113] The selection of quotes below demonstrates that a significant section of this demographic is unlikely to change their behaviour anytime soon. Stating that *The Spirit Level* says everyone is happier in a more equal society is likely to be as successful as pointing out to alcoholics that they would feel better if they didn't drink. Chrystia Freeland notes that in the age of globalisation, plutocrats have more in common with each other that their fellow citizens, thus weakening incentives for them to support policies of inclusion.

> '**I would call attention to the parallels of fascist Nazi Germany to its war on its "one percent", namely its Jews, to the progressive war on the American one percent, namely the "rich"'.**
>
> —US investor Tom Perkins, 2014

> '**There is no monopoly on becoming a millionaire. If you're jealous of those with more money, don't just sit there and complain. Do something to make more money**

---

[113] R. Edward Freeman, Jeffrey S. Harrison, Andrew C. Wicks, Bidhan L. Parmar, and Simone De Colle, Stakeholder Theory: The State of the Art (Leiden: Cambridge University Press, 2010).

yourself—spend less time drinking or smoking and socialising, and more time working.

—Australian billionaire heiress (!), Gina Rinehart

'It's a war. It's like when Hitler invaded Poland in 1939'.

—Private equity boss Stephen Schwarzman about
a proposed tax hike on carried interest profits

The next richest 9 percent could be described as the professional classes, doctors, lawyers, and the like. Most of their income comes from salary, and their wealth tends to be invested in property and savings, from which some also derive income.[114] Higher taxes on salaried income could reduce inequality between this sector and those below, but these taxes are, in many countries, already quite high, and they would probably widen the gap up to the top 1 percent. Better to move some burden of taxation on property, which will also affect the top 1 percent.

Those at the bottom rely on wages and welfare payments for their income. Indeed, a modern phenomenon is in work benefits, where a salary can be too low to support a family and requires topping up with welfare payments. This clearly places a large burden on government finances. Additionally, many people in this demographic are unemployed or underemployed, settling for a part-time job when they would like a full-time one. No one in this sector, in fact up to the bottom 40 percent of society, has much wealth to speak of, and actually

---

[114] Piketty, Capital in the Twenty-First Century, ch.8.

may be in debt. Policies on employment, wages, and credit are key to raising the incomes of this sector. Given that the poorest spend most of their income, we need to look at what it is they are spending it on.

A study of expenditure in the United Kingdom shows that the lower decile income groups spend more as a percentage of income on food and drink, alcohol and cigarettes, housing, housing goods, and utilities and communication (mostly mobile phones).[115] By far the largest item for the poorest households is housing, usually in the form of rent payments. If we can ensure that markets in these goods are competitive, if we can boost supply of these items or reduce any taxes on these items, we can mitigate the effects of inequality somewhat. Retirees, who have the greatest propensity to vote, and median households also spend heavily on these items, so prioritising them should be politically popular.

At the top of the income structure, there is greater percentage expenditure on transport, education—mostly in the form of university fees—leisure items, and 'other' items, which are mortgage payments, local property taxes, and insurance premiums. (In the United States, with more sparsely distributed population centres, car and gas costs affect all income levels, which is one reason why fuel taxes are so low there.) The suggestion here is that these items should not be tax advantaged or subsidised, which is especially interesting where university fees are concerned, as these tend to be heavily subsidised currently. We may wish to subsidise some of these

---

[115] Office for National Statistics, 02 December 2014. http://webarchive.nationalarchives.gov.uk/20160105160709/http://www.ons.gov.uk/ons/dcp171766_383471.pdf. Table A1.

items, however, if they have positive spillovers economically or environmentally.

The median voter is, in fact, in the income bracket slightly above the median income, as the propensity to vote generally increases with income. This means, politically, we cannot skew product taxes and subsidies too heavily in favour of the poor and against the rich. For example, in the United Kingdom, taxes on petrol have hit a ceiling politically, as they affect the median voter quite strongly. When thinking about income taxes, the fact that incomes are distributed on what resembles a power-law schedule means that unless tax hikes are targeted at the top decile, where very high incomes are concentrated, the median voter is likely affected by any rise, or very close to being affected by it. This is especially true for dual-income households. We must consider these political constraints when setting tax policy.

4.04. A Holistic Approach to Reducing Inequality

Reducing inequality, given the combined challenges of globalisation and technology, and the splintering of traditional working-class communities and voting blocs can seem an insurmountable problem. While many great books and texts diagnose the extent and adverse effects of inequality, they tend to be light on solutions. Piketty admits as much in describing his call for a global tax on capital 'utopian'. Meanwhile, traditional socialist solutions are probably unworkable politically and economically, and although the third way overcomes those hurdles, it does not seem to reduce inequality on the scale required to counteract the structure of the global economy today.

There is however a unified and coherent set of policy solutions to these problems, if we can combine the lessons of the third way about electability and 'what works' while directing policy to specifically benefit and appeal to the traditional working-class voters of the left. From a technical point of view, we can view policy questions as a form of a constrained optimisation problem. The optimisation goal is reduced inequality, while the constraints are economic efficiency and maintaining a large enough political coalition to be electable. First, let us look at some areas where some of our goals and constraints seem to be in conflict and see if we can resolve them.

What is our attitude, for example, to policies that increase growth and increase incomes at the bottom but also increase inequality? A Rawlsian analysis would accept these policies, which was also the decision taken under third-way governments. However, with the evidence of *The Spirit Level*, we would now perhaps reject such policies, as unequal growth is seen to be socially damaging. The decision here should probably be based on the strength of growth against the extent of the increases in inequality and environmental damage. While the evidence in *The Spirit Level* is compelling, it is not conclusive, and it has not been generally accepted. Therefore, where the rate of growth increase arising from a policy is likely to be large, the effects on inequality are unclear or marginal, and there is no environmental damage, the policy should be accepted. Here the political damage of being seen to reject such policies dominates the marginal inequality effect. Conversely, where the effect on growth is small but the increase in inequality large, we should reject the policy.

What about growth-enhancing policies that do not increase inequality but do environmental damage? The classic example here would be decisions on using coal for energy production. The coal mining and oil extraction industries can be large employers in traditionally working-class communities, and they are seen as growth enhancing, although we challenge this assumption. Here the environmental damage must dominate the decision process, as the long-term effects of climate change will fall on the poorest in society and the world. In some working-class communities, especially in the United States and Australia, environmental policies are unpopular, which means we will have to draft policies very carefully and put resources into making the long-term case for environmental protection to these communities.

Some environmental activists are against all growth, arguing that even 'clean' growth will merely lead to the proceeds of that growth being consumed in environmentally damaging ways. We should reject this thesis on several grounds. Firstly, it seems an overly pessimistic take on human behaviour and technological progress, and damage can be countered by increasing taxes on damaging economic choices. Secondly, growth-reducing policies are not currently politically saleable. Lastly, we see from Piketty that reducing growth implies that income from wealth will dominate income from wages, thereby increasing inequality.

Globalisation and technological change often fall into this policy grey area of conflicting goals. Globally, growth and inequality can be seen to have been improved by these forces, and the owners of capital and consumers have benefited greatly. However, workers in developed countries have seen wages stagnate as a result, and the environment in developing nations has suffered. The net effects, globally at least, seem to be positive, leading to the conclusion that these changes should be managed rather than reversed. We saw earlier that Andrew Smithers contends that technological change leading to increased inequality is actually a function of corporate governance and management remuneration, and this is where we should direct our fire, as well as ensuring future trade deals incorporate rigorous standards for working conditions and the environment to level the playing field.

While the net effect of these changes on workers in developed countries is a trickier problem, which we examine in detail later, there are two important things to note on this subject. Firstly, many low-paid jobs are in nontradeable sectors of the economy, meaning action on wages can be taken now without affecting international competitiveness. Additionally, at some point unit labour costs in tradable sectors, which allow for productivity differences, will approach parity between the developed and developing worlds, at which point wages in developed countries could begin to rise again without harming competitiveness. As we see manufacturing activity moving out of China to Vietnam, Bangladesh, and other lower cost countries, we may be approaching that point.

We would reject policies that reduce inequality but also reduce growth, unless the reduction in growth is small and the reduction in inequality is large and therefore clearly meets the utilitarian criterion. For example, a 100 percent tax on incomes over a certain level would reduce inequality but likely reduce growth, as capital and skilled labour would flee. The perceived unfairness of very high marginal rates would likely prove politically unpopular also. Surveys often claim that hiking the top rate of tax is a popular policy, but this is rarely borne out in real elections. Nevertheless, as the damage of climate change and inequality become apparent, some of the more utopian policies may become feasible politically.

A political dilemma for the left is the divergent views of the traditional working class and the liberal elite. The political left, at least in the United Kingdom, has historically been a coalition of these two sections of society, with the Labour Party being formed by the trade unions and the Fabian Society, whose members included George Bernard Shaw and H. G. Wells. Recently these two sections have found themselves on opposite sides in many policy debates, with the liberal intellectual left seeming to dominate, and disillusioned working-class voters leaving for the Tea Party in the United States and UKIP in the United Kingdom. This shift in the balance of power has to be reversed for a couple of simple reasons. Firstly, the original purpose of most parties of the left was to represent working people, and the intellectual left was there to support them through policy prescriptions and raising finance. If we are to reduce inequality, the supposed beneficiaries should be on board. Secondly, the working classes are a larger and more loyal voting bloc, while the liberal left can be notoriously fickle. Therefore, where we have a marginal policy choice, we should most often come down in favour of the view of the working classes unless it crosses ideological red lines.

This framework for analysing policy choices, while necessary, could seem a bit technical and cold. How do we frame these policy choices to form a coherent whole? Here we introduce the holistic concept, most famously practiced in traditional Chinese medicine. Holistic medicine treats the body as an interconnected whole and seeks to treat the root causes of illness as well as its symptoms while avoiding damage to the rest of the body. Conversely, Western medicine often attempts to temporarily suppress the symptoms of an illness with drug therapies, and these drugs may often have harsh side effects. Similarly, optimal policies to reduce inequality will attempt to treat the causes of inequality while simultaneously alleviating its symptoms and minimising any negative side effects. For example, hiking marginal tax rates to high levels could temporarily reduce inequality. However, it does nothing about the pretransfer level of inequality, there may be negative side effects on growth, and the effects may be temporary if a subsequent government reverses the hike.

Additionally, policies should be complementary, building on the success of others, and yet independent, so that they are effective in isolation. The policies implemented in the '80s and '90s, although we may disagree with their goals, were very successful in achieving these outcomes. For example, anti–trade union and privatisation policies were argued to have increased economic efficiency while empowering the individual over the collective. They reinforced each other, but they would have worked separately. They also changed the narrative and collective consciousness of society, and the success of earlier policies meant that stronger policy prescriptions could be introduced later. Margaret Thatcher began with mostly incremental changes at first and implemented stronger policies after electoral success. For example, she did not attempt to introduce the controversial poll tax or rail privatisation until towards the end of her premiership. So, while for some the policy solutions we are about to introduce may seem more timid than they would like, they are actually stronger than they seem in terms of getting to the root causes of inequality and, if successful, will open the door to stronger policies later.

5. The Holistic Manifesto

5.01. The Size of the State (1)

> 'For my part, I think that capitalism, wisely managed, can probably be made more efficient for attaining economic ends than any alternative system yet in sight, but that in itself it is in many ways extremely objectionable'.
>
> —J. M. Keynes

The starting point for the analysis here is the assumption that, for most product and service markets, the traditional capitalist system is the most efficient means of producing and distributing those goods. It is rare that the conditions for economic perfect competition are met 100 percent, but in most markets, private provision is still generally superior to the alternative of a centrally planned economy. As we have seen, the distributional implications of these markets may not be desirable, but we hope to find policy solutions to this other than the government taking over production decisions.

Given this assumption, the historical role for the state has been to oversee and regulate the smooth operation of markets through antimonopoly legislation and financial regulation and to provide 'public goods' (goods that everyone benefits from) such as national defence and policing. This was the role of the state in the United Kingdom, and other industrialised countries, up to World War I, and it involved the state spending just above 10 percent of GDP.

After World War I, the government began to provide more quasi-public goods, such as free education, and limited means-tested insurance against unemployment, sickness, and old age, which private markets had failed to provide at competitive enough a price for the poor. At this point, government spending was around 25 percent of GDP. After World War II, National Insurance was made universal and many key industries were nationalised, such that UK public spending reached around 45 percent during the 1970s. The privatisations of the 1980s brought this level back to the 35 percent level. Spending ranged from 35 percent to 40 percent until the 2008 financial crisis, when government stimulus measures, coupled with a drop in GDP, led to a temporary spike in spending as a percentage of GDP. Most other industrialised countries followed this pattern, although each with slightly different timeframes and levels of spending.

What goods and services should the government provide and what level of government spending to GDP is optimal for the twenty-first century? The government will inevitably continue to provide public goods such as defence and education and step in where there are market failures, such as in social insurance markets. However, there are many grey areas, such as utilities, where it is unclear whether private or public provision is superior.[116] In these cases, the burden of proof is on the public sector to show that taking over provision of these

---

[116] Wren-Lewis, 'The State, Corporations, and Markets'

goods will be more efficient and will reduce inequality. There are several reasons for saying this.

> **'The Republicans are the party that says government doesn't work, and then they get elected and prove it'.**
>
> —P. J. O'Rourke

Looking first at the efficiency argument, after the poor performance of nationalised industries in the 1970s coupled with forty years of antistate propaganda, the reputation of the government is at all-time lows in many developed economies. We need to rebuild the brand of government before we can expand its role. This means that anything central government is doing poorly should be passed to either local government or the private sector to provide. In the United Kingdom, there is some public support for renationalising the railways. It is not clear, however, that the government would do a better job running them, and a poorly run state railway would again tarnish the image of the government.

How about the distributional arguments for nationalisation? If the argument here is to reduce fares or fees such that the industry runs at a break-even level, the effect is not always obvious. For example, lowering rail fares would benefit many business commuters from the suburbs of large cities. If the argument is to pay workers in the state industries higher wages than those in the private sector, this will merely cause resentment in the private sector and amongst taxpayers who will be footing the bill. The main argument for rail nationalisation is probably the environmental impact of increased use of trains and decreased use of cars, but do subsidies to private rail companies not achieve the same result?

While the ideal may be to judge what the government should provide and tax accordingly, as we get up to ratios of 40 percent of spending to GDP, the taxes to pay for this spending will inevitably start to fall on the middle class, given that the poor cannot pay large amounts of tax and the very wealthy are few in number and good at minimising their tax bills. US economist Brad DeLong argues that the optimal size of the state will be bigger in the twenty-first century than it was in the previous one.[117] This is because technological progress will require greater spending on education to train workers, and increased life expectancy will require greater spending on healthcare and pensions. These arguments indeed seem plausible, and the trends can already be seen in Figure 6, which implies we must reduce the role of the state now where it is not needed or useful to make room for these future necessary expenditures.

The same analysis should be used to determine the provision of government services. Where the private or charitable sector or local government can do a better job of providing government services, they should do so. Outsourcing like this can have adverse distributional effects, as the private sector will often bear down on the wages and benefits of workers, but we can deal with that separately through changes to the tax system and minimum wages and the reform of corporate governance. At the moment, it seems voters have a strong

[117] Brad DeLong, 'Rethinking Macroeconomics', Bradford-delong.com, 5 April 2015, http://www.bradford-delong.com/2015/04/draft-for-rethinking-macroeconomics-conference-fiscal-policy-panel.html.

preference for efficiency over equity in the provision of goods and services, and this needs to be reflected in policy. To keep services in the government sector on distributional grounds implies that workers in those sectors are being paid more than their private counterparts, which will again only breed resentment.

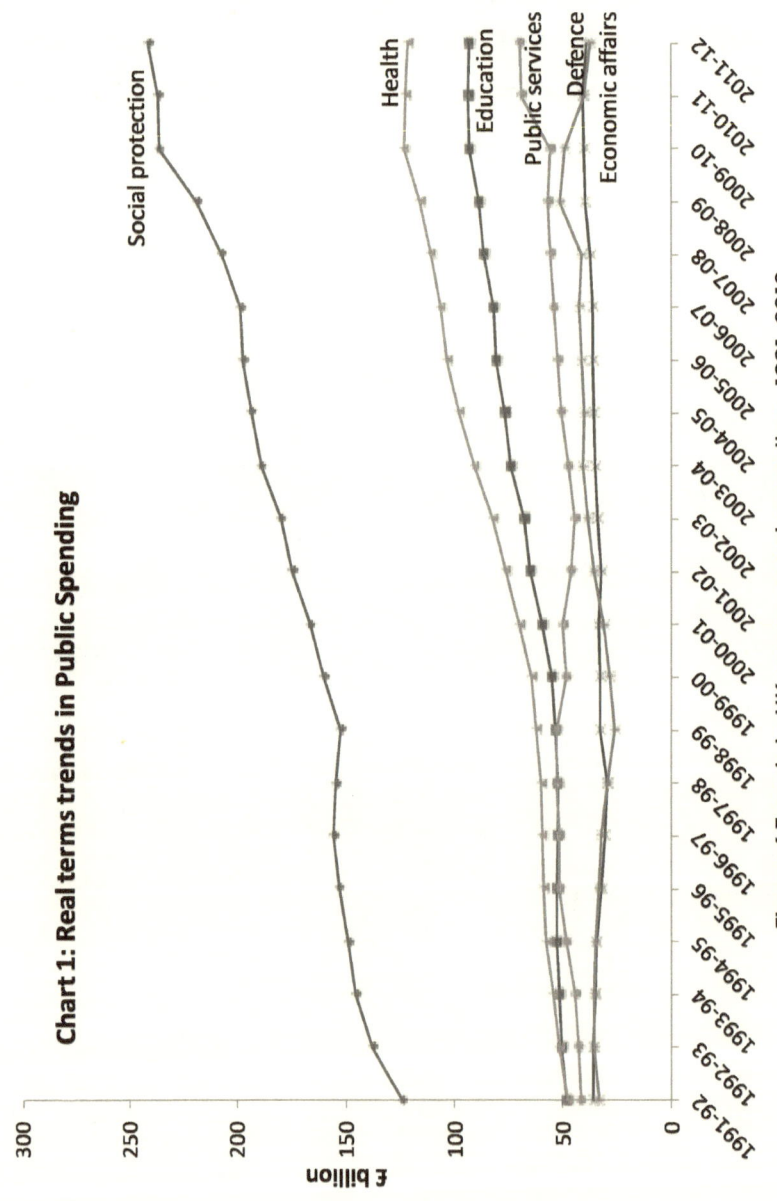

Chart 1: Real terms trends in Public Spending

Social protection

Health

Education

Public services

Defence

Economic affairs

£ billion

300 250 200 150 100 50 0

1991-92 1992-93 1993-94 1994-95 1995-96 1996-97 1997-98 1998-99 1999-00 2000-01 2001-02 2002-03 2003-04 2004-05 2005-06 2006-07 2007-08 2008-09 2009-10 2010-11 2011-12

Figure 6 Trends in UK government spending, 1991–2012

Source: HM Treasury, 'Public Spending Statistics April 2013'

Having said this, we must be careful that where the private sector claims to provide a more efficient service, this does not simply entail a worse or more expensive service for customers. Anyone who has had to renew a passport or visa for the United Kingdom recently will have seen this in action. Essential government services should not be used for revenue generation.

To demonstrate parts of the economy where the government should be involved, it may be useful to look at sectors where the government seems to do a good job and there is popular support from voters. We look at these in the next three chapters.

5.02. Healthcare Policy

Comparing different healthcare systems can be controversial because the results depend on the criteria used. A simple comparison is life expectancy against spending, as in the OECD study in Figure 7. This shows that taxpayer-funded models of healthcare ("Medicaid for all" in US parlance), such as those in Japan and the United Kingdom, demonstrate much better value for money than the free-market insurance system, pre-Obamacare, in the United States. In 2014, the United States–based Washington Fund named the UK National Health Service as the world's best healthcare system.[118] A year earlier, another report, *US Health in International Perspective*, laid bare the failings of the US system.[119]

This result would be expected under economic theory, as healthcare is a market that demonstrates many instances of market failure, the main one being asymmetric information, where healthcare providers have much better information than the typical patient does. In a market-based healthcare system, medical practitioners will often overprescribe procedures, sometimes to cover all the bases for fear of litigation and sometimes just to milk the insurance provider. Those for whom medical insurance is unaffordable do not receive the care they need, often until it is too late. This places large cost pressures on the government-funded hospitals that provide treatment of last resort in the United States, who often receive patients at an advanced stage of illness.

---

[118] Karen Davis, Kristof Stremikis, David Squires, and Cathy Schoen, Mirror, Mirror on the Wall: How the Performance of the U.S. Health Care System Compares Internationally (New York: The Commonwealth Fund, 2014).

[119] Steven H. Woolf and Laudan Y. Aron, U.S. Health in International Perspective (Washington, D.C.: The National Academies Press, 2013).

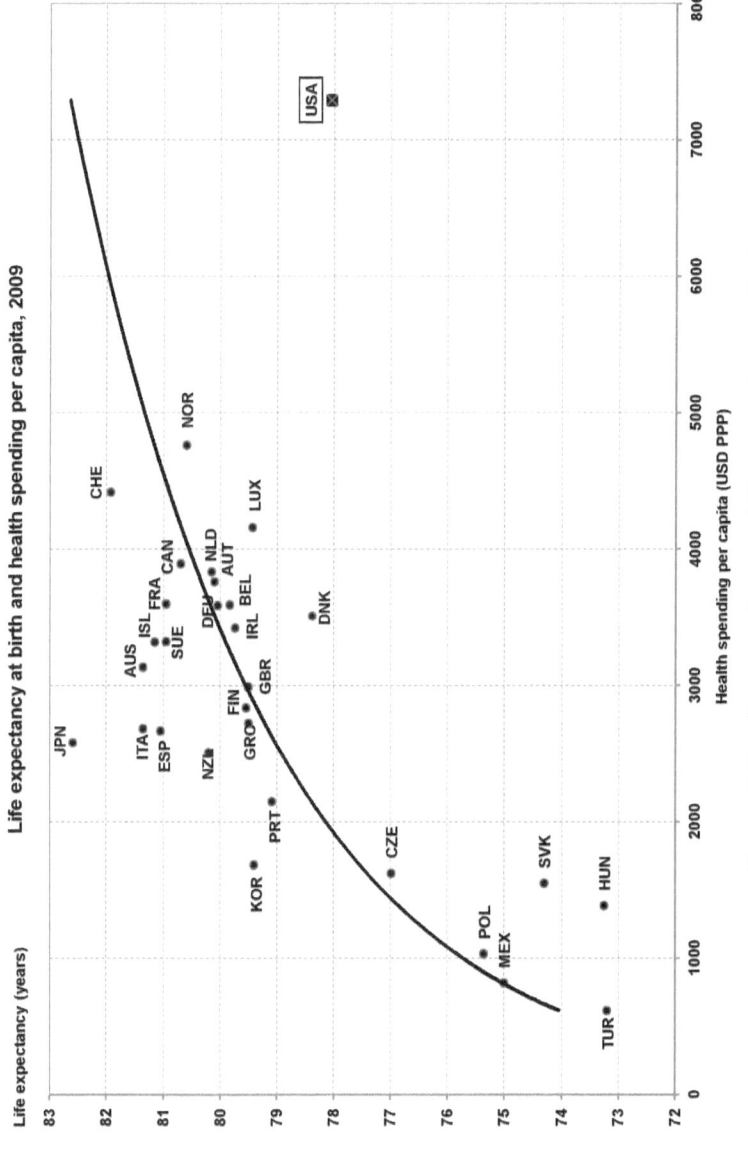

Figure 7 Health spending and life expectancy, 2009
E. P. Anthony, 2016. Data: OECD

The government-run health systems of the United Kingdom, Canada, and Japan are very popular with the majority of the electorate—in 2012, sixty-one percent of those polled in the United Kingdom were satisfied with the NHS.[120] There are obvious positive externalities to the economy of having a healthy workforce. They are universal services, where every household contributes to the system via the tax system, and all citizens can use the service when needed. It is difficult for anyone to overconsume medical services, and there are small copayments on certain items, such as prescription drugs. Bulk purchases by the state can lower the cost of prescription drugs, and a government-run healthcare system can take advantage of the economies of scale of a large insurance pool (the whole population) and can plan resources accordingly. The system is quite redistributive, as the poor tend to fall ill more often, although this is offset somewhat by the fact that the wealthy tend to live longer.

Opponents of single-payer healthcare often try to rebut these arguments by cherry picking certain illnesses, especially cancers, where they say the US system has better outcomes. These outcomes are to be expected for a couple of reasons. Firstly, a system based on ability to pay rather than need will put more resources into illnesses prevalent among wealthier patients, and cancer is that rare illness that is more prevalent in the well-off.[121]

[120] John Appleby, Ruth Robertson, and Eleanor Taylor, British Social Attitudes 32: Health, (London: NatCen Social Research, 2015), http://www.bsa.natcen.ac.uk/media/38925/bsa32_health.pdf.
[121] J. Banks, M. Marmot, Z. Oldfield and J. P. Smith, 'Disease and disadvantage in the United States and in England', Journal of the American Medical Association (2006) 295 (17) pp. 2037-2045

Secondly, the focus amongst opponents of government-run healthcare is often on the survival rates of diseases rather than the mortality rates. Survival rates measure what percentage of people with a disease are still alive a certain number of years after diagnosis. Mortality rates measure the percentage of people that die of that disease. Survival rates can be improved simply by earlier screening, with little influence on mortality rates. For example, in 2001, US women were screened for breast cancer at age forty and in the United Kingdom at age fifty. The five-year survival rate for breast cancer was 8.8 percent better in the United States than in the United Kingdom. However, the mortality rate was only 1.7 percent better. Thus, the superior 'survival' rate in the United States merely reflects that US women were diagnosed with breast cancer earlier than women in the United Kingdom were.[122]

This is not to say that publicly funded universal healthcare does not need to change or can be expanded without limit. It must constantly be reformed to keep up with new developments and changing demographics. Aging populations and the coming obesity crisis will put a huge strain on resources, so increasing copayments or limiting certain treatments will have to be considered. There will need to be a shift of emphasis to preventative measures, such as taxes on sugar, and a focus on quality rather than length of life. This system is, however, a template for policies with redistributive effects that command public support. The concept of universal contribution and access seems fair to the electorate, and the system, by correcting

---

[122] Aaron Carroll, 'Survival Rates Are Not the Same as Mortality Rates', The Incidental Economist, 31 August 2010, http://theincidentaleconomist.com/wordpress/survival-rates-are-not-the-same-as-mortality-rates/.

for market failures, is more efficient than the private-market alternative. The idea that this is a service rather than a cash payment also seems popular, as recipients are not perceived to overconsume or waste the funds. We now look at another area of public policy that has some similar characteristics.

5.03. State Pensions

Otto von Bismarck introduced the world's first state pension in Germany in 1889. It contained numerous elements still seen in many state pensions today, with contributions made by workers out of tax, topped up with contributions from the federal government. Although several other aspects of pension policy differ globally, such as incentives for adding to the pension and differences in how the funds are invested, the principal of a contributory system, coupled with universal, non–means-tested payments upon retirement, mean that state pensions carry popular support in most countries that have them.

Prior to the introduction of state pensions, poverty amongst the old was widespread, as it would no doubt still be in their absence. Financed out of taxation or mandatory social insurance payments that tend to have a progressive structure, state pensions seem highly redistributive. One significant caveat to this is that the wealthy tend to live longer than the poor and so on average will claim more in pension benefits. Life expectancy is increasing for all income groups in the United Kingdom, but the disparity between different income groups is growing.[123] In the United States life expectancy is actually falling for the least-educated whites.[124] This is why simply raising the retirement age as means to save money can be

---

[123] Sabrina Bushe, 'Deprivation, Gender and Health Inequalities in England', New Policy Institute, 26 July 2013, http://npi.org.uk/blog/income-and-poverty/deprivation-gender-and-health-inequalities-england/

[124] Sabrina Tavernise, 'Life Spans Shrink for Least-Educated Whites in the U.S.', The New York Times, September 20, 2012. http://www.nytimes.com/2012/09/21/us/life-expectancy-for-less-educated-whites-in-us-is-shrinking.html?_r=0

quite regressive, as citizens in low-paying manual jobs tend to die much earlier than other groups. If an efficient means of adjusting retirement age according to occupation could be found then this would be a way to save money in a progressive way.

State pensions also benefit from an insurance pooling effect, whereby actuarial mortality statistics for the population as a whole can be used for planning purposes. Individual life assurance policies can be expensive, as the insurance company has to allow for uncertain mortality dates for individuals and make a profit.

In the absence of forced pension saving, people, especially the young, would tend to underinvest in retirement funds. *The Norm Chronicles* by Blastland and Spiegelhalter documents how ineffectively individuals assess risks, especially ones that are far off in time or unlikely.[125] In this sense, state pensions can be seen to correct a market failure of inadequate information and economically irrational behaviour.

Increasing the level of the state pension could be seen as good policy, as it is redistributive and electorally popular because the old vote in large numbers. There are, however, large financial obstacles to doing this. Many advanced economies have a demographic 'time bomb' in the structure of their population. Longer life expectancy coupled with lower birth rates mean that in many developed countries, a smaller working age population is having to fund the pensions of a growing retiree population. Given that the old fall ill more frequently than the young do, this also puts a strain on state healthcare systems. So to increase the state pension above

---

[125] Michael Blastland and D. J. Spiegelhalter, The Norm Chronicles: Stories and Numbers About Danger (London: Profile Books, 2013).

the general level of growth would place a large financial burden on the young, who are already losing out financially to the old.[126] Governments have to become better at long-term demographic management, as this will have a significant effect on inequality in the future. This means having demographically planned policies on birth rates and immigration, which we look at later in chapter 5.15.

Another issue that is coming increasingly to the fore is final-years care for the elderly. Many pensioners live longer but are unable to care for themselves in their final years. Historically their children would take care of them, with the responsibility in many societies falling upon the eldest son or daughter. As societies become richer, the children of the old and infirm seem to be increasingly eschewing this responsibility, which could be a symptom of affluenza, or simply of increased economic mobility, and the burden is falling on the state. Currently many pensioners have to sell or remortgage their properties to pay for their own care. In the United Kingdom, a proposed policy is to cap the amount pensioners spend on their care, which could be seen as a subsidy to wealthier pensioners who live longer. A fairer alternative would be to pay the state pension up to a certain age and then use the monies to fund universal–care home provision for those who want it. Whatever the policy solution is, it will be expensive, which again makes demographic management all the more imperative.

---

[126] David Willetts, 'Pensioners Prosper, the Young Suffer. Britain's Social Contract Is Breaking', *The Guardian*, 24 October 2015, http://www.theguardian.com/commentisfree/2015/oct/24/young-bear-burden-of-pensioner-prosperity.

5.04. National Defence and the Military

Funded through general taxation, this sector of the economy is run almost completely by the government, with little private sector involvement; it employs many from the poorest neighbourhoods in the country and has popular support, especially amongst working-class communities. For those on the left, what's not to like? When it comes to defence, quite a lot it seems. Conversely, the military can do no wrong in the eyes of the right.

The military is an example of a pure public good, as it is nonexcludable—everyone shares in the protection from the military—and inexhaustible in that to protect one extra citizen has effectively zero marginal cost. In economic theory, price should be set to marginal cost, and marginal cost here is zero, so the state needs to provide public goods for free. If these goods were provided privately, we would encounter the 'free-rider' problem, where people who didn't pay for the good would still benefit from it anyway.

Why is military spending often unpopular on the left? There are probably two main reasons: There is an understandable fear that the military will be used in conflicts that are not widely supported, such as the second Iraq War, or that military hardware will be sold to repressive regimes. There is also a concern that military spending will crowd out more important social spending.

These concerns can be overcome through legislation, however. Military intervention can be put to a referendum or a free vote of the legislature, and the legislature can impose export bans on military hardware. As for crowding out other spending, of the major developed economies, only the United States spends much over 2 percent of GDP on the military, and there are probably large positive externalities to having the world's best military.[127] Additionally, there are often positive economic spillovers from research into military technology—the Internet was originally developed by the US military. The military often draws its personnel from poorer neighbourhoods, so there is a redistributive element to defence spending. The officer class, especially in the British military, often comes from the elite schools and universities, so there should be positive discrimination legislation, based on income, to ensure that officers are drawn from poorer communities.

The first job of any government is the defence of its people, and the military is very popular with many of the disaffected former supporters of centre-left parties. NATO has called for its members to allocate 2 percent of GDP to defence spending, and this target should be adhered to, both for its redistributive element and its electoral appeal.[128]

[127] Wikipedia, s.v. 'List of Countries by Military Expenditures', last modified February 2016. https://en.wikipedia.org/wiki/List_of_countries_by_military_expenditures.

[128] North Atlantic Treaty Organisation, 'Wales Summit Declaration', NATO, 5 September 2014, http://www.nato.int/cps/en/natohq/official_texts_112964.htm.

5.05. GDP and Measuring Social Welfare

In information technology, the acronym GIGO stands for 'garbage in, garbage out'. It implies that if the data input to a system is flawed, the results will be similarly flawed. The same acronym could be applied to the use of gross domestic product (GDP) statistics to measure increases in the welfare of society. The evidence in *The Spirit Level* and *Affluenza* suggests that much of the growth in GDP over the past thirty years has been associated with an increase in many social ills, and various surveys of happiness suggest that above a certain level of GDP per head, happiness stops increasing.[129]

GDP is a flawed measure of social welfare for several reasons. As we have already seen, GDP growth that is unequally distributed may actually reduce social welfare. GDP does not measure aspects of life that are important but subjective, such as friendship, community ties, or a pleasant environment. Nonmarket work such as childcare, housekeeping, and community and charity work is similarly ignored. Workers choosing to take more leisure time, as opposed to being forcefully unemployed, will be negative for GDP, when in reality the worker presumably feels better off. GDP tends to favour the short term at the expense of the long term. Depleting natural resources boosts GDP, whereas welfare has really increased only if those resources were previously unextractable, if they can now be used more efficiently, or if they can be sold at a

---

[129] Gerald Guild. 'Happiness as Measured by GDP: Really?'.. Gerald Guild. 23 May 2012. http://geraldguild.com/blog/index.php?s=gdp+and+gpi+growth.

higher price than before. Most importantly, GDP ignores the long-term environmental consequences of actions.[130]

Alternative measures to GDP have been suggested, two of the more practical of which are the index of sustainable economic welfare (ISEW) and the genuine progress indicator (GPI). Both measures make monetary adjustments to the traditional GDP measure to compensate for some of its flaws.[131] Nonmarket work such as childcare is included, while the future costs of current production and consumption, such as resource depletion and pollution, are deducted. Increased income inequality has a negative effect on the reading. GPI is a broader measure that includes adjustments for leisure time and criminality. Even broader measures exist such as green GDP, genuine savings (GS), and the nonmonetary human development index (HDI) calculated by the UN.[132]

We should move away from using GDP as a measure of social welfare but in the short run it is probably more practical and politically feasible to move to a narrower measure of social progress, such as ISEW or GPI. If there is too much detachment of the new statistic from the traditional GDP measure of growth, the new metric could seem meaningless or unrepresentative to many. For this reason, it is important the figures be compiled by a body independent from the

[130] Mijin Cha, 'What's Missing from GDP?' Demos, 29 January 2013, http://www.demos.org/publication/whats-missing-gdp.

[131] Tejvan Pettinger, 'Genuine Progress Indicator GPI v GDP', Economics Help, 22 February 2011, http://www.economicshelp.org/blog/2666/economics/genuine-progress-indicator-gpi-v-gdp/.

[132] A. B. Atkinson, Atkinson Review: Final Report: Measurement of Government Output and Productivity for the National Accounts (Basingstoke: Palgrave Macmillan, 2005).

government. Also, at the moment, it tends to be parties of the right who try to use accounting tricks or gut the statistical departments of government. In the United Kingdom, cuts to items such as flood defences and tax inspectors are used to 'reduce' debts levels without recognition of the long-term costs. In the United States, the Republicans are attempting to corrupt the independent Congressional Budget Office by forcing it to codify trickle-down economics into their results by using a measure called dynamic scoring.

A criticism of these newer measures of growth and social welfare is that the adjustment for income inequality implies hidden preferences, so the adjustment for inequality must be explicit and calculated independently. As more research is done on the link between social wellbeing and inequality, the explicit metric can be adjusted, but we should begin with a conservative measure until the results of research begin to come in and until the preferences of the electorate between growth and inequality are better understood.

Figure 8 shows US GDP and GPI over fifty-four years since 1950. Note that from the late 1970s, GDP and GPI begin to diverge. The main reasons for this divergence are a fall in non-market activities, especially childcare, as more women entered the labour force, and increased inequality, resource depletion, and environmental damage. The ISEW measure shows a similar pattern. Note that the graph displays GDP and GPI on a per capita basis. This is important, as the headline level of GDP or GPI can be boosted simply by increased immigration.

Therefore, what seems like a technical change to the measurement of growth can have huge consequences and can help resolve some of the tensions and contradictions in policy discussed previously. The trade-off between the growth de-manded by poorer working-class communities and the environmental damage feared by green activists can be calculated, and policies can be geared to more sustainable sectors of the economy. GDP-reducing decisions such as workers taking more leisure time or a parent taking time off to raise a child could be welfare enhancing under ISEW or GPI due to increased nonmarket benefits.[133]

[133] Nick Hanauer and Eric Beinhocker, 'Capatilism Redefined', Democracy, Winter 2014, http://democracyjournal.org/magazine/31/capitalism-redefined/

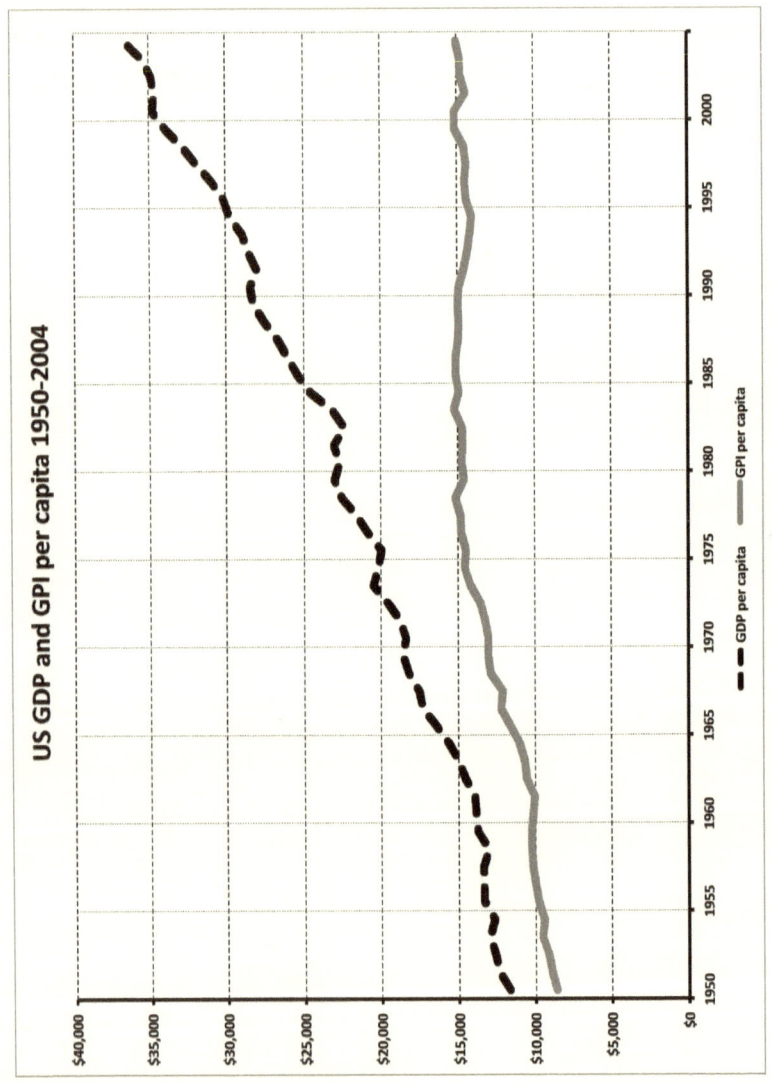

Figure 8 GDP and GPI, United States, 1950–2004
E. P. Anthony, 2016. Data: Redefining Progress

Producing an explicit trade-off between growth and inequality gives us a framework within which to construct policy to maximise that trade off, and calculating the present value of the long-term costs and benefits of policies will let us avoid false economies, such as defunding tax collection agencies, while encouraging investment and research. It also sets up a framework where the costs and benefits of immigration can be weighed, and, crucially, immigration that uses resources and drives down wages at the bottom of the income scale may be rejected under these new measures of social welfare.

Correcting the flawed measure of GDP leads to improved policy. As another example, tighter fishing quotas, which would depress traditional GDP, would likely increase ISEW or GPI, which take into account the long-term environmental effects of the policy. This is also an example, however, of why we do not want welfare measures that stray too far from GDP. The fishermen affected by the tighter quotas will be worse off in the short term, while the benefits of this policy may not accrue for years. To focus too strongly on the long-term will likely come at a political cost, and it runs the risk of the long-run models being overoptimistic. This is why we should begin with incremental change in the measure of social welfare away from GDP and more conservative inputs for the inequality and long-term environmental adjustments to GDP. As the new measures become accepted, we can adjust the models to be more aggressive in their focus on inequality, the environment, and the long term.

5.06. Productivity and Growth

There are two ways to increase output and, therefore, growth in a country. Given that output is the product of working-age population and the average output per worker, we can increase either the population or the productivity of the average worker. We study the latter option in this chapter.

The study of productivity in economics is the equivalent of Fermat's last theorem in mathematics, with the key difference that Fermat's last theorem has been solved. Many economists have studied productivity over the years, but no single key factor has been identified, and these studies often veer into the realms of anthropology and sociology. For most of the last 100 years, the United Kingdom's productivity has been disappointing, especially so since the 2008 crash; thus, many of the studies focus on the UK economy.

Ray Dalio, the founder of Bridgewater Associates, one of the world's largest and most successful hedge funds, has produced one interesting recent study. His model of the 'economic machine' is unusual because it appears to be a synthesis of the theories of Keynes, Minsky, and supply-side economics.[134] Within the study, there is extensive research on the drivers of productivity for major economies going back over one hundred years. We can use these studies of productivity and cherry pick the policies that enhance growth in an equitable and sustainable way. It is still vital to increase productivity and growth where possible, as Piketty shows that in the long

---

[134] Ray Dalio, 'How the Economic Machine Works', Economic Principles video, 30:59, 2015, http://www.economicprinciples.org/.

run growth must be higher than the return on capital (*g>r*) for inequality to fall.

In nearly all studies of productivity, improving the education and skills of workers comes close to the top of recommendations. Dalio points out that most of the competition globally is between workers educated below college level, so this is where most of the resources should be concentrated. Increasing resources for technical colleges and apprenticeship schemes for low- to middle-skilled workers will help to increase productivity and reduce inequality simultaneously.

Most studies also focus on the benefits of innovation. Professor Jonathan Haskel of Imperial College London claims there is a rate of return of around 20 percent on basic scientific research in the United Kingdom.[135] He suggests that governments simply spend more directly in grants for scientific research, especially for those in partnership with the private sector. Low research and development spending in the private sector of the United Kingdom has been cited as a factor in the country's productivity deficit.[136] Firms generally finance long-term investment and research out of profits and equity capital, so shifting corporate tax breaks away from debt and towards equity should help to encourage innovation and growth.

Increasing innovation and research would seem to imply increased spending on education at the university level. As we have already recommended improving education below

[135] Tim Harford, 'The Economists' Manifesto', *Financial Times*, 17 April 2015, http://www.ft.com/intl/cms/s/2/7da2852c-e3af-11e4-9a82-00144feab7de.html.

[136] Anna Valero and Isabelle Roland, Productivity and Business Policies (London: LSE Centre for Economic Performance, 2015).

degree level, this would seem to suggest an across-the-board rise in education spending. In constrained economic times, this may not be feasible. We examine how to resolve the conflict between school and university spending in chapter 5.10 on education.

A third area in which there is general agreement in studies of productivity is that increased investment in capital and infrastructure improves productivity over the long term. It is obvious how poor transport and energy networks and insufficient housing can slow the productive potential of an economy. Dalio emphasises that this investment must be wisely spent, however, and that much of the infrastructure spending by the Japanese government in the 1990s did not seem to have many productivity benefits. To ensure investments produce a good return, Professor John Van Reenen of the London School of Economics argues that an independent infrastructure strategy board (ISB) should develop investment strategies, and a planning commission should implement them.[137] This board would be independent, but the legislature would approve its members, in the same way members of monetary policy boards often are. The UK government created an ISB in 2015, though with a major flaw, which we look at in the next chapter on stabilisation policy.

There are two potential problems with increased infrastructure and capital spending. Firstly, large infrastructure projects can have a negative adverse environmental effect in the short term. Generally, however, they will have large long-term

---

[137] John Van Reenen, 'Profiting from Productivity: Ensuring investment and productivity growth feed through to wages', 30/03/2015, Resolution Foundation, http://immersive.sh/resolutionfoundation/3CNr4MvOb

environmental as well as productivity benefits and will increase employment, which can reduce inequality. The new measure of economic welfare outlined previously will be able to assess this objectively. Secondly, infrastructure spending is an easy target when reducing budget deficits, as the costs are immediate and the benefits longer term. We actually want to reverse this tendency, and we examine how and why to do this in the next chapter.

5.07. Stabilisation Policy

Probably the most damaging aspect of recessions is the associated rise in unemployment. Obviously, this has negative implications for inequality in the short term, as large numbers of workers suffer large drops in income. There is also the longer-term problem of hysteresis discussed previously, with pockets of long-term unemployed workers finding that their skills atrophy. Depressions lead economies into an even worse long-term equilibrium, as there is not only mass unemployment but also a loss of business and consumer confidence, such that employers and consumers delay purchases for fear of further economic contraction and due to the belief that goods and services will be cheaper in the future due to deflation.

Recessions must be avoided if possible, and when they happen, any rise in unemployment must be minimised. The government should commit itself to a policy of full employment where everyone who wants a job has one and, crucially, people work all the hours they want. A recent phenomenon is that of underemployment where many part-time and self-employed workers would like to work more hours if they were available, or where skilled workers are stuck in low skilled work.[138] The government and monetary authorities should focus on a measure of unemployment that includes these workers.

---

[138] David,Bell and David Blanchflower. 'Quarter 3 2013 Underemployment'. *Underemployment*. 10 February 2014. https://bellblanchflowerunderemployment. wordpress.com/2014/02/10/quarter-3-2014-data/.

5.07.1. Monetary Policy

Since the early 1980s many governments have relied on monetary policy, through the adjustment of interest rates to hit an inflation target, as the main lever of macroeconomic and stabilisation policy, often with policy set by an independent central bank. What is the mechanism by which interest rates stabilise the economy? The main channels are through the different effects of interest rates on debtors and creditors and by the effect on business confidence and investment. In a recession, inflation usually falls, and the central bank reacts by cutting interest rates. Debtors benefit through lower interest payments giving them more disposable income, and creditors lose out, possibly forcing them out of investments in safe assets such as cash and bonds and into riskier assets. Both these effects should boost the economy. In reality, the biggest effect in most developed economies comes through the housing market, which is usually the largest debt item of middle-income households.

What are the potential problems of leaning mostly on monetary policy for economic stabilisation? An obvious one is that monetary policy is a blunt and slow instrument for reducing unemployment. It relies on lower interest payments on mortgages to feed into consumer confidence and spending and then cycle back into business expansion and job creation. This can take a long time, and the regions with high unemployment are often not areas with large numbers of homeowners, thus creating or exacerbating a mismatch between poorer high-unemployment areas and wealthier areas that benefit from increased house values.

A second problem touched on above is that monetary policy has distributional implications. Most creditors are wealthy and most debtors are poor, but there are significant and important exceptions to this. The very poorest in society do not own their houses and often have little debt, although those who do tend to be charged usurious interest on it.[139] For someone paying 20 percent per annum on a credit card, a 0.25 percent cut in the central bank rate is not going to help much. The second-round effects of the interest rate cut may help to alleviate unemployment for this sector over the medium term, but in the meantime, the wealth gap between middle-income homeowners and poorer renters will increase. On the creditor side, lower interest rates can hurt pensioners with savings but no housing assets. These distributional questions are an even greater concern under the recent policy of quantitative easing (QE), where central banks print large amounts of money at zero interest rates. While these policies have probably stabilised the housing markets and the economy in the short term, it is argued that many of these funds have flowed into financial assets held mostly by the very wealthy, thus increasing inequality.[140]

The third criticism of relying mostly on monetary policy to target inflation is that it actually leads to economic instability in the long term. Martin Wolf suggests policymakers have conflated price stability with economic stability, whereas the

[139] Frederick Wherry, 'Payday Loans Cost the Poor Billions, and There's an Easy Fix', *The New York Times*, OCT. 29, 2015 http://www.nytimes.com/2015/10/29/opinion/payday-loans-cost-the-poor-billions-and-theres-an-easy-fix.html?_r=0
[140] Claire Jones, 'Did QE only boost the price of Warhols?', *Financial Times*, October 18, 2013. http://www.ft.com/intl/cms/s/0/6f219ba8-327d-11e3-91d2-00144feab7de.html#axzz43tinrFJf

current global monetary framework has created huge imbalances in the world economy and large, unstable capital flows.[141] During the Great Moderation of the 1990s, growth was strong but inflation was subdued, which allowed interest rates to be kept low, sowing the seeds for the housing crash in 2008.

Michal Kalecki foresaw the potential problems of relying on inducing private investment for stabilisation policy in his 1943 paper 'Political Aspects of Full Employment':

> The rate of interest or income tax is reduced in a slump but *not* increased in the subsequent boom. In this case the boom will last longer but it must end in a new slump: one reduction in the rate of interest or income tax does not, of course, eliminate the forces which cause cyclical fluctuations in a capitalist economy. In the new slump it will be necessary to reduce the rate of interest or income tax again and so on. Thus in the not too remote a time the rate of interest would have to be negative and income tax would have to be replaced by an income subsidy.[142]

We see this result today, with negative interest rates in Europe and Japan, and earned income tax credits in the United Kingdom and United States.

[141] Martin Wolf, The Shifts and the Shocks: What We've Learned—and Still Have to Learn—from the Financial Crisis (London: Penguin Books, 2015).
[142] Michal Kalecki, 'Political Aspects of Full Employment', Political Quarterly, 1943.

For these reasons, we need to reintroduce fiscal policy into the toolbox of stabilisation policy. There already is some degree of fiscal adjustment during recessions through the 'automatic stabilisers' of increased spending on unemployment benefits and reduced tax revenues, which swing the government budget naturally towards deficit. Nevertheless, fiscal policy should be even more countercyclical, and we discuss how below in section 5.07.2..

As for monetary policy, there have been several suggestions in response to the 2008 financial crisis. To avoid deflation, it has been suggested that central banks should have a higher inflation target, say 4 percent instead of 2 percent. Then, if there is a large negative shock to the economy, there is a larger margin before we reach deflation. A concern with this idea is that it implies that interest rates would have been even lower during the Great Moderation and the associated imbalances even larger. Another suggestion is that the central bank should target nominal GDP (NGDP) growth instead of inflation.[143] This is essentially a combined growth and inflation target. If we think the long-term potential growth rate of an economy is 2 percent and the target rate for inflation is 2 percent, then the authorities would target 4 percent NGDP growth. During the Great Moderation, when growth was well above trend and inflation slightly below, this implies interest rates may have been slightly higher than otherwise, possibly reducing some of the overexuberance during that time. After the 2008 crash, targeting NGDP would have implied faster and

[143] Simon Wren-Lewis, 'The UK as a test case for NGDP targets', Mainly Macro, 7 September 2015, http://mainlymacro.blogspot.sg/2015/09/the-uk-as-test-case-for-ngdp-targets.html

deeper cuts in interest rates. This is an interesting idea, but a relatively new and untested one that requires more analysis.

In the meantime, a simple dual mandate, like the Federal Reserve has in the United States, should be instituted. The central bank could be tasked to maintain growth and price stability in that order of priority. For those concerned about deflation or high inflation, a constraint of 1 percent to 5 percent for inflation could be added to the mandate. This broad mandate gives the central bank lots of room to optimise policy rather than having to hit an arbitrary inflation target that does not stabilise the economy in the long term anyway. As Keynes said, 'It is better to be roughly right than precisely wrong'. The prioritisation of growth over inflation has an inequality reducing bias. To ensure long-term economic stability, the central bank would have macroprudential tools that could target specific imbalances in the economy without the need to adjust interest rates. Macroprudential regulation is no panacea, however, and it is better to target financial instability at its source; we examine this in chapter 5.14 on corporate policy and the financial sector.

5.07.2. Fiscal Policy

We wish fiscal policy to be more countercyclical than it is currently, where we only have the automatic stabilisers of increased welfare spending and reduced tax revenues. How much more countercyclical we want it to be and how this should be implemented are questions we hope to answer now.

One countercyclical measure was introduced implicitly in the last chapter. The infrastructure strategy board (ISB) studies which long-term investments generate a suitable return relative to the funding costs. In a recession, interest rates usually fall, reducing funding costs, which should make more projects viable (although maybe some of the projected returns will fall also). Thus, more infrastructure investments will be made during economic downturns when they are cheap to implement and fewer during boom times when they are expensive. This is as it should be, but, unfortunately, it is the reverse of what actually occurs at the moment. We can, and should, make this even more countercyclical by requiring a greater margin of return on investments during booms and a lower return during slumps. This infrastructure spending reduces inequality by increasing employment during slumps, and the infrastructure itself produces a long-term flow of returns that benefit the economy. For the same reasons, extra tax breaks for capital investment should be given to private-sector firms during downturns.

What this will entail is larger swings in budget deficit than is currently typical. The European Union, in one of many policy errors, has a strict budget deficit constraint of 3 percent of GDP, and the measures suggested here will sometimes involve deficits and surpluses greater than that. We saw in chapter 2.13 why austerity during a downturn is self-defeating. Nevertheless, if the government runs a deficit of greater than 3 percent, we would still no doubt hear commentary involving the comparison of government debt to household debt, and statements to the effect of 'you cannot replace debt with debt'. This is an economically illiterate point of view. In a downturn, interest rates fall, but debt-laden households and businesses are constrained, with no one willing to lend to them. Meanwhile, investors want to lend to the government by purchasing government bonds because they are seen as safe assets, and this is exactly the time the government should borrow to invest. By doing so, the government increases its debt, but the increased economic activity allows the private sector to pay down its debts. In this case, we have successfully replaced one type of debt with another.[144]

The main problem with this approach is that there is scepticism amongst the electorate that the government will generate an equivalent surplus during a boom. For this reason, Jonathan Portes and Simon Wren-Lewis suggest explicit fiscal policy rules overseen by an independent fiscal council.[145] The fiscal council would decide what stage of the cycle the economy is at and set a budget surplus or deficit accordingly to hit a medium-term debt target. These budget targets would be for current spending or spending excluding investment. George Osborne, the former UK chancellor, has suggested something similar, although he has perversely included investment spending in the deficit target, exactly the opposite of what optimal policy would suggest.

Historically, government finance heads did have control over both fiscal and monetary policy, but the ability to set interest rates was given to independent central banks to stop political considerations trumping economic ones and interest

---

[144] James Montier, 'Market Macro Myths: Debts, Deficits, and Delusions', GMO, January 2016, https://www.gmo.com/docs/default-source/research-and-commentary/strategies/asset-allocation/market-macro-myths-debts-deficits-and-delusions.pdf?sfvrsn=2.

[145] J. Portes and Simon Wren-Lewis, Issues in the Design of Fiscal Policy Rules (London: NIESR, 2014), http://www.niesr.ac.uk/sites/default/files/publications/dp429.pdf.

rates being set too low, resulting in higher inflation. Fiscal policy seems similarly manipulated currently, with finance secretaries loosening policy just before elections and tightening it just after. With fiscal and monetary policy now in the hands of independent but legislatively approved bodies, they can coordinate to optimise policy. This is especially important in periods of stagflation or periods of very high inflation, where in the absence of coordination, fiscal and monetary policy could work against each other; and in depressions, where fiscal and monetary policy should complement each other.

Fiscal as well as monetary policy should have the goal of full employment. If during a recession the increased investment by the ISB does not fulfil that goal, then direct action should be taken. Professor Anthony Atkinson, in his book *Inequality*, suggests the government should be the employer of last resort by offering jobs, retraining, or education to the unemployed on a voluntary basis.[146] There are two concerns about the political viability of this policy. The voluntary aspect of the scheme goes against the framework of universal contributions, universal benefits, and universal responsibility that the voting public favour. The idea that a job or training is available to someone but they turn it down in favour of benefits would strike many voters, rightly, as unjust. The scheme should be made mandatory.

The idea of the government directly creating jobs is also unpopular in surveys. Voters believe that many of these jobs would be unproductive and are therefore essentially make-work schemes. The funds would be better used directly

---

[146] A. B. Atkinson, Inequality: What Can Be Done? (Cambridge, Mass.: Harvard University Press, 2015), ch.5.

subsidising wages for employers that hire unemployed workers in the private sector. There is a risk here of a deadweight loss, where employers who were going to hire anyway receive a windfall gain in the form of the subsidy, but this is outweighed by the efficiency gains from the fact that the most productive firms are the ones that will take up the subsidy. Subsidies can be used on a long-term basis or regional basis to reduce pockets of long-term unemployment. We look at this policy in more detail in chapter 5.09 on welfare and wage subsidies.

5.08. Tax Policy

In this section we discuss taxes in general terms. Countries have different funding requirements and different cultural attitudes towards certain taxes, so it would be pointless to recommend specific tax rates and allowances here. Instead, we begin by examining the general principles of an efficient tax system.

Neutrality

Taxes should not discriminate for or against any economic choice. An obvious exception here is for 'sin taxes', where we wish to skew incentives away from harmful activities such as smoking and polluting.

Efficiency

The cost of paying the tax and the cost of collecting the tax should be small relative to the revenue raised.

Simplicity

The average taxpayer should easily understand the tax system. Most modern tax systems fail on this metric. One exception here is Singapore, where most taxpayers' personal income tax can be completed online in ten minutes. Historically some thought that a complex and opaque tax code favoured larger tax revenues and larger government. The reverse is now the case.

In a complex system, taxpayers lose sight of the connection between their taxes and the services they fund, and the principle of universality is undermined. In such a system, people fear they will be liable for taxes that in reality will have no effect on them, and opponents of those taxes can play upon these fears. In the United States for example, estate taxes paid by a tiny percentage of the richest taxpayers upon their death have been called 'death taxes' by the political right and used to frighten moderate-income families into thinking they also could be liable for them. In the recent UK election, some minimum wage voters were concerned by the Labour Party's proposal to raise the top rate of income tax to 50 percent. They thought either, incorrectly, that the tax would affect them or that the overall principal of 50 percent tax was unfair.

At the other end of the income scale, complexity encourages aggressive tax management by the superwealthy, who can afford to pay for tax advisors to minimise their tax liabilities and exploit any loopholes the complex tax system throws up. In the twenty-first century, a simple tax system can help to reduce inequality by strengthening the link between taxes and services and reducing avoidance.

Effectiveness and Fairness

Double taxation should be avoided where possible. In broad terms, this may be difficult, as income and consumption are both taxed, and it is likely that some taxed income will be taxed again when making a purchase of a good or service. However, it should be avoided for specific items. For example, if housing is taxed locally, it should not be taxed again nationally via a wealth tax, for example. This was one criticism of the Labour Party proposal for a 'mansion tax' during the 2015 UK election. Just as importantly, there should not be unintended nontaxation.

Horizontal Equity

Taxpayers in similar circumstances should pay a similar amount of tax. Again, most tax systems fail on this count, as income from different sources are taxed differently.

Vertical Equity

This is a subjective measure describing how progressive the tax system should be. If we wish to reduce inequality, we should wish the tax code to be strongly progressive, though the degree of progressivity is clearly a subject for debate. One thing is certain, however, and this is that regressive taxation should be avoided at all costs. Famously, during the 2014 US presidential election, it emerged that billionaires Mitt Romney and Warren Buffett paid a much lower tax rate than the average taxpayer because most of their incomes were derived from investments.[147] In the United Kingdom, the local council tax, used to fund local services and based on property values,

---

[147] Pat Garofalo, 'Buffett On Why Romney Should Pay Higher Taxes: He's Just 'Shoving Around Money,' Not 'Straining His Back", thinkprogress, JAN 23, 2012. http://think-progress.org/economy/2012/01/23/409332/buffett-romney-money-shoving/

is a regressive tax, as the more valuable the property is, the smaller the percentage charge against it.[148]

5.08.1. A Holistic Tax System

Now that we have established the principles of taxation, let us examine how existing tax systems stack up against these measures and our goal of reducing inequality. We examine taxes on companies in chapter 5.14 on corporate policy.

Figure 9 shows the sources of tax revenues in the United Kingdom for 2014. It can be seen that the majority of revenue comes from taxes on work income, consisting of income tax plus NIC (National Insurance contributions). Another large percentage comes from taxes on goods and services in the form of VAT (value-added tax), sin taxes on alcohol and to-bacco, and fuel duties. In the United Kingdom in 2015-16, seventy-one percent of tax revenue came from income and consumption. Other developed economies are similar but with a different mix between income and consumption taxes. Contrast this with the amount raised by taxes on property (council tax, 5 percent) and capital gains (1 percent). We saw earlier that the top 1 percent earn most of their income through investments in financial instruments and capital gains, and the top 10 percent often earn income from property. To reduce inequality and to increase fairness in the tax system, we need to skew taxes more towards capital and property.

---

[148] Thomas Pope and Barra Roantree, 'A Survey of the UK Tax System', Institute for Fiscal Studies, November 2014, ch.3.9

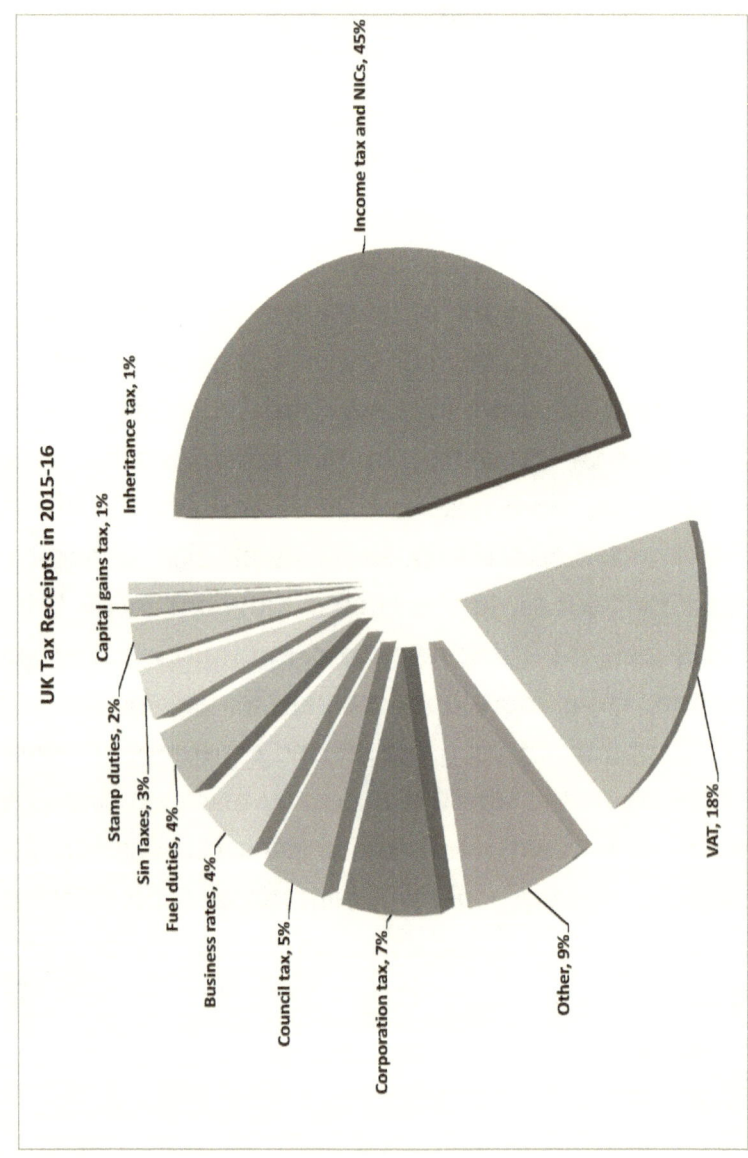

UK Tax Receipts in 2015-16

Income tax and NICs, 45%

Inheritance tax, 1%

Capital gains tax, 1%

Stamp duties, 2%

Sin Taxes, 3%

Fuel duties, 4%

Business rates, 4%

Council tax, 5%

Corporation tax, 7%

Other, 9%

VAT, 18%

Figure 9 Composition of UK tax revenue, 2015-16
E. P. Anthony, 2016. Data: Office for Budget Responsibility

5.08.2. Taxes on Income

In many tax regimes there is a separation of income taxes and social security taxes that are earmarked for specific benefits, such as pensions and unemployment insurance. Over the years, the link between the specific taxes, such as NICs in the United Kingdom, and benefits has been broken, in that the tax revenue is not ring-fenced or earmarked for specific benefits. In the United Kingdom, the combination of these two separate tax systems has kicked up some very strange marginal tax rates at various points on the income scale, and some employees avoid paying NICs altogether.[149] These two taxes should be combined into a single simplified income tax.

To fulfil the tax principles of neutrality and horizontal equity, all forms of income should be treated equally. At the moment, income from capital and certain gifts and inheritances are treated more favourably. There may be a good reason for this in certain circumstances, which we look at below, but in general, all income should be taxed at the same rates. As for the structure and level of income taxes, there should a simple and generous tax allowance for individuals, meaning that low-paid workers would earn a lot of tax-free income. The tax system should always incentivise work over claiming benefits, and having a large tax-free allowance helps to do this while helping to minimise the incidence of any poverty trap, which we study in the next chapter. Most other tax allowances should be limited, as they favour mostly the wealthy. There

[149] Richard Dyson, ; The chart that shows there are 12 rates of income tax', *The Telegraph*, 07 jul 2015. http://www.telegraph.co.uk/finance/personalfinance/tax/11544301/The-chart-that-shows-there-are-12-rates-of-income-tax.html

should then be a standard rate of tax as well as an upper rate that applies to the top 10 percent or so of income earners.

Where should the top rate of tax be? Anthony Atkinson suggests a 65 percent rate, close to the peak of the Laffer curve, the optimal rate to maximise revenue, in some economic papers.[150] Evidence suggests a lower rate for several reasons. Firstly, we noted earlier that the recent 75 percent top rate of income tax in France was not successful politically nor did it raise much revenue. Secondly, as argued earlier, many taxpayers, even less wealthy ones, would view rates of over 50 percent as government requisitioning. Lastly, it is frequently pointed out, correctly, that many of the current superwealthy, especially in the United States, did not come from privileged backgrounds. High marginal rates of tax on income can be seen as a form of economic trawler fishing where you capture the financiers and other rentiers but also cause a lot of damage by taxing genuine entrepreneurs and other professions. It is better to target the rentiers directly through changes to financial sector regulations and specific taxes on rent-seeking activity, such as the land value tax.

Conversely, the case for very low marginal top rates of income tax is weak also. As discussed previously, the Laffer curve almost certainly peaks above 40 percent, even in the longer term. In response to the argument that higher rates of tax would curtail entrepreneurial activity, Warren Buffet said, 'Maybe you'll run into someone with a terrific investment idea, who won't go forward with it because of the tax he would

---

[150] Atkinson, Inequality, ch.7.

owe when it succeeds. Send him my way. Let me unburden him'.[151]

Therefore, the top rate of tax on income should be somewhere between 40 percent and 50 percent and should kick in at a level of income linked to a multiple of the median wage income. Currently, three times the median wage income would mean the top 10 percent to 15 percent of households pay the higher rate on some of their income in the United States and United Kingdom. Linking this top-rate level to the median wage gives everyone an interest in seeing median wages rise. At the bottom, there should be a tax-free allowance up to the point of the minimum wage income, and then a low initial rate of tax up to the income of someone being paid the living wage, so that everyone in employment is contributing to the system. The main rate of tax can then be set at a level to raise the requisite amount of revenue.

5.08.3. Taxes on Property and Land

The wealth of the top 10 percent is often held in the form of property, and the very richest are often significant landowners.[152] To reduce inequality, the burden of taxation needs to be shifted towards land and property. Land value taxation (LVT) has been supported historically by economists, even free-market advocates such as Adam Smith and Milton Friedman, as one of the best forms of taxation. This is because LVT taxes pure

---

[151] Warren E. Buffet, 'A Minimum Tax for the Wealthy', *The New York Times*, Nov 25, 2012. http://www.nytimes.com/2012/11/26/opinion/buffett-a-minimum-tax-for-the-wealthy.html

[152] Piketty, Capital in the Twenty-First Century.

rentier income and does not distort decision-making, as the amount of land is fixed and land rent prices depend upon demand, so the burden of the tax falls entirely on the landowner. The tax can encourage the development of underutilised land, as it would be expensive for the landowner to leave it idle.

Property taxes are an efficient tax from a collection perspective, as houses are difficult assets to move or hide. Taxes can be levied at a certain percentage of the latest valuation of the property, and properties should be revalued regularly, possibly concurrently with census collections. As discussed above, property wealth is usually correlated to income, so taxing property tends to be redistributive. However, allowances need to be made in the form of discounts for householders who are income poor, such as pensioners and the temporarily unemployed.

One issue with taxing property is that properties can be very expensive in and around large, wealthy cities and generally very cheap in rural areas or in towns and cities that have fallen on hard times. If property were taxed nationally, we would face the situation of poorer homeowners in rich cities facing very large property tax bills, while wealthy owners in rural areas would pay little. In addition, those living in rich cities tend to have higher living costs than those elsewhere. For this reason, it is better for property taxes to be implemented as a local or regional tax to fund local services.

5.08.4. Taxes on Capital

We stated above that all income should be treated equally. In practice, capital gains, the realised profit when an asset is sold, are often treated more favourably. One argument for this is that inflation can increase the nominal value of an asset without increasing its real value, and it is unfair to tax this inflation gain. This objection is easily overcome, however, by indexing the asset to inflation and only taxing the real gain. The main argument for lower capital gains taxes is that they encourage saving and entrepreneurship and therefore boost economic activity.

The empirical evidence for these effects is weak.[153] Many capital gains are from speculative investments in shares or property that are not entrepreneurial. Owning Apple shares does not mean you had a hand in developing the iPhone. As for encouraging saving, we do indeed wish to do this, but for the poorer taxpayers who currently save too little and not the wealthier ones who already save a much greater share of their income. Additionally, from Piketty we know that the very wealthy generate most of their income from capital and that this trend is likely to strengthen. So from the perspective of encouraging saving and reducing inequality, it is preferable to treat capital gains the same as other income and to have a large tax-free allowance rather than lower marginal tax rates This is precisely the tax regime we describe above.

J. E. Meade in the 1950s and James Kwak more recently proposed overhauls of the system of taxation of capital gains. Meade proposed adjusting the tax rate according to the recipient's lifetime inheritance income[154]; Kwak proposes a ret-

---

[153] James Kwak, 'Reducing Inequality with a Retrospective Tax on Capital', Cornell Journal of Law and Public Policy (forthcoming), published electronically 18 May 2015, p.30. http://papers.ssrn.com/sol3/pazumpers.cfm?abstract_id=2607699.
[154] Meade, Efficiency, Equality and the Ownership of Property.

rospective tax on capital which would tax only the risk-free return on capital.[155] While desirable in reducing inequality and encouraging entrepreneurship respectively, both suffer from complexity and a large administrative burden. We do indeed want to encourage true risk-taking behaviour, but we can do this in a more simple and binary manner. Individuals who start their own enterprises and investors in start-up or ethical businesses should be subject to a lower rate of tax on disposal of these assets.

A possible objection to such a scheme is that tax is levied only on disposal of assets or on death, and as such, individuals can accumulate large capital gains during their lifetimes without paying any tax on these assets. For this reason, some people would prefer to implement an annual wealth tax. Such a tax could be administratively burdensome and could lead to capital flight, as assets are taxed even if they do not appreciate. We can accept individuals accumulating wealth over their lifetimes if they cannot use that wealth to influence the political process and if upon death the assets are taxed so intergenerational inequality is reduced.

5.08.5. Inheritance Taxes

Taxes on inheritances can be an emotive subject. However, they are one of the most important taxes if we are to reduce inequality and level the playing field for each subsequent generation. For this reason, inheritances and gifts (large transfers before death) should be treated equally with other income.

---

[155] Kwak, 'Reducing Inequality with a Retrospective Tax on Capital'

Historically, large tax-free allowances have been made for primary residences and even larger allowances for farms and family businesses due to the emotional bond families feel for the family house or business. It is unfair however, from a horizontal equity position, that farms and businesses are treated more favourably than family homes. It also is open to manipulation, where the wealthy could invest in a farm or set up a shell company prior to death. The allowance for farms and businesses should not be any greater than that for primary residences.

Politically, however, we must take account of the emotional bond to certain inherited assets. There is also the shock of a large tax bill soon after the death of a loved one. For this reason, assets such as primary residences, businesses, and farms that have been in possession for a certain time could have their tax liability spread over a lengthy period, say the next twenty years. This would mean the beneficiaries would not have to sell an asset in a fire sale and would give an inheritance tax advantage, twenty years of the tax-free income allowance, to the assets. If the surviving family members do sell the asset sooner, it suggests the asset was not of such huge sentimental value, and the residual value should be taxed fully in that tax year. In France, all surviving children are entitled to a minimum percentage of the deceased's assets. This means, for example, in a family of two or more children, all the assets cannot go one child. This means estates are usually split, which can help to reduce concentration of wealth. We should adopt this policy.

5.08.6. Taxes on Goods and Services

Taxes on goods and services, especially in the form of value-added tax (VAT), have become an increasingly important revenue generator in most developed countries over the last thirty years, with the exception of the United States, which does not have such a tax at the federal level. Governments like these taxes, as they are efficient to collect and produce fairly stable revenues.

These taxes are criticised as being regressive, stemming from the fact that the poor spend most of their income, whereas the wealthy tend to save a lot. An OECD study, *The Distributional Effects of Consumption Taxes in OECD Countries*, examines these effects.[156] The authors conclude that VAT is indeed regressive when measured against income but progressive when measured against expenditure. As most people have a lifecycle of income—earning most in the middle of their lives and with low income around periods of studying, unemployment, and retirement—over the average lifecycle, VAT is better considered on an expenditure basis and is therefore slightly progressive. Obvious exceptions here are for the permanently poor and permanently rich, but the general conclusion is that lowering VAT rates is not the quick and easy means to poverty alleviation that is often suggested.

The study also examines the effects of excluding certain goods and services from VAT. In chapter 4.03, 'The Structure of Inequality', we note that the poorest households tend to spend

[156] Organisation for Economic Co-operation and Development, 'The Distributional Effects of Consumption Taxes in OECD Countries', OECD Tax Policy Studies 22 (Paris: OECD/Korea Institute of Public Finance, 2014).

a greater proportion of income on food, housing, and utilities. The OECD supports this by concluding that exemptions from VAT for food, energy, and water do have a progressive effect. Even here, the picture is not completely clear, as we may not wish to exempt energy and water for environmental reasons, and certain foodstuffs may be enjoyed more by the rich than the poor. Some countries' VAT systems also exempt items for educational, cultural, or leisure and tourism reasons. Examples here are books and magazines, theatre and cinema tickets, and flights and hotel accommodation. Here the study is unequivocal: despite the possible good intentions behind these exemptions, they are very regressive in their nature, favouring expenditure by the rich.

Luxury taxes attempt to do the opposite of VAT exemptions by taxing 'luxury' goods favoured by the wealthy at a higher rate of VAT. The problem here is defining what a luxury good is. Once those have been classified, there is the very real possibility that people switch to alternatives or don't buy the good at all. There is also the problem of stopping the smuggling of these goods from abroad. A 10 percent luxury tax introduced in the United States in 1991 on watches, expensive furs, boats, yachts, private jet planes, jewellery, and expensive cars was repealed in 1993 due to its lack of success.

The conclusion here is that VAT exemptions should be limited to specific food staples such as fresh fruit and vegetables, bread and milk, and so on. Other exemptions should be rescinded and the revenues used to lower the overall rate of VAT or the main rate of income tax, or to improve welfare services, which will have a greater effect on inequality.

5.08.7. Transactions Taxes, Fees, and Sin Taxes

Sin taxes are excise duties on goods to discourage their use due to their harmful effects or externalities. Typical examples are taxes on alcohol, tobacco, and gasoline. (We examine other environmental taxes in chapter 5.11.) Singapore is a country with very high levels of sin taxes. One problem with these taxes is that they tend to be very regressive, falling more on poor and middle-income households, and this is confirmed in the OECD study cited above. Over the years, governments have found it easier to raise these taxes than others, to the point where they have become revenue generators rather than sin taxes.[157] To restore the principles of tax neutrality and progressivity, these taxes should be set to the level that compensates for the harm they cause, no higher or lower. Similarly, regressive fees for use, such as parking charges at municipal buildings, which have actually become revenue-generating taxes, should be cut to equal their economic cost.

We wish to introduce some new sin taxes at this point. To ease the future pressures on the healthcare system, we need to focus on preventative measures, which means that unhealthy sugars and fats in food and drink must be taxed, and such foods must be made unavailable in schools. As with other new taxes there will be a suspicion that they will just be used to fund bigger government, so these taxes should be earmarked to cut other taxes.

To tackle affluenza at its source, we also wish to introduce

---

[157] *The Guardian*, 'George Osborne: low taxes, high pay – and high charges', 18 November 2015, http://www.theguardian.com/commentisfree/2015/nov/18/the-guardian-view-on-george-osborne-low-taxes-high-pay-and-high-charges

an advertising tax. As described previously, much advertising is insidious, deliberately creating feelings of inadequacy in viewers, listeners, and readers. For consumers who wish to research purchases, there are many sources of independent consumer research online and in print. An advertising tax has been mooted for years but never implemented, possibly because of lobbying by media outlets who rely on advertising revenues. Since the rise of digital media, much content is now available only on a subscription basis, and this seems to be the way valuable content will be distributed (advert free) in the future, lessening some of those objections. Adverts that are merely informative could be exempt from the tax. This will be a difficult tax to implement, but we must try for the reasons listed above.

At the higher end of the income scale, certain transaction taxes have become revenue generators, especially stamp duties (transfer taxes) on properties. While these taxes can be highly progressive, they fail badly on the tax principles of neutrality, efficiency, fairness, and horizontal equity. A household that needs to relocate for work or changing family circumstances is hit with a large stamp duty tax liability, whereas a similar household that stays put pays nothing. This is unfair and inefficient, as it reduces economic mobility. It is better to charge a transaction tax equivalent to the registration costs and instead increase the progressivity of property and land taxes directly.

5.08.8. Tax Avoidance and Evasion

The first step to minimising tax losses through avoidance and evasion is to make the tax code as simple as possible and to tax all forms of income and wealth similarly. A complex tax and benefit system has a regressive bias, as the wealthy can afford tax advice and the poor often underclaim what is due to them.[158] This is true for individuals and companies. Complementary to the goal of simplicity is transparency. Taxpayers should have to justify a good reason for complex company structures, and beneficial owners of assets or income should always be named. Complex company structures with unnamed owners often have little purpose other than tax avoidance or money laundering.

A general antiavoidance (GAA) law legislates against tax avoidance by stressing the spirit, rather than the letter, of tax law. The punishment for tax avoidance should be asset seizure, and in egregious cases imprisonment for the tax avoiders and their advisors. The very wealthy may choose to gamble on the former if they do not fear the latter. Measures similar to these have just been introduced in the United Kingdom.[159] Whistle-blowers should be supported legally and financially, and we look at this in the section on criminal justice. Nevertheless, we should not pretend, as opposition politicians often do when drawing up budgets, that there is a large and perpetual

[158] Ros Wynne Jones, 'Up to £20bn of benefits are UNCLAIMED every year', The Mirror, 15 JUL 2015. http://www.mirror.co.uk/news/uk-news/exposing-figures-government-sweep-under-6067450

[159] Simon Bowers, 'Osborne targets multinationals and tax evaders in budget crackdown', *The Guardian*, 18 March 2015, http://www.theguardian.com/politics/2015/mar/18/osborne-targets-multinationals-and-tax-evaders-in-budget-crackdown

stream of undertaxed income ready to come on stream at the turn of a tap. Unless the current government has been totally captured by vested interests, which is a possibility, especially in the United States, they will have already attempted to capture most of the revenue they can.

5.08.9. Tax Exiles

The ultimate form of tax avoidance is for an individual to move tax domicile. How much notice of this threat should we take when setting tax policy? We discussed earlier why tax rates over 50 percent could be considered unfair, and we will in chapter 5.14 on corporate policy show how we will tax advantage real 'job-creators' as opposed to speculators and rentiers. Even then some individuals will shop around for better tax deals with marginal tax rates at well below 40 percent.

Society needs to draw a line in the sand at these levels of taxation and not cave in to bullying or threats from the wealthy. Entrepreneurs and business owners rely heavily on the state sector, from legal protection to having an educated workforce, an affluent consumer base, and good infrastructure. In *The Entrepreneurial State: Debunking Public vs. Private Sector Myths*, Mariana Mazzucato points out the role of government research and investment in high-risk technologies.[160] For example, the majority of the technology in the smartphone originated from government-funded research.

Countries should charge citizens tax on their global earnings as the United States does. If a high net worth individual

---

[160] Mariana Mazzucato, The Entrepreneurial State: Debunking Public vs. Private Sector Myths (New York: Public Affairs, 2015).

wishes to change tax domicile to save a few percentage points in tax then they will have to relinquish their citizenship. This will force people to consider all the costs and benefits of citizenship, for themselves and their families. Currently many of the wealthy are able to pick and choose their tax domicile like diners at a buffet while keeping many of the benefits of citizenship, such as military and diplomatic protection and the right of abode for their children.

Much as there is an economic theory of the marginal worker, in many senses there can also be a marginal business owner or entrepreneur. Commentators often talk as if when a wealthy individual leaves a country, the whole of their economic value leaves with them, but who is to say another entrepreneur or businessperson will not step into their shoes with little economic loss? In addition, as Lawrence Summers noted, we are now in an age where considerations of inequality are becoming more important than questions of overall wealth.

5.09. Welfare Policy

Earlier we studied popular government programmes and noted their common features. Those features are universality, in the sense that everyone contributes to the programme and that everyone benefits, and a preference for services over cash payments where possible. Some may disagree with this perspective, but it is borne out in most surveys of the voting public.[161] [162] We do indeed argue in this book for a reversion to the universal, contributory principle that all citizens should pay into the system to receive the benefits. This is distinct, however, from a defined contribution system, whereby the amount paid in determines what can be paid out. The current level of inequality makes such a system unviable, for example, for the many who require tax credits on top of their salaries to enjoy a decent standard of living. So what we propose in this book is a welfare system where everyone pays *something* into the system, but the amount paid in depends on ability to pay, and everyone takes out of the system, but the amount taken out depends on need: from each according to his ability, to each according to his needs.

Universal benefits are preferable over means-tested ones. Under means testing, as those on low incomes earn more, people earning low incomes are not only taxed more but benefits also are withdrawn, creating very high implied marginal

---

[161] Stephan Shakespeare, 'Voters Prefer Spending on Services to Cutting Borrowing', YouGov UK, 14 January 2013, https://yougov.co.uk/news/2015/01/14/voters-prefer-spending-services-cutting-borrowing/.

[162] Peter Kellner, 'Welfare Reform: Who, Whom?' YouGov UK, 7 January 2013, https://yougov.co.uk/news/2013/01/07/welfare-reform-who-whom/.

tax rates, sometimes close to 100 percent. This is sometimes called the poverty trap or welfare cliff. The original Beveridge report in the United Kingdom that was the basis of the modern welfare state favoured universal benefits for this reason. The problem with universal benefits is that they are expensive, as they are paid to everyone regardless of income, so any cash benefits should be made taxable to claw some revenue back.

Figure 10 shows the projected spending on benefits in the United Kingdom for the 2015 tax year. What is noticeable is that nearly 50 percent of the expenditure is on pensions and pension credits, and these are popular programmes in contrast to the public perception that much of the welfare spend is wasteful. The situation is similar in the United States, with Social Security and Medicare for seniors consuming a large portion of the budget. We now look at the other items in turn.

5.09.1. Housing Benefit

Housing benefit, known as Section 8 in the United States, is paid mostly to households on low income to help pay for private rented accommodation, and we look at this in more detail in chapter 5.12 on housing policy. For the moment, note what a large budget item this is in the United Kingdom, and even in countries without direct housing payments other benefits have to be increased to enable the recipients to afford accommodation.

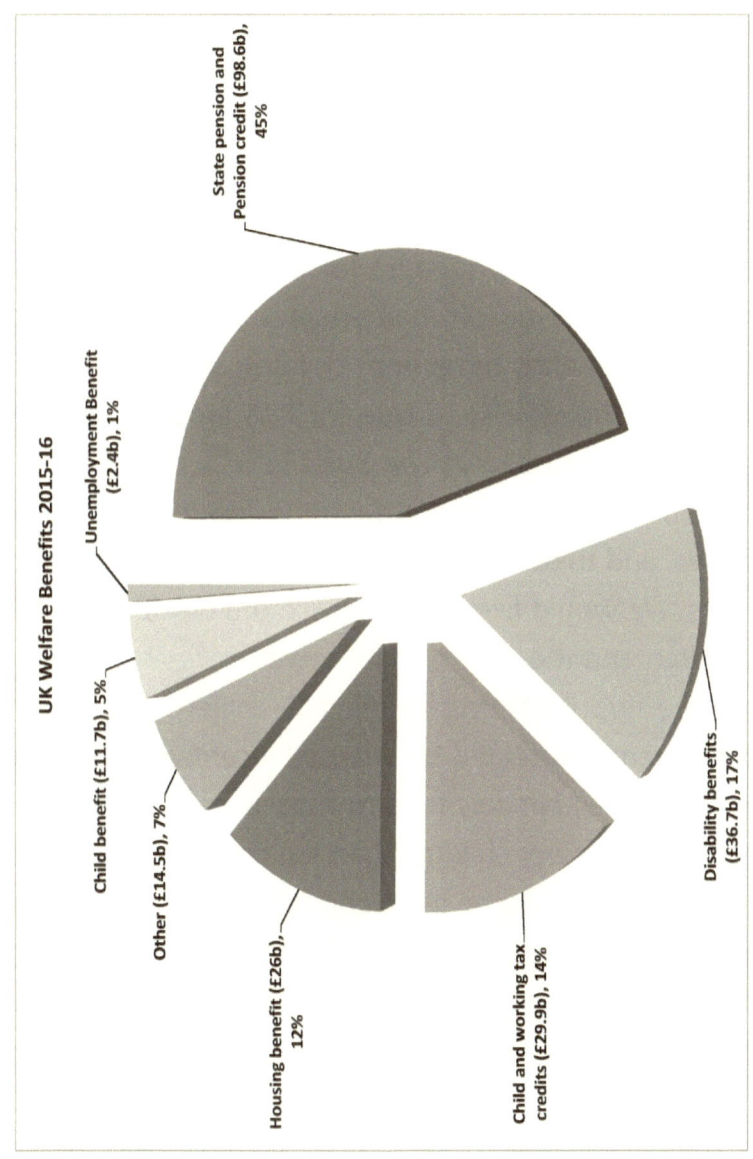

UK Welfare Benefits 2015-16

State pension and Pension credit (£98.6b), 45%

Unemployment Benefit (£2.4b), 1%

Child benefit (£11.7b), 5%

Other (£14.5b), 7%

Housing benefit (£26b), 12%

Child and working tax credits (£29.9b), 14%

Disability benefits (£36.7b), 17%

Figure 10 Composition of UK welfare budget, 2015–16

E. P. Anthony, 2016. Data: Full Fact, 'Benefits and Tax Credits'

5.09.2. Child Benefit and Child Working Tax Credits

Child benefit is a universal cash payment made usually to a mother for each of her children. Child tax credits are a form of welfare payment made to working parents with children, and these are means tested.

From the perspective of inequality, we would prefer the wealthy to have large families and the poor to have smaller families. This is not an argument for eugenics but simply a statement of fact based on mathematics and empirical observation. If the wealthy have many children, inherited wealth is diluted, and the reverse is true for less wealthy families. Additionally, as discussed in *The Spirit Level*, children of the very poorest in society often grow up in less than ideal circumstances, and their development suffers relative to that of their peers. We would like to incentivise the wealthy to have more children and the poor to have fewer.

There are two problems in trying to achieve this. Firstly, birth rates seem unaffected by financial incentives. As societies become richer, families tend to have fewer children, and the wealthy have fewer children than the poor.[163] The wealthy are often asset rich but time poor, and no amount of tweaking of the tax system seems to have the desired effect, as demonstrated in Singapore, which has many family-friendly policies and one of the lowest birth rates in the world.[164] At the other

---

[163] The Economist, 'More or less', Sep 1st 2012. http://www.economist.com/node/21561112

[164] Tyler Cowen, 'Why does Singapore have such a low birth rate?', MarginalRevolution, December 28, 2013. http://marginalrevolution.com/marginalrevolution/2013/12/why-does-singapore-have-such-a-low-birth-rate.html

end of the income scale, evidence presented in *The Spirit Level* suggests that reducing child benefit appears to have little effect on birth rates amongst the poor, while it punishes their children and stores up expensive societal problems for later.[165]

One possible solution to both problems is to transfer funds from child benefit and child tax credits to fund free kindergarten for children from the age of two or three and to fund free childcare and parent-and-child centres for younger kids. This would help wealthy families, where often both parents wish to return to work after childbirth, and poorer single mothers who, at the moment, are very restricted in what jobs they can take. It would also help the very poorest children by getting them into a supportive and caring environment and give their parents resources they may lack otherwise. Such a system could also help to break down barriers and bring rich and poor families together, a theme we develop in the chapters on education and housing.

Some child-benefit cash payments would no doubt have to still be paid to cover other expenses, and parents in remote areas may need the full payment if they cannot access childcare facilities easily. The net effect of these changes is likely to be to increase welfare spending on younger children. Some revenue can be clawed back by limiting cash benefits to two children per family and by taxing these benefits, though obviously this change should not be done retrospectively. Additionally, we can change priorities in the education budget, as we see later.

---

[165] Wilkinson and Pickett, 'The Spirit Level', p.143.

5.09.3. Unemployment and Disability Benefits

We have grouped these two benefits together because there is perception in the public mind that many people have moved from unemployment to disability benefits, either prompted by the authorities to massage the unemployment statistics or to claim more generous benefits. It can be seen in Figure 10 that the disability benefit bill is much larger than the cost of unemployment benefit.

It should be noted, however, that governments have been aware of this perception for many years and so have been working to reduce the number of disability claimants. In the United Kingdom, controversial tests of fitness to work have been in place for five years, so any easy savings here should have been made. It should also be noted that it is understandable that being unemployed for a period of time can lead to depression and other mental illnesses, alcoholism, poor diet, and lack of exercise. Poverty.org.uk notes that in 2010, forty percent of out of work disability claimants had mental and behavioural disorders and that most of the claimants were in areas of high long-term unemployment.[166]

The main policy solution to the problem of long-term claims for unemployment and related disability benefits is the commitment to full employment detailed in the chapter on stabilisation policy and especially aggressive demand management to prevent severe depressions. Even government make-work schemes are preferable and cheaper than allowing pockets of long-term unemployment to build. In addition, the

---

[166] Poverty.org.uk, 'Working-age out-of-work benefit recipients',February 2009. http://www.poverty.org.uk/13/index.shtml

evidence presented in *The Spirit Level* demonstrates that policies to reduce inequality can have favourable consequences for the physical and mental health of the nation. Both these benefits should also be made countercyclical. At the moment, savings are sought during recessions, when government budgets are tight. Instead, savings and reforms should be sought out during economic expansions, when jobs and opportunities are plentiful, helping to build up a large budget surplus.

5.09.4. The Minimum Wage

In recent years, government policy in many developed economies has focussed on 'making work pay', and therefore on policies aimed at the working poor. The two main policies used to support the wages of the low paid are the minimum wage and earned income tax credits (EITCs). In the absence of these policies, the market-clearing wage would probably be too low to give the worker a sustainable standard of living. We consider the pros and cons of both of these measures before examining an alternative policy proposal.

A minimum wage is a price floor for wages, and the minimum can be set lower for younger workers and the long-term unemployed to encourage hiring them. The main benefit flows to the employed low-wage workers, who see their incomes rise. This policy has obvious positive distributional benefits, so what are the criticisms of it, and why not just raise the minimum wage to reduce inequality?

The traditional criticism of minimum wage policy comes from classical economic theory of competitive labour markets. The theory states that if wages are raised above their market level, employers will demand less labour and unemployment will increase. Empirically, this theory has not materialised, at least for modest increases in the minimum wage, for several reasons. Increases in wages can reduce absenteeism and increase productivity, offsetting the increase in costs for the employer. Additionally, many low-paid workers are in sectors where the competition is local rather than global.[167] A MacDonald's franchise is in competition with the Subway down the street rather than a fast-food outlet in Asia, so increased business costs from a higher minimum wage are common across the sector and less likely to cause unemployment.

In the absence of increased unemployment, the costs of an increased minimum wage tend to be borne by the employer in lower profits and by the consumer in increased prices for goods and services. When Walmart unilaterally increased wages for its employees in 2015, its financial results were affected, sending its share price lower.[168] However, if the wage costs are passed mainly to consumers, this could have negative distributional effects, as many of the sectors that employ minimum-wage workers, such as the fast-food and retail sectors, are used heavily by the poor. Some government-funded sectors, such as healthcare, employ low-wage workers, and they would find their costs rising, placing the burden on taxpayers. Another potential problem of high minimum wages is wage compression. The wages of low-skilled workers are

[167] Alan Manning, 'Why Increasing the Minimum Wage Does Not Necessarily Reduce Employment', LSE US Centre, 27 January 2014, http://blogs.lse.ac.uk/usappblog/2014/01/27/minimum-wage-employment/.

[168] Kevin McCoy, 'Walmart plunges on lower earnings forecast', *USA Today*, October 15, 2015. http://www.usatoday.com/story/money/2015/10/14/walmart-shares-plunge-lower-earnings-forecast/73921190/

pushed up by the minimum wage to close to the wages of more skilled workers, reducing the incentives for the low skilled to upskill via training or education.

The minimum wage can be a useful tool in reducing inequality, and carefully calculated increases need not have large adverse effects. Indeed, if companies are earning monopoly rents, increasing the minimum wage can improve efficiency. Nevertheless, if the level of the wage is raised too high, it is possible we would start to see increases in unemployment, inflation in the prices of goods and services, and wage compression. Additionally, Ben Chu, in *The Independent*, points out that many of the benefits of increases in minimum wages in the United Kingdom flow to minimum wage second earners in nonpoor households.[169]

In the United Kingdom, the Low Pay Commission is tasked with setting the appropriate level of the minimum wage to avoid the undesirable effects outlined above. In the 2015 budget, then UK Chancellor George Osborne hiked the minimum wage well above the advised level to partially offset a cut in tax credits. It will be interesting to see if some of the negative effects described appear, in which case the fear is that many low-paid workers will be worse off via unemployment and inflation. It is also interesting that a politician who seems to believe in a classical model of the economy when it comes to debt and government spending ignores the negative effects this economic theory indicates this policy change will have.

---

[169] Ben Chu, 'Why Doesn't a Higher Minimum Wage Help the Poor More?' The Independent. 14 July 2015. blogs.independent.co.uk/2015/07/14/why-does-a-higher-minimum-wage-help-the-better-off-more.

5.09.5. Working Tax Credits

Working tax credits (WTC) in the United Kingdom and earned income tax credits (EITC) in the United States are means-tested payments to working-poor households, and they have many of the opposite pros and cons to the minimum wage. They do not affect the hiring decision of the employer or add to costs that are passed on to consumers.

There are several problems with these schemes. The burden here falls on taxpayers to fund the schemes, which have become increasingly expensive. The responsibility falls on the employee to claim the tax credit, which many fail to do, and it has been claimed that employers can pay below market wages in the knowledge that tax credits will make up the difference, so that the employer captures some of the tax credit. The means-tested element of the credit means many low-wage workers face very high marginal tax rates, sometimes over 100 percent, as discussed at the start of this chapter.

5.09.6. Direct Wage Subsidies

Oren Cass of the conservative Manhattan Institute for Policy Research suggests converting tax credits into a wage subsidy paid directly to the employee and with a subtly different method of calculation.[170] The major benefit of the direct subsidy is its transparency, and the employer could advertise jobs with the wage subsidy included, making the job more attractive to unemployed workers. Cass claims that the funds

[170] Oren Cass, 'The Wage Subsidy. A Better Way to Help the Poor', Manhattan Institute for Policy Research 37 (August 2015).

currently directed to tax credits could pay the cost of a wage subsidy scheme in the United States. A disadvantage of this direct payment is the administrative burden, so the administration of this scheme should belong to the government, who is better placed organisationally to deal with it.

The subsidy works by closing 50 percent of the gap between the market wage and a target wage. So if the market wage is $8 per hour and the target wage is $12, the worker will receive a subsidy of $2 per hour, bringing the hourly wage to $10. There would be no phaseout of the subsidy for working longer hours, so there is no disincentive to working harder. Instead, the subsidy would be phased out as the per-hour wage increased, and once the target wage was reached, no subsidy would be paid. In the example above, if the market wage rises to $10 per hour, the subsidy would fall to $1, giving the worker an hourly wage of $11. This is an implicit marginal tax rate of 50 percent, which is a lower rate than most low-wage workers currently face.

Cass would make all workers eligible for the wage subsidy based on their hourly wage. The WTC and EITC currently target certain households. He argues that if policymakers wish to target certain households, they should do so directly, not through wages and wage subsidies. For example, families with children can be helped with childcare and universal child-benefit payments, as described above, and not through credits or subsidies, which inevitably create very high implicit marginal tax rates. Wealthier families with low-paid second earners could also benefit from wage subsides, so Cass suggests making the subsidy taxable. In this way, second earners in wealthy households would face a high effective marginal tax rate (the 50 percent subsidy taper plus the top rate of tax), and so this policy could free up some of these jobs for poorer families, who would face lower marginal rates (50 percent plus the lower rate of tax).

5.09.7. A Minimum Wage plus a Wage Subsidy

A problem with a stand-alone wage subsidy, the same as with tax credits, is that the employer captures some of the subsidy. Cass estimates that 25 percent of the subsidy is captured in this way. We should couple a wage subsidy with a minimum wage policy to ensure that employers share the burden of higher wages. A low-pay commission would set the minimum wage annually, at a rate that does not create unemployment or raise the prices of key goods needed by poorer households. A lower minimum wage could be set for different worker groups to encourage their hiring, such as the long-term unemployed and those with criminal records. Different minimum wages could be set for different sectors of the economy, lower for sectors that face foreign competition and higher for sectors that appear to enjoy monopoly rents. The minimum wage could even be adjusted to counter economic cycles, being lowered during recessions to keep workers employed and raised during booms. If the living-wage level is not affected by the economic cycle, then the compensating wage-subsidy bill would rise during slumps and fall during good times, adding to the countercyclical nature of the government deficit.

The target wage could be set at the level of the national living wage, again set by the low-pay commission. The living wage is a vague concept, representing the per-hour wage needed for employees working the average number of hours to have a decent life; the definition would have to be more specific in practice. The subsidy would, as described above, pay 50 percent of the difference between the minimum or market wage, whichever is the higher, and the living wage. This necessarily implies that low-pay workers who receive a subsidy will be paid less than the living wage.

Why not set the target wage over the living wage, so that the 50 percent tapered subsidy on top of the minimum wage reaches the living wage? So, if the minimum wage is $8 per hour and the living wage is $12, then the target wage would be set to $16, so that minimum-wage workers would receive a net $12 per hour. This could indeed be a long-term goal, but in the short term, this would be prohibitively expensive, requiring large tax hikes. In addition, the wage levels just described imply that workers earning above the living wage of $12 per hour but below $16 would receive a wage subsidy, which could be viewed as wasteful. As with other policies in this book, we favour an incrementalist approach, first proving that policies are effective before expanding their scope. To go straight to the end point, with the associated tax hikes, would be politically difficult.

To reduce the expense of the system, one solution would be to hike the minimum wage above the recommended level, making the subsidies paid lower. The UK government seems to be taking this approach by hiking the minimum wage and reducing tax credits. There are two problems with this approach, however. Setting the minimum wage above the recommended level could result in the increased unemployment and other problems we outlined earlier. Moreover, the United

Kingdom plans to cut the level of tax credits by more than is offset by the rise in minimum wage, making many of the poorest workers worse off, while making minimum-wage second earners in wealthy households better off.[171] This policy could make inequality worse, and it is potentially the worst of all worlds.

In the short term, we may have to tolerate that some workers are paid below the living wage. Having a job must be preferred to having no job, and the minimum wage plus wage subsidy system, with other benefits being universal in nature, ensures this is the case. Furthermore, in keeping with the holistic nature of this book, we wish to make long-term, lasting changes to corporate policy that will encourage employers to prioritise employee welfare and wages; we look at this in chapter 5.14 on corporate policy.

---

[171] Ben Chu, 'Why Doesn't a Higher Minimum Wage Help the Poor More?' *The Independent*, 14 July 2015, blogs.independent.co.uk/2015/07/14/why-does-a-higher-minimum-wage-help-the-better-off-more.

5.10. Education Policy

The Spirit Level and *Affluenza* both document how important the first few years of children's lives are to their future development. Studies have shown that by the age of three, children from poor backgrounds can be a year behind their peers, with half the vocabulary.[172] A study of high-quality preschool programmes in some US states found they closed this attainment gap, with the benefits even increasing lifetime earnings.[173] This suggests that early-years education should be a priority.

Ray Dalio's 'Economic Model' paper suggests that the educational attainment of workers, allowing for wages, is the major driver of productivity and growth in one country relative to another. Given that most workers are educated to high school level, we can argue this should be the area of focus. Many other studies of productivity suggest that high-level research at universities, especially in the sciences, is a key driver of innovation. Thus, an argument can be made for increasing resources at every stage of education. How can this be achieved without large spending rises and the associated tax rises, or cuts to other areas?

This can be done by redirecting resources from university education to early-age development, without necessarily diluting the positive effects of university research in certain areas. There are two clear arguments for this. First, the current

---

[172] Betty Hart and Todd R. Risley, 'The Early Catastrophe: The 30 Million Word Gap by Age 3', American Educator Spring (2003): 4–9.

[173] Greg J. Duncan and Aaron J. Sojourner, 'Can Intensive Early Childhood Intervention Programs Eliminate Income-Based Cognitive and Achievement Gaps?' Journal of Human Resources 48, no. 4 (Fall 2013): 945–68.

focus of educational spending is unstable, in the same way an inverted pyramid is, where more resources are used in later-years education to try to correct for the failings in early years. We need to correct this pyramid so that young children reach school age better equipped academically and socially. This will make them easier, and possibly cheaper, to teach leading up to their high school and university years. Secondly, focussing resources on all children at an early age will obviously do more to reduce inequality than subsidising university education for the minority that attend, even if some of them are from poorer backgrounds. We describe in the chapter on welfare how we wish to use some of the funds for child benefit and child tax credits to fund universal childcare and pre-school provision. Some extra funds would likely be needed, however, to make this a reality.

What is the optimal form of education from primary to high school? We have a role model in the education system of Finland, which is consistently the top Western country in the OECD PISA (Programme for International Student Assessment) tests of education and sometimes the top country globally.[174] The Finnish model is a comprehensive system from seven to sixteen years old. Tests are used for diagnostic rather than streaming purposes, and teaching emphasises creativity and group learning, offering much better preparation for the world of work. Children are separated into vocational and academic streams from the age of sixteen, which must

---

[174] Organisation for Economic Co-operation and Development, 'PISA 2012 Results in Focus: What 15-Year-Olds Know and What They Can Do with What They Know', OECD, 2014, http://www.oecd.org/pisa/keyfindings/pisa-2012-results-overview.pdf.

be superior to doing so at eleven, as is done in parts of the United Kingdom, when some children will still be disadvantaged by their early-years experiences. In addition, removing the brightest poor kids from their peers at age eleven must have a detrimental effect on those left behind in terms of the schooling received, their self-worth, the absence of role models, and the perceptions of future employers. *The Economist*, in a study of the Scandinavian model, notes that the Finnish system is not particularly expensive.[175] Teachers are paid moderately well but are given a lot of respect and autonomy. Class sizes are average by Western standards, demonstrating that reducing class size is not always the solution to poor educational attainment.[176] Many high-achieving Asian countries have large average class sizes. Indeed, there are diminishing returns to reducing class sizes, as accomplishing this involves hiring more teachers. The extra teachers added are likely to either be expensive, if we want good ones, or inexperienced, if the budget is not increased enough.

One of the easiest ways to reduce inequality would be to ban the private provision of education. Investment in children's education is one of the ways inequality is perpetuated and social mobility is restricted. It is not just about the quality of the teaching, although the better pay at private schools must attract the better teachers. Private schools also specialise in passing exams, which is not the same as educating; in instilling confidence in their pupils; and in creating valuable

---

[175] The Economist, 'Special Report: The Nordic Countries'.
[176] Amelia Thomson-DeVeaux, 'Should States Spend Billions To Reduce Class Sizes?', *FiveThirtyEight*, Dec 11, 2014, http://fivethirtyeight.com/features/should-states-spend-billions-to-reduce-class-sizes/.

networks of alumni. They also reinforce an 'us-and-them' dynamic, where many wealthy, privately educated pupils often have little contact with children from poorer backgrounds, and so their perspectives and problems are alien to them. Giving a few children from poor neighbourhoods scholarships simply diminishes the education of those left behind in the same way streaming does. It is for this reason that Singapore makes it very difficult for local children to attend the expensive international schools on the island, as they want Singaporean children from all backgrounds to mix. This is also evident in their housing policies, as we see later.

Banning private provision of education, at this moment in time, will likely meet political or legal resistance. Nevertheless, there should be no subsidies or tax advantages for these schools as currently exist in the United Kingdom, where private schools have charitable status. Labour MP Tristram Hunt has suggested that private schools in the United Kingdom should collaborate with local state schools and help to develop methods of best practice if they are to keep their charitable status.[177]

5.10.1. Further Education Policy

Many baby boomers credit the expansion of university places after World War II for their own personal success and the increase in social mobility in the 1960s and '70s. In countries

---

[177] Patrick Wintour, 'Tristram Hunt warns private schools to help state pupils or lose £700m in tax breaks', *The Guardian*, 25 November 2014. http://www.theguardian.com/education/2014/nov/24/private-schools-labour-warning-tax-breaks-tristram-hunt

where university tuition fees were once free for students but are no longer, many parties of the left have promised to reverse these changes once in power. This may not be the best use of resources. We argue at the start of this chapter that inequality is better tackled by moving resources to early-years care and education. The children of the very poorest in society rarely go to university, whereas large numbers of wealthier kids do, so subsidising tuition fees for everyone could actually increase inequality. Additionally, there appear to be decreasing returns to higher education, where the future benefits may not justify the cost, whether it is borne by the individual or the state.[178] There is an argument that, for many, a university degree is simply a signalling mechanism to employers, with little intrinsic value. This is especially marked in Japan, where, for many, gaining entry to a prestigious university is often more valuable than what is learnt there. We have also seen how the future of employment may rest on whether a task is predictable and repeatable rather than whether it is manual or cognitive. There are, however, positive externalities to having a well-educated population, and there are some subjects, such as science and IT, where the economic benefits are potentially large and there is a lack of skilled workers in most developed economies. How do we reconcile investment in key subjects with reducing costs and promoting social mobility?

First, the government should subsidise 50 percent of

---

[178] Paul Krugman, 'Degrees and Dollars', *The New York Times*, March 6, 2011. http://www.nytimes.com/2011/03/07/opinion/07krugman.html?rref= collection%2Fcolumn%2Fpaul-krugman&action=click&contentCollection= opinion&region=stream&module=stream_unit&version=search&content Placement=1&pgtype=collection

tuition fees in key subjects where there are large spillover benefits and skill shortages. This subsidy would apply to all students. Next, we can introduce a form of means testing for up to another 50 percent of the tuition fees, with the poorest students fully subsidised. Although we have tried to avoid means testing for most welfare benefits, parents are unlikely to adjust their behaviour in the labour market for the three- or four-year period while their children are at university. These targeted subsidies focus attention on the most needed areas and students while avoiding the large costs associated with a blanket subsidy for all tuition fees. The poorest students studying key subjects will have 100 percent of tuition fees covered, and those studying nonkey subjects will have 50 percent of fees covered. Wealthier students taking key subjects will benefit from a 50 percent subsidy, and those taking nonkey ones will have no subsidy. Any funding shortfall for students should be filled by low-interest student loans from the government.

Allied with these measures, the cost of further education must be reduced. Degree courses should be cut by a year where possible. Full advantage should be taken of advances in technology, with online lectures and tuition reducing costs further. Universities that discriminate in admissions against children from poorer neighbourhoods or state schools should expect the same sanctions as if they had discriminated based on race, religion, gender, or sexual orientation, and there should be no bias in favour of the children of alumni.

Lastly, some resources should be shifted from academic centres of education to technical or vocational colleges, as this is where many students will end up and where the largest productivity gains for the majority of the workforce can be made. The McKinsey survey on the future of work suggested it is important that nonroutine skills be taught here. These skills can be furthered by apprenticeship schemes. At the same time, companies offering unpaid internships that favour the children of the wealthy should be forced to pay at least the minimum wage, which, along with the wage-subsidy scheme outlined earlier, would allow poorer students to gain entry into many of the industries which currently use internships as entry level jobs. To help pay for the expansion of vocational training, welfare benefits could be restricted to those above the age of eighteen or twenty-one. We do not want the first experience of 'work' for young people to be claiming benefits, and we do not want students leaving school without sufficient skills to prepare them for the job market.

5.11. Environmental Policy

US politician Upton Sinclair once famously said, 'It is difficult to get a man to understand something, when his salary depends on his not understanding it'. The Showtime series *Years of Living Dangerously* demonstrates that sometimes it is hard to get people to understand something even when their livelihoods depend on understanding it.[179] In a rancher town in Texas decimated by drought, the population rejects climate change theory and instead prays for divine intervention in the form of rain. It is obvious why coal miners in West Virginia would be climate change sceptics but hard to see why these ranchers are. A partial explanation can be found in the book *Merchants of Doubt*, which documents the playbook of climate-change-denial think tanks and their wealthy backers.[180] However, even people who accept that manmade greenhouse gases, primarily carbon dioxide (CO_2), are causing climate change have not altered their behaviour much, possibly thinking that something will turn up. Unfortunately, what may turn up is millions of refugees fleeing famine or flood.

One of the simplest and easiest policies to reduce carbon emissions is a tax on carbon, which by increasing the cost of carbon-intensive goods, should lead consumers and corporations to alter their behaviour in the same way as taxes on cigarettes do. There is political resistance to such a tax, however, as many see this as just another path to more taxes and bigger government. Ex–Australian PM Tony Abbott successfully campaigned to repeal a carbon tax, focussing on promised

[179] Years of Living Dangerously, season 1.
[180] Oreskes and Conway, Merchants of Doubt.

reductions in fuel bills while seemingly implying the revenue from the tax disappeared into a black hole. To avoid this scenario, a carbon tax should be introduced and the revenues committed to lowering other taxes, either goods and services taxes or the main rate of income tax.

A tax on carbon production is the major policy needed to reduce the demand for energy produced by carbon. To further reduce the demand for energy, we would need to reduce the global population or reduce growth, neither of which is likely or desirable in the short term, or increase the efficiency of the use of energy. In his book *Sustainable Energy—Without the Hot Air*, David MacKay notes that, in the United Kingdom, two of the largest uses of energy are for transport and temperature control in the home.[181] Efficiency improvements here will have the greatest effect on CO_2 emissions while creating desirable cost savings for consumers; the same is also true in most other developed economies.

In terms of the environmental effects of residential energy use, savings can be made in the production of heat and the preservation of heat through insulation. The simplest and easiest change that can be made immediately is simply to turn the thermostat down in winter and up in summer. Following the Fukushima nuclear disaster in Japan, all nuclear facilities were closed and an energy shortage ensued. In response, the Japanese government instituted 'cool-biz' in the summer months, advising homeowners and offices to set the thermostat to twenty-eight degrees Celsius and to wear loose casual clothing instead of formal work attire. A reverse

[181] David J. C. MacKay, Sustainable Energy—Without the Hot Air (Cambridge, England: UIT, 2009).

policy of 'warm-biz' in the winter months would also make sense. The carbon tax, with its effect on heating bills, should encourage these changes, plus the use of appliances that are more energy efficient. Using electricity-powered heat-pumps to generate hot and cool air, as opposed to the gas-fired water heating systems that currently dominate some markets, is one such efficiency saving.

Although we cover transport policy in more detail in chapter 5.16, for the moment we note that there are three main ways to reduce the energy expenditure of travel. One is to travel less. International air travel is one of biggest contributors to CO_2 emissions, but global competition plus the tax-free status of jet fuel means one country acting alone is unlikely to reduce emissions. Domestic air travel is somewhere action can be taken though, with taxes ensuring that the ticket price covers the pollution cost. Other energy savings can be made by travelling in less energy-consuming vehicles. Public transport fulfils this role by carrying multiple passengers in single vehicles. (We look at the economics and redistributive aspect of public transport in the chapter on transport.) The third way to reduce the energy consumption of transport is through the electrification of the transport system. This is because the internal combustion engines in most vehicles tend to be four or five times less efficient than vehicles powered by electricity produced on a large scale. If, as many fear, people are unlikely to travel less, and public transport will never be attractive to some and cannot cover some areas of the country, a push for the electrification of private motor vehicles seems to be the only route to reduce CO_2 emissions from transport.

David MacKay examines the possible energy savings on

the consumption side and then asks whether that amount of energy could be supplied by 100 percent renewable sources. His conclusion, for a country such as the United Kingdom, is probably not. This is partly because some renewable sources are too expensive; some, such as wind energy, are viewed as eyesores by local communities; and due to space constraints. Countries such as the United States and Australia, with more space and more extreme climatic conditions than the United Kingdom, could probably generate more from solar and wind. Nevertheless, most countries are going to solve their energy problems through a mixture of efficiency savings, renewables including solar, wind and tide, and some contributions from lower-carbon traditional sources such as gas and nuclear. Nuclear suffers from the same NIMBY concerns as wind turbines, especially after the disasters at Chernobyl and Fukushima. Advances in small modular reactors (SMRs) of various types could overcome these concerns. SMRs produce electricity at a slightly higher cost than large nuclear plants but have the huge benefits of flexibility in their construction and placement, lower capital costs, fewer safety concerns because they can be self-cooling, and significantly less polluting by-products.

The other thing to note about green technology is that there are large first-mover advantages to embracing it. EDF, the French state-owned energy utility, is able to export electricity, and expertise, from its nuclear power plants. Japan is a world leader in energy-efficient cars and appliances, a result of an efficiency drive after the oil price spike in the 1970s. For this reason, plus that global CO_2 levels are currently at historic highs, the move to efficiency and green energy must be made sooner rather than later.

5.12. Housing Policy

Housing is a policy area in which we can have a significant influence on inequality, unemployment, health, and the environment. We note previously that housing is one of the largest expenditure items for the poor and one of the most important assets for the wealthy, and we advocate increasing land and property taxes. Housing can also be a large drain on government revenues if welfare benefits need to be paid so the poor can afford private-sector rents. Housing benefit is one of the larger items in the United Kingdom welfare budget.[182] Living in squalid conditions contributes to ill health and can negatively affect the educational and economic attainment of families.

We saw in the previous chapter that residential energy use is a major contributing factor to CO_2 emissions. Subsidies for insulating houses and the use of heat-pump climate control systems, perhaps in the form of zero VAT for insulating products and services, coupled with a carbon tax should encourage more energy efficient choices from consumers.[183] Social housing should be retrofitted with the latest insulating materials, and building codes for new properties should demand full insulation of walls, roofs, windows, and doors.

The biggest influence we can have is in cities. Cities, especially when designed and planned well, are much more efficient environmentally than suburbs and towns are because of energy savings in buildings, with more dense, multistorey,

---

[182] Hilary Osborne, 'Private landlords gain £26.7bn from UK taxpayer, says campaign group', *The Guardian*, 9 February 2015, http://www.theguardian.com/money/2015/feb/09/private-landlords-gain-26-7-billion-uk-taxpayer-generation-rent.
[183] MacKay, Sustainable Energy, ch.21.

and smaller property units; savings in transport, with greater emphasis on public transport, cycling, and walking; and better waste management.[184] High-growth cities are where the majority of job growth and innovation occur in modern economies due to concentrations of capital, networks, information, and skills. It is usually easier to move people to where the jobs are than to move jobs to pockets of unemployment. Years of large fiscal transfers to the regions in Japan have failed to reverse the movement of young workers into the large cities.[185]

However, there are problems associated with high-growth cities. Oliver James notes in *Affluenza* that people living in cities are more stressed than those living in the countryside are. Secondly, these 'global cities', as described by Saskia Sassen, tend to concentrate wealth in the hands of a few, sucking in wealth from the surrounding regions while spitting out the poorest who can no longer afford to exist in these megacities.[186] We need policies that harness the positive economic and environmental effects of cities while reducing the inequality and stress within them.

One solution that has been floated is rent caps in expensive cities. While there should be legislation preventing large annual changes in rent, which landlords sometimes introduce knowing the large fixed costs of moving for tenants, rent caps

---

[184] New Climate Economy. 'Estimates of Emissions Reduction. Seizing the Global Opportunity: Partnerships for Better Growth and a Better Climate'. New Climate Economy. 2015. http://newclimateeconomy.report/misc/working-papers.

[185] Jun Hongo, 'Tokyo Keeps Growing as Japan's Population Falls', *The Wall Street Journal*, Jun 26, 2014. http://blogs.wsj.com/japanrealtime/2014/06/26/tokyo-keeps-growing-as-japans-population-falls/

[186] Saskia Sassen, The Global City: New York, London, Tokyo. (Princeton, N.J.: Princeton University Press, 2001).

are not a viable long-term solution because, as with many price caps and floors, there will be unintended consequences, and they work against the fundamental problem of a lack of supply of housing. Investors are unlikely to want to invest in housing in rent-restricted areas.

The solution lies in the creation of 'urban garden cities' or 'climate-smart cities', as described by the Global Commission on Climate and Economy.[187] We need to reverse the social cleansing that has begun in wealthy cities by creating mixed-income estates; given that land is expensive in these cities, we have to build high-rise apartments. Singapore's Housing Development Board (HDB) estates are an example of how this can be done successfully. Here housing for different income groups is mixed in estates to prevent social stratification. Subsidised long-term rent-to-buy schemes, where a portion of the rental is diverted to a payment on the property, should be introduced for lower-income residents to help them to purchase their properties. In this way, poorer citizens accumulate a valuable asset in a high-growth area, and this policy coupled with land-value and property taxes can be a force for reducing the inequality of capital.

There will be numerous objections to such a policy. The image of high-rise social housing is poor in many Western countries, but this need not be the case. Building design and technology has advanced greatly since the postwar period, and these new buildings would be designed to the highest environmental standards. Mixing different income groups

[187] Future Spaces Foundation, 'Vital Cities not Garden Cities: The Answer to the Nation's Housing Shortage?' Future Spaces Foundation, 2015, http://www.futurespacesfoundation.org/our-work/garden-cities-report/.

within each building, plus the commitment engendered by long-term rent-to-buy schemes for poorer residents, should mean these estates are more successful than previous efforts where these buildings were only for the poorest. The sale of the prime properties in the building to wealthier owners can be used to subsidise the units for the rent-to-buy tenants. Some will object to high-rise buildings on aesthetic grounds. For this reason, these estates should be built in clusters in run-down neighbourhoods, and good transport links should be added. This is the approach in Tokyo and Singapore, which are often voted two of the most liveable cities in the world. Indeed, by building up, space can be created at ground level for parks and recreation areas, which can improve the quality of life for residents.

Not everyone will be able to, or will want to, live in cities. Where cities can no longer expand, a second-best solution is to connect other major towns or cities to them, either through transport using high-speed rail or through technology using high-speed fibre networks that allow people to work remotely; we study the pros and cons of creating these transport links in chapter 5.14 on transport policy. Advances in modular housing, which can be built in factories and assembled on site, are a potential solution to providing low-cost housing in towns and suburbs

Housing could also provide a cheap solution to homelessness. While this may seem like a superfluous statement, the current policies in the developed world to deal with homelessness that involve a mixture of poor-quality homeless shelters, neglect, and jail time are incredibly expensive for the healthcare, social welfare, and criminal justice systems. The city of

Medicine Hat in Alberta, Canada, where previously treating homelessness could cost up to $100,000 per person per year, decided to conduct an experiment and gave homeless people free modest but safe and individual housing costing $20,000 a year. The current pervasive thinking, insisting that the homeless get off drink and drugs and deal with mental issues before being granted housing, is the wrong way around, as it is very hard to do those things while living on the streets. Once the homeless in Medicine Hat were granted housing, the scheme saw police and hospital time dealing with the homeless fall, saving the city money and no doubt saving several lives.[188] While as radical a policy as this may be difficult to implement in less forward-thinking cities, it is more evidence that providing good quality and affordable housing has so many positive spillovers that it must be made a policy priority.

[188] CBC Radio, 'Medicine Hat Becomes the First City in Canada to Eliminate Homelessness', CBC Radio, 14 May 2015, http://www.cbc.ca/radio/asithappens/as-it-happens-thursday-edition-1.3074402/medicine-hat-becomes-the-first-city-in-canada-to-eliminate-homelessness-1.3074742.

5.13. Size of the State (2)

So far, we have argued that expenditures on pensions and healthcare are likely to increase with an aging population. We have moved resources from higher education into early-years care, but the net effect is likely to be an increase in spending, and we wish to maintain defence spending at 2 percent of GDP. We wish to embark on a large house-building project and spend more on investment. Meanwhile, we have introduced a carbon tax, a sugar tax, a land-value tax, increased taxes on capital and property. A typical leftist, large-state, tax-and-spend agenda then?

Well, yes and no. We must acknowledge, as Brad DeLong has argued in his *Equitablog*, that with an aging population and a globalised economy with little job security, citizens will want the state to play the role of insurer of last resort more frequently. Insurance is used to cover uncertain events in the future, and healthcare and pensions certainly fall into this category. These expenditure items are likely to increase, and these are already major expenditures for the state, so if these increase the overall spending is likely to increase.[189]

If the scale of these programmes is likely to increase, then maybe we can limit their scope somewhat. John Hill notes in his book *Good Times, Bad Times* that the wealthy, because they live longer on average, draw on pensions and healthcare resources quite heavily.[190] Additionally, because their children are more likely to attend university, they are more often the

---

[189] DeLong, 'Rethinking Macroeconomics'.
[190] John Hills, Good Times, Bad Times: The Welfare Myth of Them and Us (Bristol: Policy Press, 2015).

beneficiaries of student subsidies. If we are to limit the growth of the state, any welfare benefits or subsidies that flow to the wealthy need to be limited. Tax breaks for pension top-up schemes should be limited, and universal cash benefits should be made taxable.[191] Once state pensions are at a level where seniors can live free of the fear of poverty, the level of the pension should be tied to median wages, which will align the interests of pensioners with those of workers. The wealthiest students should have to fund the costs of their university education, as outlined in chapter 5.10 on education.

As for healthcare, in most state-run schemes there has been a sense of 'mission creep' over the years, whereas the original purpose was to cater for those with chronic or emergency needs. Some procedures, such as some cosmetic surgery and fertility treatments, could be left to the private sector to supply. Small co-payments for nonessential visits should remind people that they are using a service that costs money to run. The focus of healthcare policy should shift from prolonging life to improving the quality of life. Sanctions for people making poor health decisions should be introduced. This is not a nanny-state policy, but simply a moral-hazard clause that can be found in all private insurance contracts. If a house-insurance policy holder leaves doors and windows open and is then robbed, the policy will not pay out. We need to reduce the moral hazard implicit in public universal health care policies.

This ties in with the other measure to reduce healthcare

---

[191] Michael Johnson, 'Costly and Ineffective: Why Pension Tax Reliefs Should be Reformed', Centre for Policy Studies, 03/03/2015, http://www.cps.org.uk/files/reports/original/121123104830-costlyandineffective.pdf

costs, which is an aggressive push to prevention. The coming obesity epidemic threatens to overwhelm healthcare systems in the West. Sugar taxes, trans-fat taxes, and taxes on other harmful foods and drinks should be introduced. Meanwhile, fresh fruit and vegetables should be free from VAT or GST. Schools should be banned from serving sugary drinks and fast food, and sports and exercise should be expanded in the curriculum. The use of antibiotics in food production should be banned and minimum pricing for alcohol introduced. This again may seem like nanny-state policymaking, but a free universal healthcare system requires that citizens act responsibly, or they are burdening costs on other taxpayers.

In terms of taxation, note that many of the new taxes we have proposed are being used to lower other taxes and make overall taxation more progressive. The taxes on carbon and sugar can be used to reduce VAT or income tax, and the increased taxes on land, property, and capital are partially used to reduce lower rates of income tax or fund the wage-subsidy scheme. The house-building scheme and increased spending on infrastructure are investments, with large outlays now bringing large future benefits, and it should be recognised as such. The changes to stabilisation policy, emphasising full employment, should lead to lower unemployment and higher wages and, therefore, lower unemployment and disability welfare expenditures.

Therefore, we can see this is not necessarily a big-state agenda. It will be difficult to reduce the insurance and public-good functions of the state, however, and for that reason we should look for savings in other areas of government. We should try to reduce debt over the medium term, so that expenditure on debt interest can be diverted to productive uses. We must also try to reduce government expenditure in areas where there do not appear to be many redistributive benefits, and we look, in forthcoming chapters, at policies on transport, criminal justice, and cultural items.

There are areas where the government can reduce inequality without spending any money. If an aging population has so many negative effects on growth and government budgets, then why choose to have an aging population in the first place? Good demographic management can increase growth and save money, as we show in chapter 5.15. Lastly, we must be wary of nationalising industries unless the case is compelling from an economic efficiency and distributional perspective. As discussed previously, the rail industry does not look like the best candidate for nationalisation based on these criteria. Lowering water and energy prices would have larger benefits for the poor and so are better candidates for nationalisation. Even without outright nationalisation, we can have a positive effect on these industries, and others, by making changes to rules on corporate governance, and we look at this next.

5.14. Corporate Policy

In the 1950s, tobacco companies suppressed information on the harmful effects of tobacco. In the 2000s, General Motors failed to replace a faulty ignition switch, deciding it would be cheaper to settle with victims' families after accidents.[192] It recently emerged that ExxonMobil was concerned as long ago as 1981 about the effect of CO_2 on the climate but carried on funding climate change denial for the next three decades.[193] If an individual had been responsible for the direct damage and deaths these decisions caused, the person would have been charged with crimes against humanity. Indeed, in a study of psychopaths, author Jon Ronson found that CEOs of public companies are four times more likely to be psychopaths than the general population.[194] Clearly there is something sick in the corporatist model of capitalism we find ourselves with.

Activist groups or individuals working alone in areas in which they are experts and about which they felt passionate exposed many of the crimes listed above, and others like them. Centre-left parties should be partnering with these groups to expose criminal, immoral, and unethical behaviour on the part of large corporations. This can help in the fight

---

[192] Michael Moore, 'The Price of Human Life, According To GM', Huffington Post, 4 April 2014, http://www.huffingtonpost.com/michael-moore/gm-recall_b_5070492.html.

[193] Suzanne Goldenberg, 'Exxon Knew of Climate Change in 1981, Email Says—But It Funded Deniers for 27 More Years', *The Guardian*, 8 July 2015, http://www.theguardian.com/environment/2015/jul/08/exxon-climate-change-1981-climate-denier-funding.

[194] Kamelia Angelova, 'Why CEOs are 4X more likely to be psychopaths', Business Insider (video interview with Jon Ronson), May 8, 2015, http://www.businessinsider.sg/psychopath-jon-ronson-ceo-traits-2015-5/#.VuKspZx96Uk

against environmental damage and inequality by highlighting where multinational corporations pollute or treat workers badly in undeveloped countries, situations that domestic consumers may be unaware of. It helps by forcing corporations to maintain good environmental and employment standards overseas, which levels the playing field for domestic workers

There will be the usual complaints from plutocrats and media barons that the centre left is being antibusiness. Campaigning against pollution and poor working conditions is not antibusiness, it is prohuman, and this is a debate the left should embrace, as there is widespread distrust amongst the voting public of large corporations.[195] Allied with increased scrutiny and pressure, lobbying by industry groups should be restricted or even banned, think tanks should reveal their sources of funding, and all meetings with ministers, legislators, and regulators should be declared publicly. These policies could run into legal objections on the grounds of freedom of speech, but if trade union legislation can trample on individual rights so successfully, then it should not be beyond the wit of lawyers to draw up suitable legislation.

Having said all that, we must acknowledge that public corporations can be a force for good in many ways, delivering innovative products and services cheaply and efficiently to consumers while providing employment for millions. If we place too many restrictions on public corporations, we may push the owners into taking the businesses private. There is little evidence that this will help to reduce inequality, while there is some evidence that privately held companies, especially

---

[195] Gallup, 'Confidence in Institutions', June 2-7, 2015. http://www.gallup.com/poll/1597/confidence-institutions.aspx

family-run businesses, are less well managed than public ones are and have less access to finance.[196]

5.14.1. Corporate Governance

We have identified several connected problems with the current structure of the corporate sector in the developed world, especially in the United Kingdom and the United States. There is a focus on the short-term share price over the long-term good of the firm; there is the disregard for other stakeholders in businesses, especially employees, society as a whole, and the environment; and then there is a problem of rent extraction by senior executives. These problems arise from the concept of limited liability, the extent to which shareholder value maximisation (SVM) theory is accepted, and flowing from that, existing corporate governance rules and how they are interpreted.

Looking at limited liability first, there are reasons why we would wish to keep this in place. With the mass ownership of shares seen today, such a dispersed and varied group of shareholders are unlikely to have the time, or inclination, to monitor the day-to-day running of companies they own shares in. To remove limited liability would be to effectively make share ownership the preserve of the very wealthy or large funds, unless small investors were willing to take on potentially catastrophic risks. This would in turn limit the ability of companies to raise equity capital. Additionally, where shareholders have unlimited liability, this incentivises other stakeholders in the

---

[196] Valero and Roland, Productivity and Business Policies.

business to pursue their own interests and push the corporation to take risks, as the financial burden in the event of a negative shock will fall mostly on shareholders.

Problems arise from the combination of limited liability with SVM. This combination gives shareholders the best of both worlds, in that they expect companies to be run for their benefit and can use their voting rights to this end, while accepting none of the responsibilities that ensue. Lynn Stout notes in *The Shareholder Value Myth* that many of BP's shareholders did not feel any responsibility for the Deepwater Horizon oil spill but did complain when BP later cut dividends to pay for the clean-up and damages.[197]

SVM theory rests on false assumptions. The first is that shareholders are the owners of the corporation. Legally the shareholder and the corporation are separate entities, and a share of stock is simply a contract between the shareholder and the corporation in which the shareholder expects some share of the company's future profits. Next is the ridiculous assertion that shareholders are locked into the future performance of the company in the way other stakeholders are not. The reverse is in fact true, as it is much easier to diversify a share portfolio, or sell shares in a company, than it is for an employee to change jobs or a bank to sell a loan. Third is the idea that shareholders are a homogenous group who wish to maximise profits at the expense of everything else. Shareholders are also consumers, workers, and citizens with

---

[197] Lynn A. Stout, The Shareholder Value Myth: How Putting Shareholders First Harms Investors, Corporations, and the Public (San Francisco: Berrett-Koehler, 2012).

differing perspectives, who may well care to some extent about society, the environment, and employees' well-being.

Lastly, SVM theory rests crucially on the efficient markets hypothesis (EMH) that states that financial prices immediately, and efficiently, process all available information about a financial instrument. In the case of shares, this means the current share price is the discounted value of all expected future profits, and this in turn implies that if you maximise the current share price of a stock you are maximising the long-term profits of the firm. The problem here is that the EMH is not correct in theory or practice. There is a large body of empirical evidence against the EMH, while Nassim Taleb's books, *Black Swan* and *Fooled by Randomness*, demolish the theory.[198] [199] If the EMH does not hold true, then maximising short-term share prices can come at the expense of the long-term health of the company. Evidence for this can be seen in the share structures of many public technology companies, such as Google (Alphabet), who have dual share classes, with those issued to outside investors carrying zero voting rights. The founders of these companies clearly did not believe the traditional shareholder model would permit them to invest over the long term or take risks in new products and services.

We need to realign the control shareholders have over a company with their responsibility and commitment to a firm, and to move corporations away from SVM. We can do this using tax policy and corporate governance legislation. As

---

[198] Nassim Nicholas Taleb, Fooled by Randomness: The Hidden Role of Chance in Life and in the Markets (London: Penguin, 2007).

[199] Nassim Nicholas Taleb, The Black Swan: The Impact of the Highly Improbable (London: Penguin, 2008).

stated earlier, however, we do not wish to push companies into private ownership nor do we want to give company insiders too much power and make them wholly untroubled by scrutiny from outside shareholders, as is often the case in the Japanese model of governance. If we cannot make shareholders responsible for their actions by removing their limited liability, we can get them to commit to the firm by limiting voting rights to long-term shareholders.[200] The problem here is that we need voting shareholders to commit to the firm by being long-term shareholders *after* any important vote, not before. A simple way to implement this would be to legislate that shares that have been used in a vote cannot be sold until a few years after the vote. A tax break could be given to those who commit in this way when they do finally come to sell or pass on their shares. Hostile takeovers of underperforming firms by activist shareholders would still be possible, but the activist shareholders, and those voting for them, would have to commit to the firm for years afterwards.

Legislation should be passed so that large, long-term institutional holders of shares, such as investment and pension funds, would have a strengthened fiduciary duty to the long-term interests of their investors in the broadest possible sense, recognising that these investors have considerations other than profit maximisation. Until recently these funds have tended to vote passively in favour of the board and management, especially where executive compensation is concerned. Executive compensation should not be in the form of share options, which give management one-way financial incentive

---

[200] Colin Mayer, Firm Commitment: Why the Corporation is Failing Us and How to Restore Trust in It (Oxford: Oxford University Press, 2013).

to excessive risk taking. It is not even clear that they should be paid in shares, as share price performance can often simply be a function of the general direction of equity markets, for good or bad. Instead, executives should be paid based on specific financial targets (and perhaps some nonfinancial targets such as employee satisfaction), and the payment should be a mix of deferred cash and shares that can be clawed back if company performance deteriorates in subsequent years.

We noted above that if limited liability was removed from shareholders this would effectively give power to other stakeholders. The reverse is true for companies that are heavily debt financed, because shareholders gain the most when a highly-leveraged company does well, whereas other stakeholders, mainly creditors and employees, suffer the most if that company does badly. In many jurisdictions, company debt finance is tax deductible, while equity capital is not, skewing financing decisions towards debt and in favour of shareholders. Debt and equity finance should be treated equally, possibly by making both 50 percent deductible against tax.

One way to ensure the interests of other stakeholders are protected would be to mandate it in company law. The problem with a vague and broad remit such as this is that it suggests a return to the so-called agency problem, where management have a lot of discretion and no clear targets. As a solution, the corporate governance model that exists in Germany is preferable. In this model, there is a two-tiered board structure with a management board, made up entirely of company insiders, and a supervisory board, made up of shareholders and other stakeholders, such as bank and employee representatives. The supervisory board appoints and fires members of the management board and advises them on strategy, and the management board is responsible for the day-to-day running of the company. In this way, the stakeholders give the management the clear strategy they want implemented rather than leaving the prioritisation of stakeholders at the discretion of management. In Germany, the size of the supervisory board and the number of employee representatives on it is set by law. To impose this system in the English-speaking economies could cause many public companies to become private, so in the short term, this structure should be voluntary but tax advantaged. Another benefit of the dual-board structure is that the supervisory board can have a different mix of stakeholder representatives depending on the characteristics of the industry. This is relevant when we discuss monopolies later in this chapter.

In the United States, benefit corporations (B corps) are 'for-profit companies certified by the nonprofit B Lab to meet rigorous standards of social and environmental performance, accountability, and transparency'. Instead of imposing these standards, companies that meet these benchmarks and that adopt the board structure described above should be given preferential tax treatment over their peers. Over time, if we are right that this framework produces superior long-term returns, other companies will adopt these standards.

5.14.2. Utilities and Natural Monopolies

Massimo Florio, in *The Great Divestiture*, notes that the privatisations of the last thirty years in the United Kingdom has had a mixed record in terms of efficiency but a negative effect on inequality. This does not mean, nevertheless, that renationalising these industries will reverse this, as the private sector will have to be compensated for their shares of the businesses unless the government simply requisitions the businesses, which would be politically unpopular, legally contestable, and have dire consequences for business confidence and investment.

To nationalise an industry there would have to be clear efficiency and equality gains in doing so. The water industry could fall into this category. Water is a major item in the expenditure of the poor, and since privatisation in the United Kingdom, water usage prices have risen sharply; it is not an obvious sector where private sector 'innovation' has aided efficiency, as evidenced by frequent hosepipe bans. Perhaps the main question here is a political one. Would this policy be popular, and would it look like a politically regressive step for a centre-left party to make? This is important because a policy such as this could colour voters' perceptions of the rest of the policy platform.

Electricity and gas utilities and the railways are other obvious candidates for nationalisation. Rail nationalisation we discussed, and rejected, in the chapter on transport, and we can argue against nationalising the energy industries on environmental and efficiency grounds. Energy is an area of expenditure we wish to discourage due to the large CO_2 emissions currently generated in its production. Nationalising energy markets and driving prices down to cost will have the opposite effect. Additionally, energy efficiency and green technology are areas where private sector innovation can add value.

The current method of ensuring privatised monopolies do not extract monopoly rents in the United Kingdom is for powerful regulators to monitor that prices are what they would be if the market was competitive. There is a lot of room here for subjectivity and for regulatory capture by the industry. There is also something morally dubious about private shareholders profiting from vital goods and services produced by natural monopoly industries. This is especially so where an industry, such as the railways, benefits from taxpayer subsidy, as some of this subsidy will inevitably be captured by shareholders and management.

The dual board structure described earlier gives us a way to combine private sector efficiency with concerns about equality and the environment. Consumers, employees, taxpayers, and environmental experts should all have representation on the supervisory board of companies in these industries in addition to shareholders. We hope such a board will strike a better balance between efficiency and the concerns of other stakeholders than currently exists. In the water and rail industries, due to their distributional importance and taxpayer subsidy respectively, we can go even further and legislate that the supervisory board should be run based on a not-for-profit trust. If these models prove successful, the energy industries can follow suit.

5.14.3. Taxes on Corporations

We discuss tax avoidance in the chapter on tax policy. The same principles of simplicity and transparency should apply to corporate taxes. Beneficial owners of companies should be named, and there has been much progress on this recently with the introduction of the Foreign Account Tax Compliance

Act (FATCA) legislation in the United States, which is likely to be copied in the European Union. This helps the fight against tax avoidance and is a useful weapon against embezzlement, terrorism funding, and organised crime. Progress is also being made against transfer pricing and tax shopping. All these measures require strong international cooperation, and persistent budget deficits have prompted governments to act.

More can be done here. Whistle-blowers, whether individuals or companies, must be protected and compensated. Limits can be placed on accounting losses being rolled forward as future tax allowances, and international generally accepted accounting standards (GAAS) should be made mandatory to stop creative accounting shifting profits from one year to another or one tax jurisdiction to another. Accountants and auditors who collude or turn a blind eye in tax avoidance should face financial sanctions and criminal proceedings. However, as with personal taxes, we should not fool ourselves into believing this will create a large and permanent stream of income for the government. It is more likely that there will be a one-off windfall, which would still be welcome, financially and morally.

There are two problems with the current way corporation tax is implemented. In some countries, there is the problem of double taxation, where profits are taxed and then dividends paid out of profits are taxed again as individual income. Then there is the recent development of corporations making large profits but choosing to add to large cash holdings rather than reinvesting them or paying them out to shareholders. A solution to these problems, suggested by Financial Times journalist Martin Wolf, is that we increase the tax on retained earnings (profits not paid out), while making dividends and investment in research, infrastructure, and training fully deductible against corporation tax.[201] This solves the problem of double taxation and encourages firms to invest rather than hoard cash. We can also give preferential tax treatment to companies that have stakeholder representation on the board and uphold high social and environmental standards. A more radical solution that should be considered in the future is not to tax corporations at all but to tax the owners (shareholders) directly.

The other major tax paid by corporations is their contribution to the social security system on behalf of their employees, sometimes referred to as payroll taxes. This is usually based on the employee's income, but in many countries, this tax is regressive or at best flat relative to the employee's income. The structure of these employer payroll taxes seems to be a throwback to the defined contribution system of welfare. If we make employer payroll taxes more progressive, it makes it cheaper for firms to hire and retain lower-paid workers, while making them think twice whether they are getting value for money from highly paid senior executives. Large CEO salaries would be possible but would cost a lot more in payroll taxes and have to be justified to shareholders and other stakeholders.

5.14.4. Private Monopolies

A recent development in the global economy has been the emergence of digital monopolies who take advantage of huge

---

[201] Martin Wolf, 'Corporate surpluses are contributing to the savings glut', *Financial Times*, November 17, 2015, http://www.ft.com/intl/cms/s/0/b2df748e-8a3f-11e5-90de-f44762bf9896.html#axzz42ao8q8ko

economies of scale and network effects. Services and apps such as Google, Facebook, Uber, and Amazon dominate their markets, and the more they dominate their markets, the better off consumers are in using them. The market shares of these companies are definitely at monopoly levels, as are the profit margins at Google and Facebook.[202] Should we consider breaking up or regulating these companies and industries?

Peter Thiel, one of the founders of PayPal, argues that the monopoly profits these firms make allow them to take risks and innovate. Ironically, this argument for digital monopolies is as old as the hills, and it was used by monopolies such as Standard Oil in the nineteenth century and also by Austrian economist Joseph Schumpeter. There is implicit in this line of thought a strong statement about economic efficiency. What Thiel is effectively saying is that we should allow these firms to dominate their markets, stifle competition, and cross subsidise other businesses, because they will use their monopoly profits more efficiently than their competitors or the government would if the market was broken up. The case for this is certainly not proven.

A more important consideration is the distributional effects of these monopolies. Do the benefits of these network effects to consumers outweigh the negative effect they may have on suppliers and competitors? In many markets this is not obviously the case. Some digital monopolies have taken over start-up companies merely to close down potential competition or for the monopoly rents from patents, and many use transfer pricing to avoid taxes. One of the best ideas in

---

[202] Barry C. Lynn, 'Killing the Competition', Harper's Magazine, February 2012.

Anthony Atkinson's book, *Inequality*, is that antitrust regulators should prioritise the distributional effects of monopolies and oligopolies in making their decisions.[203] We should adopt this policy proposal.

A common concern with going after digital monopolies is that they can threaten to withdraw their products or investment a country, leading to an economic loss. There are several counter arguments to this. If these companies are abusing their monopoly position, then economic theory tells us this is inefficient, so breaking up the monopoly increases economic efficiency. The taxes they pay are often derisory as a percentage of revenues, and the sum of taxes from smaller competitors that could take market share from them may exceed what the monopolies are paying. There is also the idea of the marginal entrepreneur discussed earlier. If Google pulls out of a market, consumers can use Bing instead, with little economic loss. If Amazon pulls out of a market, another competitor would no doubt step in, with little loss to consumers. We should not be afraid of taking action on digital monopolies where necessary.

5.14.5. The Financial Sector

The financial sector was responsible for two of the biggest recessions in the last hundred years. It is no coincidence that these two crashes coincided with record levels of inequality in developed countries. In times of increased inequality, there is often deficient aggregate demand in an economy, as

---

[203] Atkinson, Inequality, ch.4.

the wealthy save a large percentage of income and the poor cannot spend any more of theirs. One temporary fix for this problem of inadequate demand is a credit boom. Credit creation by banks leads to asset bubbles, which in turn lead to the creation of more credit and, eventually, a financial crash.[204] As Martin Wolf notes, after a crash it becomes apparent that the banking sector is actually a ward of the state. Banks receive implicit subsidies in the form of cheap funding and liquidity insurance from central banks and deposit and capital insurance from taxpayers, and so he argues banks should be viewed as part of the state.

This is not to say banks should be nationalised. The financial sector plays an important role in attempting to efficiently allocate savings to their most productive uses and in granting credit to companies or individuals. Where banks and savings institution do fall under state influence, the credit process often gets hijacked by politicians and vested interests, who divert funds to inefficient pet projects. An example of this was the Japan Post Bank, whose savings were said to be used by Japanese politicians as a piggy bank, leading to a large-scale misallocation of resources.

The solution to financial instability after the great financial crisis (GFC) was to increase regulation in an attempt to prevent another crash in the future. There are a few problems with this solution. Regulators tend to be like generals fighting the last war, and the next crash will no doubt be different from the last. The increased regulatory burden in the Dodd-Frank legislation has driven smaller banks out of many markets,

---

[204] Wolf, The Shifts and the Shocks, pp.277-278

concentrating market share in the biggest banks, who are now even bigger than when they were considered 'too big to fail'. Complex regulations often give the biggest players opportunities to find loopholes and game the system to their advantage. Separating the risk-taking parts of banks from their retail divisions may help somewhat, although in the GFC it was the 'shadow', off–balance sheet parts of banks that contributed to the crash, while other banks were brought down by simple old-fashioned poor lending practices.

The simplest solution in the short term would be to require banks to hold much more equity capital as a buffer against shocks, meaning shareholders and junior creditors shoulder more of the burden long before depositors and taxpayers are put at risk. The Basel III regulations on banks attempt to do this but in a flawed form by not requiring enough equity capital and by basing the amount of equity capital required on the value of risk-weighted assets the bank holds. Deciding which assets are risky or not is clearly a subjective process, and if the wrong assets are classified as safe, the potential for trouble in the future is huge. Mutual banks and building societies, which are owned by their members and can make only conservative investments, should be granted more favourable terms for regulation and tax.

Other simple changes could be very effective. Senior management and risk-takers should not be paid bonuses in share options, which gives them an incentive to take excessive risks, but instead with cash and shares deferred for a long period and which can be clawed back if the bank gets into difficulty. A financial recklessness law should be introduced for those whose actions threaten their institutions, or the whole system, with jail time and asset seizure for individuals as part of the punishment. As for consumers, a simple fix suggested by Professor Frederick Wherry, is that regulations for small loans from banks should be made less onerous. This would mean the poor could get credit at reasonable interest rates from their banks, rather than paying the usurious rates on credit cards or going to payday lenders.[205]

5.14.6. Agriculture and Food Policy

We tackle two of the major problems of food and diet in modern society when we advocate for taxes on sugars and harmful fats in food and for healthier school meals. There are two further potential time bombs lurking in the modern industrial food system, highlighted in the documentary *Food Inc.*[206] As with the 2008 financial crisis, there have been plenty of warnings about these problems, but they will probably reach public consciousness only when it is too late.

The first is caused by the dominance of a few huge agricultural conglomerates in the food production system. This has led to a lack of biodiversity in crops, as farmers are forced by the agri-businesses to use their patented crop seeds exclusively. This makes agriculture very vulnerable to new strains of bacteria or breeds of parasites to which these crops do not have resistance, which could wipe out a large percentage of the world's production of any affected crop. This is like having only one password for all your various online activities; once the password is cracked, your whole system is vulnerable.

---

[205] Wherry, 'Payday Loans Cost the Poor Billions'.
[206] Food, Inc., directed by Robert Kenner (Los Angeles: Participant Media, 2008).

The second problem is in the production of cheap protein demanded by the modern consumer. Animals are fed unsuitable grains and hormones to promote rapid growth. This can lead to E. coli outbreaks, so the animals are then given antibiotics or the meat is 'washed' with ammonia. Bacteria build resistance to the antibiotics in the animals, and these new strains can cross over to affect humans. New antibiotics rarely come to market, as there is more profit in other types of drugs. The runoffs from industrial farms often pollute local water systems, and intensively farmed cattle are a large source of CO_2 emissions. The food industry is a microcosm of the modern capitalist system, having delivered mass produce cheaply to consumers but with a damaging focus on the short-term and environmentally harmful side effects.

At the other end of the food distribution chain sit the supermarkets; we previously discussed some of the problems with their market power in forcing down prices for farmers, undercutting local merchants, and confusing consumers with complex pricing and loyalty schemes.

When tackling these problems in the industrial food chain, we must be careful, because modern farming techniques have increased yields and eliminated food poverty in much of the developed world to the extent that excessive calorie consumption is now a bigger problem than hunger. Food and drink items are also one of the major expenditures for poorer households, so we have to be careful not to increase costs too much in this area. Antibiotic and hormone use and unnatural feeds for animals should be banned. These measures, plus the carbon tax, will push up the prices of some meats, especially beef, but other protein sources can be easily substituted into the diet. The carbon tax should also push up the prices of inefficiently produced or imported foodstuffs, leading to consumers and restaurants switching to more local and seasonal sourcing of food.

These measures will, on balance, push up prices for certain foods, so we need to find countermeasures that can reduce prices. Supermarkets should be banned from confusing pricing practices and from pricing items below cost. In the long term, this will help local small outlets to compete with the supermarkets and give consumers clearer pricing and more choice. Fresh fruit and vegetables should be exempt from goods and services taxes. Subsidising small farms is likely to fall foul of international trade agreements, so instead small, independent food merchants should be given tax breaks to help them compete with the supermarkets, as they are more likely to source their produce from local producers. These measures will improve diets and help smaller local farms and the environment.

5.15. Demographics and Immigration

The demographic profile of Japan has a top-heavy structure, indicating a large dependency ratio where the taxes of a smaller percentage of younger workers are required to pay for the benefits of a large retired cohort. Japan has this structure due to high life expectancy, low birth rates, and low levels of immigration. This structure is a problem due to the high dependency ratio and also because countries with older populations tend to invest and innovate less, thereby slowing economic growth.[207] Mainland Europe is starting to look more like Japan and may experience the same problems of persistent slow growth and large government deficits, as will many other developed economies unless they make proactive changes to demographic policy.

To prevent a high dependency ratio, a country must reduce life expectancy, increase birth rates, or increase the immigration of young people. Decreasing life expectancy is clearly undesirable and not a vote winner. Our policies for increased provision of early-years childcare and nursery education may have a small influence on birth rates, but the inescapable fact is that wealthier societies tend to have lower birth rates. Therefore, we need to talk about immigration.

Immigrants are on average younger and have more children than the indigenous population in developed countries, and therefore increasing immigration can help to solve the

---

[207] Matthew C. Klein, 'Aging, Real Rates, and Labour Bargaining Power: The Case of Japan', FT Alphaville, 8 December 2015, http://ftalphaville. ft.com/2015/12/08/2147125/aging-real-rates-and-labour-bargaining-power-the-case-of-japan/.

demographic problem faced by most of these countries. Studies have shown that immigrants tend to be hard working and innovative, and this contributes positively to growth in the economy.[208] So shouldn't we just increase immigration for a younger, faster-growing economy?

Obviously, things are not that simple, especially as, to keep an ideal demographic profile, a country will have to keep attracting immigrants until average life expectancy plateaus. The first problem is that much of the immigration experienced by the developed economies of the West in the last twenty years has been of low-skilled, low-wage workers. The common refrain is that these immigrant workers do the jobs the locals do not want to do. This is a subtly misleading statement. The immigrants do the jobs that the locals do not want to do *at the offered wage*. Without immigrant labour, employers would have to increase wages until they could attract workers of sufficient quality. So, it can be seen that low-skilled immigration is in effect an employer subsidy, keeping wages down, which is partly why the business lobby is so keen on it. There is an exception to this subsidy argument, and that is in jobs where the output is subject to strong foreign competition, such as in the agricultural sector. In these sectors, if wages were raised, the cost of the finished product may not be competitive in global markets. However, as discussed previously, most low-wage jobs are in the nontradeable sector, so, from a distributive perspective, we should wish to restrict low-skilled immigration to those filling jobs in the tradeable industries.

The second problem with immigration is that many of the

---

[208] Pomeroy, 'An Age-Old Question'.

native population object to it on social grounds. Common objections are that new immigrants do not integrate culturally, do not speak their language, and put strains on public services such as hospitals and schools. These concerns are valid where there is large-scale immigration and must be addressed. Immigrants should be able to speak the local language and must pledge to uphold the customs and laws of the land before they are granted visas or residency.

In Singapore, applicants for permanent residency or citizenship are tested for HIV and TB, as these are hugely expensive diseases to treat, and there is no reason why Singaporean taxpayers should pay for the treatment of new entrants. Likewise, there should be no expectation for immigrants to receive welfare benefits immediately. When state industries are privatised, many on the left complain, with some justification, that assets that many generations have contributed to are being sold. Similarly, the welfare system of a country has been built over many years of contributions from generations of residents, so immigrants should also have to contribute to the system before they can take from it. In truth, most immigrants are net contributors to the tax and welfare system, but perceptions amongst the voting public are vital where immigration is concerned.

It can be seen that many of the concerns about immigration are really about uncontrolled immigration. If the government can limit the scale and effects of immigration, and can pick and choose suitable applicants, people would be more comfortable with it. The left seems to have a historical aversion to listening to concerns about immigration, possibly for fears of being accused of racism, or possibly going back to

Marxist theory of international cooperation between workers. It should be noted that uncontrolled immigration affects working-class communities the most and is used by the right to drive a wedge between centre-left parties and their traditional supporters, as seen by the rise of the Tea Party in the United States and UKIP in the United Kingdom.

Remote countries, or countries with relatively secure borders such as Australia, New Zealand, and Canada, can control immigration more successfully. In the United States, the issue of the porous border with Mexico is one of voters' main concerns. Although Donald Trump's proposed policy of mass deportation is clearly unworkable, the Democratic Party's seeming laissez-faire attitude towards immigration is a potential vote loser. In the United Kingdom, the vote in 2016 to leave the European Union was heavily influenced by the negative perception of unrestricted immigration from within the EU. Without national control over borders, it is difficult to see the European Union surviving in its current form. What seems to upset voters, again, is the apparent lack of control over immigration more than the immigration itself.

Assuming immigration can be controlled, what policy should be pursued? There is a ready-made cohort of ideal candidates for immigration, who balance the demographic needs of the country but without many of the perceived negatives. Those people are overseas university students. They will be well educated and should already speak the local language in order to have qualified for the degree course. Being young adults, they are likely to be healthy and so place minimal strain on the health system, and they are likely to be relatively wealthy and open-minded to study abroad. Additionally, many overseas students end up staying in the town or city in which they were educated, and many set up companies there, creating job opportunities for the local population. There is an argument that foreign students will compete for university places with local students and possibly drive down wages in some industries upon graduation, but, from the perspective of inequality, it is preferable that this happens at the top of the income scale and not at the bottom. Overseas university students should be given priority when granting visas and citizenship.

5.16. Transportation Policy

When we earlier examined the typical expenditures of rich and poor, it could be seen that expenditure on transport, as a percentage of income, increases with wealth. Thus, government subsidy of transport could actually help the wealthy more than the poor, especially as the extremely poor travel very little. Against this, however, we must weigh up the gains in economic efficiency of getting people to their places of work or study and environmental concerns.

One of the biggest polluters and most obvious targets for restrictive action is air travel. Wealthier people and businesspersons clearly fly more than the poor do.[209] International agreements limit what can be done on international flights, but domestic air travel should be subject to carbon tax.

What about long-distance rail travel? The demographic here is again skewed to business and leisure travellers, though not as strongly as for air travel, and large ticket price differences between peak and off-peak travel can have some redistributive effect. There are significant economic and environmental benefits in reduced pollution and congestion to keeping travellers out of planes and cars, which could justify some public subsidy for long-distance rail travel. In the United Kingdom, there is currently a debate about investment in High Speed 2 (HS2), a fast rail line to link London to northern cities. The distributional effects of this investment are unclear. Will it help the northern economy or simply benefit business travellers

---

[209] Office for National Statistics, 'Table A1 Components of household expenditure, 2013 United Kingdom', http://webarchive.nationalarchives.gov.uk/20160105160709/http://www.ons.gov.uk/ons/dcp171766_383471.pdf.

and drain further talent into London? More promising is a proposed HS3 line, which would be a fast-rail link between the northern cities of the United Kingdom. This could in effect create a rival network hub to London, with the benefits more likely to accrue to the northern cities.

Long-distance car travel has a weaker pattern of income correlation, especially in countries with large landmasses, such as the United States and Australia. For reasons of political expediency, we may not wish to heavily tax long-distance car travel. However, cars are the least efficient form of transport in terms of energy use per passenger mile.[210] This suggests that not only should the carbon effect of the car be taxed into the gas price but also that long-distance expressways should not be subsidised. In the United States, with poor interstate infrastructure, a private sector solution of privately maintained and tolled highways seems like an obvious solution. In more crowded countries, such as the United Kingdom, where placing tolls on motorways could force traffic onto local roads, causing pollution and congestion, the cost of maintaining motorways should be added into the tax on petrol.

Indeed, congestion is another large contributor to CO_2 emissions from transport because of the energy wasted in repeatedly stopping and starting a vehicle. Cities should be able to implement flexible congestion charges depending on traffic conditions to encourage people to travel off-peak or use public transport to enter the city. Singapore's electronic road pricing (ERP) scheme is such a system, although evidence

---

[210] MacKay, Sustainable Energy, ch.20.

from rush hour traffic jams suggest the gap between off- and on-peak pricing is not wide enough.

So far, it seems most of the policies here are anti travel. Indeed, we do not want people to travel unnecessarily, and when they do travel, we want them to choose the most efficient form of transport. Additionally, transport is an area of policy in which we are looking to restrict expenditure. What positive steps can we take in transport policy that can help inequality and the environment?

The poor tend to use coaches for long-distance travel and buses, trams, and light rail for local travel. These are also more environmentally friendly than the alternatives, so we can subsidise these forms of transport by making them free from any goods and service taxes and by fully funding the infrastructure they use. This implies funding local rail, tram, and underground infrastructure. There is also an extremely cheap way to help the poor and the environment simultaneously through the increased provision of dedicated traffic lanes for cyclists and public transport.

Another way to reduce travel is to encourage work from home. Investment in high-speed Internet connections plus incentives to employers to allow flexible working can help in respect of this. Nevertheless, we must accept that many people enjoy the freedom of driving a car and will continue to do so. To mitigate at least some of the environmental harm from this, a push must be made towards the electrification of car use. Seventy-five percent of the energy created by the traditional internal combustion engine is wasted, whereas electric vehicles are on average five times more efficient.[211] To encourage the use of electric vehicles, their purchase cost should be tax advantaged relative to those of traditional vehicles, and gas stations should be required to have electric charging points by some date in the near future. A green transportation future does not have to be dull; the all-electric Tesla Model S can go from zero to sixty in 2.8 seconds.

---

[211] MacKay, Sustainable Energy, ch.20.

5.17. The Criminal Justice System

The criminal justice system is possibly the least successful branch of government. It is expensive, especially the court and prison system. It is unsuccessful in the sense that reoffending rates of former prisoners are high and the deterrent effect of prison seems weak. It is a large factor in inequality, as minorities and the poor are convicted at disproportionately high rates. It would probably be an improvement if we simply did the reverse of what we are doing now, and in some areas that is the approach we will take.

5.17.1. The Police

The police must be accountable to their local communities. To have largely white police forces patrolling largely ethnic minority neighbourhoods, as is the case in some parts of the United Kingdom and United States, is unsustainable if we want citizens to feel they have equal treatment under the law. Indeed where drug convictions are concerned, there is statistical evidence that there is not equal treatment for all.[212] Locally elected officials should have control of funding and oversight for local police forces, but with regular audits by an independent national body. In this way, the local community can control the scale and the priorities of the local policing to suit their needs. A national police force, such as the FBI in the

---

[212] German Lopez, 'Percent of Population Who Used a Drug in the Past Year', Vox, last modified 1 July 2014, http://www.vox.com/2014/7/1/5850830/war-on-drugs-racist-minorities.

United States, would deal with serious and complex offences such as terrorism, homicide, sexual assaults, and fraud.

5.17.2. Drug Policy

In *Drugs—Without the Hot Air*, David Nutt, a former scientific advisor to the UK government on drug policy, describes a methodology for ranking legal and illegal drugs by their harm to the user and society. Harms assessed include mortality, injury (both physical and mental), crime, and economic costs. The most harmful drugs under this methodology are alcohol, heroin, cocaine, and meth (in their various forms). [213] Cannabis, or marijuana, comes a few places further down the list, and yet a significant part of police and prison resources in developed countries is spent on the 'crime' of cannabis possession. Moreover, the poor and minorities are more likely to be imprisoned for cannabis use, even though they are no heavier drug users than the rest of the population. The best-case solution here, given that cannabis is less harmful than alcohol and tobacco, would be to legalise and tax it, as is the case in a few US states such as Colorado. This keeps people out of prison who should not be there while freeing police resources and creating a revenue stream for the state. Voters in some jurisdictions may not wish to legalise a previously illegal substance, but at the very least resources should be directed to the more harmful drugs of heroin, cocaine, and meth.

Three is an argument that cannabis is a gateway drug; in other words, its use leads to the use of harder drugs, either

[213] David J. Nutt, Drugs—Without the Hot Air: Minimising the Harms of Legal and Illegal Drugs (Cambridge, England: UIT, 2012), p.43.

because of impaired decision-making or because the canna-bis dealer will also offer harder drugs to users. The former is unproven, and the biggest gateway drug is alcohol due to the large quantities that it is socially acceptable to consume, often leading to risky behaviour. As for the latter argument, legalising cannabis would remove the dealer link between soft and hard drugs.

How do we deal with the more harmful drugs? US prohibi-tion in the 1920s showed the problems of outlawing alcohol. It turned ordinary citizens into criminals and helped to fund organised crime, and this is the pattern of all drug prohibi-tion, including the current so-called 'war on drugs'. Alcohol should be taxed commensurate to the harm it causes, but this may not be sufficient, as some users are more susceptible to its effects than others are, and drinks companies can often find ways to make strong drinks available cheaply. For this reason, British Columbia in Canada introduced a minimum alcohol tax, which successfully cut drink-related crime.[214] As for the more harmful illegal drugs, evidence from Portugal suggests that treating drug use as a public health issue rather than a criminal justice one can reduce the harm from these drugs while not significantly increasing their use.[215] This saves money on health, police, and prison expenditures. Anyway, if the authorities are serious about cracking down on drug use,

---

[214] Denis Campbell, 'Minimum alcohol pricing cuts serious crime, study reveals', The Guardian, 28 June 2015. http://www.theguardian.com/society/2015/jun/28/minimum-alcohol-pricing-cuts-serious-crime-canada.

[215] Chris Ingram, 'Portugal decriminalised drugs 14 years ago – and now hardly anyone dies from overdosing.',The Independent, 7 June 2015. http://www.independent.co.uk/news/world/europe/portugal-decriminalised-drugs-14-years-ago-and-now-hardly-anyone-dies-from-overdosing-10301780.html

they should be kicking down toilet doors on Wall Street and in the City of London on a Friday night, not arresting young working-class kids on estates for smoking a joint.

5.17.3. Fines, Whistle-Blowers, and White-Collar Crime

Between 2012 and 2013, football player Mario Balotelli was charged with up to eighteen driving offences in Italy. The fines could amount to €10,000, hardly a deterrent to a player earning more than that amount in one day. To be a fair and effective deterrent, criminal fines should be related to ability to pay. In 2015, German football star Marco Reus, on a similar salary to Balotelli, was fined €500,000 for repeatedly speeding and driving without a licence in Germany, where fines are based on annual income.[216] This is clearly more of a deterrent. A system of fines such as this could generate some very small fines for those with no income, so we may wish to add a minimum level of fine to avoid adverse publicity and to maintain a deterrent effect.

This leads into a more general debate about fraud and white-collar crime. After the financial crash of 2008, banks were fined for activities such as LIBOR rigging, and many senior bankers were fined and fired; yet almost nobody was sent to prison. Years later, banks were found to be rigging foreign exchange rates in London, and interest-rate swap rates in New

---

[216] *The Guardian*, 'Liverpool's Mario Balotelli Could Be Forced to pay €10,000 in Speeding Fines', *The Guardian*, 8 January 2015, http://www.theguardian.com/football/2015/jan/08/mario-balotelli-speeding-fines-italy.

York. This strongly suggests that banks and their employees, having seen no custodial sentences following 2008, were taking calculated gambles in continuing to break the law in various financial markets, factoring in the scale of the fraud, the likelihood of being caught, and the size of the potential fine.[217] To stop this, serious white-collar crimes should carry a mandatory minimum prison sentence along with fines and asset seizures. The perverse fact is that white-collar criminals probably fear prison more than the rest of the population, yet we fine them while jailing the poor. This tendency should be reversed, as we discuss later.

When we ask why increasing inequality is harmful, outside of material considerations, a major factor is the perceived, and real, imbalance in power and justice. The poor see themselves admonished for any misdemeanours no matter how small, whereas the rich and powerful appear to live by a separate set of rules. To further crack down on white-collar crime and fraud, laws encouraging and protecting corporate whistle-blowers should be introduced. In the United States, corporate whistle-blowers can receive 10 percent to 30 percent of any settlement. This is a necessary incentive for employees, who may find themselves unemployable after they have acted. Similar incentives should be in place for people, or companies, exposing tax evasion, and law firms could even set up departments for such a purpose. Whistle-blowing schemes

---

[217] Elliott R. Morss, 'The Criminal Acts Of Large Banks: Are Substantial Fines/ Penalties Enough?', *SeekingAlpha*, September 02, 2014. http://www.nasdaq. com/article/the-criminal-acts-of-large-banks-are-substantial-finespenalties- enough-cm386019

have produced a large revenue stream for US authorities—over $20 billion since 2009.[218]

5.17.4. Trials and Juries

The origin of the jury system is somewhat unclear. However, the intent must have been to prevent the powerful, especially royalty, dispensing arbitrary justice on their citizens. Instead, justice was to be dispensed through the legal judgement of peers, and this was formalised in the Magna Carta of 1215. A system that was originally intended to legally protect the weak from the powerful now seems to produce the opposite outcome. Corporations and the wealthy can buy the best legal advice; meanwhile, the busy and the educated can often request to avoid jury duty, hence juries are composed of those least suited to pass judgement. In cases involving complex financial or forensic evidence, the superior lawyers the wealthy can afford are able to tip the scales heavily in their favour.[219]

'LONDON—A Saudi millionaire was cleared of raping a teenager after telling the court

[218] Jana Kasperkevic, 'How Do You Make Millions by Doing Good? Become a Whistleblower', *The Guardian*, 14 May 2015, http://www.theguardian.com/business/2015/may/14/whistleblower-lawyers-corporations-us-government-awards.

[219] Erin Fuchs, 'Why America Should Ditch The Jury Trial', Business Insider, July. 3, 2014, http://www.businessinsider.sg/america-should-get-rid-of-the-jury-trial-2014-7/#.VuKxRpx96Uk

that he might have accidentally penetrated the 18-year-old when he tripped and fell'.

—*The Straits Times*, 16 December 2015.[220]

For this reason, the vast majority of cases now would be better overseen by a judge or a panel of judges, who can understand complex legal, financial, and forensic argument and see through the machinations of the top lawyers. To further rebalance the playing field, the maximum spend by one side of a legal argument should be capped as a multiple of that of the other side. The number of pretrial hearings and appeals should also be limited and the whole process sped up. This would have the effect of stopping corporations and rich individuals 'lawyering out' poorer opponents, and it would cut costs.

5.17.5. Prisons and Recidivism

Prisons fail in three main ways: They are expensive—sending someone to prison can cost as much as sending the person to college.[221] In addition, they do not generally succeed in their aim of rehabilitation. Reoffending rates of over 50 percent within three years of release are the norm in the United

---

[220] The Staits Times, 'Saudi millionaire cleared of rape after claiming he fell and accidentally penetrated teenager', DEC 16, 2015. http://www.straitstimes.com/world/europe/saudi-millionaire-cleared-of-rape-after-claiming-he-fell-and-accidentally-penetrated

[221] Brian Resnick, 'Chart: One Year of Prison Costs More Than One Year at Princeton', *The Atlantic*, NOV 1, 2011. http://www.theatlantic.com/national/archive/2011/11/chart-one-year-of-prison-costs-more-than-one-year-at-princeton/247629/

Kingdom[222] and United States.[223] Lastly, jails have been described as universities of crime, and mixing hardened career criminals with first-time offenders is unlikely to have a positive effect on the latter. Declining crime in the United Kingdom and United States has led some to say that prison 'works'. However, studies have shown that, when we allow for economic growth, aging populations, and other factors, increased incarceration has had a declining effect on crime rates over the years.[224]

It is often said the best way to turn nonviolent men violent is to send them to prison. The simple lesson from this is that we should not send nonviolent offenders to prison. The exception to this is serious white-collar criminals, for whom prison is a much greater deterrent than a fine or house arrest, and persistent offenders. A combination of house arrest, electronic tagging, community service, retraining, and rehabilitation is probably the best solution for most nonviolent offenders. If nonviolent criminals are sent to prison, the prisons should be separate from prisons for violent or persistent offenders.

Budget constraints in the United States and United Kingdom have led to a coming together of those on the left

[222] UK Ministry of Justice and National Offender Management Service, 'Transforming Rehabilitation—Policy Papers and Publications about the Transforming Rehabilitation Programme', GOV.UK, 19 December 2014, https://www.gov.uk/government/collections/transforming-rehabilitation.

[223] Matthew R. Durose, Alexia D. Cooper, Ph.D., and Howard N. Snyder, Ph.D, 'Recidivism of Prisoners Released in 30 States in 2005: Patterns from 2005 to 2010', Bureau of Justice Statistics, April 2014.

[224] Oliver Roeder, Lauren-Brooke Eisen, and Julia Bowling, 'What Caused the Crime Decline?' New York: Brennan Centre for Justice, 12 February 2015, https://www.brennancenter.org/sites/default/files/publications/What_Caused_The_Crime_Decline.pdf.

who feel minorities and the poor are disproportionately imprisoned and those on the right who feel prison is a waste of resources, leading to a push for reduced or noncustodial sentences where possible. Whereas in the US prison overcrowding and reduced budgets have led to seemingly random early releases in places such as California, the United Kingdom through its *Reoffending and Rehabilitation* white paper is seeking to incentivise rehabilitation providers by paying by results for reducing reoffending.[225] We discussed earlier how where the state is doing a poor job of providing a service it should be given to local or private sector providers, and that is exactly what we should do here.

We will likely end up with a criminal justice system that is more binary in its sentencing. For first-time offences, drug offences, and nonviolent crime, we place the emphasis on noncustodial sentences. For crimes of violence and sexual offences, which often afflict working-class communities the most, evidence in a 2013 UK Ministry of Justice report supports the view that those communities favour harsher sentencing than is currently observed.[226]

---

[225] UK Ministry of Justice, 'Transforming Rehabilitation'

[226] UK Ministry of Justice, 'Revision to Attitudes to Sentencing and Trust in Justice: Exploring Trends from the Crime Survey for England and Wales', GOV.UK, 16 August 2013, https://www.gov.uk/government/uploads/system/uploads/attachment_data/file/230186/Attitudes_to_Sentencing_and_Trust_in_Justice__web_.pdf.

5.18. Public Broadcasting, the Arts, Overseas Aid, and the Liberal Elites

State spending on the arts, public broadcasting, and overseas aid are in most developed economies, contrary to popular opinion, a small percentage of GDP. So why do we concern ourselves with them here? It is because, along with sections of the criminal justice and further education systems, they are perceived to be the bastions of the so-called liberal elite, and the parties of the right use them to drive a wedge between the traditional centre-left coalition of working-class voters and the educated middle class. This coalition may no longer be sustainable—it may be time to take sides.[227]

Thomas Frank, in *What's The Matter With Kansas*, documents the evolution of the tactics of the Republican Party in the United States in bringing cultural issues to the forefront of political debate.[228] In poor rural and postindustrial areas that have stagnated for decades, the political right downplays economic issues and can do so successfully because the citizens of these areas have not fared much better under the third-way policies of the centre left than they have under right-wing administrations. Instead they seize on cultural controversies, some manufactured but some real, over religion, education, the military, the media, and immigration, to claim that the liberal left is 'out of touch'.

---

[227] Roy Greenslade, 'Labour is Falling Apart, But Don't Blame Jeremy Corbyn for Its Collapse', *The Guardian*, 7 December 2015, http://www.theguardian.com/media/greenslade/2015/dec/07/labour-is-falling-apart-but-dont-blame-jeremy-corbyn-for-its-collapse.

[228] Frank, What's the Matter with Kansas?

These tactics can be seen from the Tea Party in the United States and UKIP in the United Kingdom. Cultural issues are used as a veil to distract voters from the fact that wealthy corporations and individuals finance many of these movements and parties, and that they have a far-right economic agenda that would harm many working-class communities. While it can be patronisingly claimed that some of their target voters are not aware of this, it is also true that many others simply don't care. For many working-class voters, cultural issues do trump economic ones and many UKIP supporters agree with redistribution of income, despite voting for a party with a far-right economic agenda.[229] In the United States, Republicans have won the white non-college educated vote for the last few election cycles.[230]

How should parties of the centre left react to this challenge to their traditional voting coalition? It has been suggested that the two election victories of President Obama in the United States show the way forward, with a broad coalition of minorities, the young, unionised workers, and the liberal elite. The problem with this coalition is that it is unstable and unreliable. Minorities and the young turn out for elections in lower numbers than other sections of society, and the number of unionised workers is falling. Minorities may tend to vote for centre-left parties, but they are not a monolithic voting block

[229] Alexandre Afonso, 'Agreement with "Government should redistribute incomes", British Election Study Wave 4', The London School of Economics and Political Science, n.d., http://blogs.lse.ac.uk/politicsandpolicy/to-explain-voting-intentions-income-is-more-important-for-the-conservatives-than-for-labour/.
[230] Asma Khalid, 'Republicans' White Working-Class Trap: A Growing Reliance' NPR, January 18, 2016. http://www.npr.org/2016/01/18/462027861/republicans-white-working-class-trap-a-growing-reliance

and with some effort can be won over, as the Conservative Party did in the 2015 UK general election.[231]

The so-called liberal elite may talk in liberal terms, but studies of voting behaviour show that votes for left-wing parties fall in a fairly linear relationship to income in most countries. This suggests there is no outsized electoral premium for the left in targeting this demographic. In addition, some liberal views repel more of the working class than they attract from the educated elites. In the 2015 United Kingdom general election, the Labour Party vote declined linearly with income, whilst UKIP ate into their vote in the second and third income deciles of the working poor.[232] Most importantly, parties of the centre left were set up with the express intent to improve the lot of working-class communities. To abandon them is to give up the very purpose of existence, which could explain why many of the centre-left parties of mainland Europe, dominated as they are by the elites[233], have been so spectacularly unsuccessful in recent elections.[234] It has been argued that the size of the working class has been falling and so to chase

[231] Ipsos MORI, 'How Britain Voted in 2015', Ipsos MORI, 26 August 2015, https://www.ipsos-mori.com/researchpublications/researcharchive/3575/How-Britain-voted-in-2015.aspx?view=wide.

[232] Alexandre Afonso, 'Agreement with "Government should redistribute incomes", British Election Study Wave 4', The London School of Economics and Political Science, n.d., http://blogs.lse.ac.uk/politicsandpolicy/to-explain-voting-intentions-income-is-more-important-for-the-conservatives-than-for-labour/.

[233] Peter Oborne, 'Europe is slowly strangling the life out of national democracy', The Telegraph, 26 March 2016. http://www.telegraph.co.uk/news/worldnews/europe/eu/10546394/Europe-is-slowly-strangling-the-life-out-of-national-democracy.html

[234] Ian Holland and Sarah Miskin, Interpreting Election Results in Western Democracies, Politics and Public Administration Group, Parliament of Australia, 27 August 2002.

their vote is to court long-term political obsolescence. This is just a factor of labelling. The old industrial working class has indeed been shrinking, but a new class of the unemployed, contract workers, and part-time and low-wage service workers have replaced them. If Piketty is correct, increasing inequality implies the numbers in these categories will grow.

Readers may have noted that this book advocates military spending of 2 percent of GDP, moving resources out of further education into early-years care, a radical shakeup of the criminal justice system, and reducing unskilled immigration. In all of these policies, we come down, in an evidence-based way, on the side of the working classes over the preferences of the so-called liberal elite, and we continue to do so in the analysis in this chapter and the rest of the book.

When it comes to cultural issues, parties of the left should side with the working-class communities they represent. Of course, there are some red lines that should not be crossed, and hard fought gains on race and gender equality should be defended, and more needs to be done in the criminal justice system. But where positive discrimination policies in the labour market or education are concerned, the emphasis should be moved from race to class and income. Marginalised ethnic minorities will still receive assistance by virtue of their low incomes, but white working-class voters and their children will benefit also. Some wealthy minority families will no longer receive assistance, which is as it should be—Barack Obama's daughters will probably not require quotas to get a good university place.

Government assistance to the media and the arts should be recognised for what it is, a subsidy for the middle-class elites, and withdrawn. This is not to say subjects in the arts should not be taught at school or university, just that these sectors should not be subsidised by taxpayers unless there are large positive spillovers as has been claimed for the film industry. In the twenty-first century, the idea of a civil servant or minister deciding that one art form is more deserving than another is patronising and ridiculous.

The purpose of public sector broadcasting was initially to educate, inform, and entertain citizens. Today, with YouTube, Apple TV, Internet content, and subscription cable, it no longer exclusively serves those functions, and there are plenty of alternatives. The BBC may make some great content, but so does HBO and the Discovery Channel. Covertly, public service broadcasting was possibly a counterbalance to right-wing media barons, but now whoever is in government tends to lean heavily on state broadcasters. The state should not involve itself in broadcasting content, except perhaps core news and information functions, and instead implement strict rules and regulations on media plurality and ownership as well as accurate and balanced news reporting.

We discuss earlier how many creative industries use internships to find future employees, which effectively discriminates against poorer candidates who cannot afford to work for free. For this reason, internships should be outlawed and instead replaced with a minimum wage apprenticeship. Many of these industries, such as broadcasting, media, and the law, include a large portion of the liberal elite and are industries where nepotism is frequently observed. If we argue for high capital gains and inheritance taxes to increase social mobility in finance and business, then it is hypocritical to allow a hereditary principle in these industries.

We also discuss earlier how lotteries are a regressive, but popular, tax on the poor, and so the revenues from them should be spent on poorer communities. If there is to be any state involvement in arts or sports, it should come from directing the lottery operators to use their funds to support the grassroots of these activities in working-class communities.

Overseas aid is often a target of those wishing to reduce state spending. It needs to be better explained how small a percentage of GDP it is (0.7 percent in the United Kingdom, 0.2 percent in the United States), but also how it is actually an investment in reducing poverty, disease, and conflict overseas that could end up costing more to treat later. This does not mean that the state need be involved directly in the delivery of the aid, something it is notoriously bad at. Instead, the money should be distributed, as decided by the legislature and with strict stipulations for use, to reputable NGOs, such as Medicine Without Borders, Oxfam, and the Gates Foundation, who have a proven track record of efficient distribution of aid.

5.19. Political Funding, Electoral Systems, and Governance

Most of the analysis so far has concentrated on reducing inequality at its economic source via changes to stabilisation policy, taxes and welfare, and corporate behaviour. We have also attempted to break the link between poverty for one generation and lack of opportunity for the next, especially through policies for housing and education. Now we turn to the final piece of the puzzle, breaking the link between wealth and power. We do this in response to the question, Why does increased inequality appear to have such negative consequences today? When reading Orwell or Dickens, it is clear that although material poverty still exists today, it is on nowhere near the breadth or scale of the prewar era.

One possible explanation is that there exists now a much deeper spiritual malaise amongst the poor than existed previously. Modern capitalism sets worker against worker and breaks community links, and modern media encourage their readers and viewers to blame the least fortunate for their problems. Previously, the church, community organisations, or trade unions filled this spiritual void and united citizens in common goals. Solutions to this problem are beyond the scope of this book, but we hope our proposed policies on housing, transportation, schooling and full employment can contribute to the healthy functioning of communities again.

'Choose a life. Choose a job. Choose a career.
Choose a family. Choose a fucking big televi-

sion. Choose washing machines, cars, compact disc players and electrical tin openers ...'

—Irvine Welsh, *Trainspotting*[235]

The other aspect of modern capitalism that is potentially more harmful today is that once a person's basic needs are met, the current capitalist system requires that, for firms to increase profits, consumers must desire more and more unnecessary material goods. Sophisticated advertising and media are used to imply that not to own these goods is a character flaw, and this no doubt feeds into the spiritual malaise outlined above. Policies such as an advertising tax and changes to corporate governance can mitigate some of these effects.

However, it is hard to believe that inequality is so poisonous today simply because the poor look jealously upon the expensive, shiny toys of the rich. This seems to be more an issue for the moderately rich, which could explain why increased inequality negatively affects some of the well-off also. The main problem seems to stem from the fact that the poor believe, correctly, that the economic game is rigged and that the rich use their wealth to buy power, a problem Albert Einstein identified as an inevitable consequence of capitalism in his 1949 essay, 'Why Socialism?'.[236] We see this evidenced in the discussion on the criminal justice system, where the poor are disproportionately sent to jail and white-collar crime goes unpunished. Similarly, in the political sphere the poor believe their voices are not heard, while the wealthy get

---

[235] Irvine Welsh, Trainspotting (London: Vintage, 2004)
[236] Albert Einstein, 'Why Socialism?' [New York?] 1949, Monthly Review 61 (2009), http://monthlyreview.org/2009/05/01/why-socialism/.

to buy policies and politicians. One study showed how US representatives respond to the wishes of the economic elites while almost completely ignoring the preferences of the average voter. [237]

5.19.1. Funding of Political Parties

The first thing to tackle is the political funding of parties, as this is the most obvious channel for translating money to power. There are three obvious ways to limit the effect of money into the political system, namely transparency, contribution limits, and spending caps. Transparency allows voters to see which special interests support which politicians and to study their voting patterns accordingly. Contribution limits stop the wealthy from dominating donations to one party or candidate so that smaller contributors become relatively more important. Spending caps can help limit the effects of money, where the first two policies have failed, by limiting the amount of media and campaign time a candidate or party can purchase. Due to the massive influence of money in politics, we must try to introduce all three policies to have any real effect. In place of large donations, there should be limited state funding of parties, with each party receiving funds for each member and voter they attract. Rules dictating minimum levels of media access (TV and radio time) are an implicit subsidy by the state to parties, and stricter rules on media plurality can also help to balance the political debate.

[237] Andrew Prokop, 'Study: Politicians Listen to Rich People, Not You', Vox, 28 January 2015, http://www.vox.com/2014/4/18/5624310/martin-gilens-testing-theories-of-american-politics-explained.

5.19.2. Electoral System

The choice of electoral system is crucial also. First-past-the-post systems such as those in the United States and United Kingdom tend towards two-party systems, where elections can often come down to a few thousand electors in a few key districts. This kind of system lends itself to being influenced by money, where huge resources can be directed at these few key voters. It also lends itself to 'pork-barrel' spending, where the state spends large sums of money to shore up key voters in key districts at the expense of the rest of the population. A further problem with such systems is that minority views are not represented at all in the legislature, leading many to abandon the political system altogether. Many on the left in English-speaking democracies favour a majoritarian system because they believe that when in power they can bring about real change. We should ask these people, how is it that countries which use first-past-the-post systems have some of the most unequal economies?

Various studies have shown more proportional electoral systems tend towards greater spending on programmes and transfers that help the poor, as parties have to appeal to the whole electorate to gain power.[238] Another advantage is that fringe opinion is represented in a purely proportional system. A problem with purely proportional systems is that they can lead to weak governance, as coalitions are nearly always required to govern; if the MPs are chosen off a party list, this

---

[238] Gian Maria Milesi-Ferretti, Roberto Perotti, and Massimo Rostagno, 'Electoral Systems and Public Spending', The Quarterly Journal of Economics 117, no. 2 (2002): 609–57.

places a lot of power in the hands of party executives who design the lists. These party executives can then be swayed my money and lobbying. Italy is a case study for the problems such a system can generate.

What is required is a hybrid system. A mixed member proportional system, as used in Germany, seems to offer the best solution. In this system, 50 percent of MPs are elected locally under the first-past-the-post system, and the remaining 50 percent are selected nationally from a party list, such that the final total of MPs is proportional to the votes cast. This system gives no great power to party bosses or to locally elected MPs, thereby diluting the influence money can have.[239] The same system could be used for local elections with the same benefits.

An issue with all forms of electoral systems is the problem of people who don't vote, most of whom are in the poorer sections of society. One solution to this is compulsory voting, as in Australia, though this would likely be tough to implement in many other countries due to constitutional freedom of expression considerations. The next best solution is to expand the voting franchise and to make registration and voting easier. Parties of the right have resisted the expansion of the voting franchise throughout history and now are trying to place restrictions on voting in the name of reducing 'voter fraud'. To realise how self-serving these arguments are, consider that in the 2014 US presidential election, roughly 93 million eligible voters did not cast a ballot, while there have been ten proven

[239] Frank C. Thames and Martin S. Edwards, 'Differentiating Mixed-Member Electoral Systems', Comparative Political Studies 39, no. 7 (2006): 905–27.

cases of in-person voter fraud since the 2000 election.[240] Not only should these attempts at disenfranchisement be fought, we need to push back the other way. The franchise should be extended to sixteen and seventeen year olds, registering to vote, early voting and voting by post or even on digital devices should be made easier, and national and local voting dates should be aligned to maximise turnout.

5.19.3. Governance

A further way to break the link between money and political power is to weaken the power of the executive. If a lot of power is vested in senior ministers, this makes them an obvious target for moneyed interests and lobbying. Instead, as much decision-making power should be given to committees and the whole legislature, for example, in choosing the heads of the fiscal council, the infrastructure board, central banks, and regulators. Patronage powers, such as the appointment of peers in the United Kingdom and presidential pardons in the United States, should be removed. Regulators should be appointed for fixed terms and not be allowed to re-enter the industry they have regulated for several years after they leave their posts to avoid obvious conflicts of interest. The much-criticised former head of the UK tax service, Dave Hartnett, left government for a role at Deloitte advising

---

[240] Janel Davis, 'Inperson voter fraud 'a very rare phenomenon'', Politifact, September 19th, 2012, http://www.politifact.com/georgia/statements/2012/sep/19/naacp/-person-voter-fraud-very-rare-phenomenon/

corporate clients on tax minimisation.[241] The Japanese even have a word for this practice, 'amakudari', which literally translates as 'descent from heaven'.

In line with this thinking, as much legislative and revenue-raising power as possible should be given to locally elected authorities. The more diffuse decision-making is made, the harder it is for vested interests to influence the decision makers, as there will be so many. Where local decision-making is concerned, it is particularly important that there is full transparency and a proportional election system. This is because the national media spotlight is often absent, and there is a danger of corrupt local fiefdoms in areas with a permanent administration of one political stripe. Sex abuse and money scandals at Rochdale and Westminster Councils respectively in the United Kingdom are examples of what can happen with an entrenched political party is permanently in charge of a local district.

5.19.4. Remuneration

The pay of representatives is a difficult issue, with voters naturally resenting pay rises for legislators after unpopular decisions are made. The UK MPs expenses scandal came about because legislators were encouraged to make up for years of stagnant pay by increasing their expense claims. Singapore has the highest-paid ministers and legislators in the world, which they justify by arguing that you want the best people

---

[241] BBC News, 'Former HMRC Boss Dave Hartnett Joins Tax Firm Deloitte', BBC News, 28 May 2013, http://www.bbc.com/news/business-22686877.

to run a country and that it reduces the possibility of corruption.[242] It is a convincing argument, and although it has bred some resentment in the city state, there is a case for having fewer but better paid legislators. Once representatives' pay is determined, it should be linked annually to median household income, which sees legislators' pay rise the most when unemployment is low and earnings are rising, and take the political sting out of annual pay rises for legislators.

5.19.5. Houston, We Have a Problem.

Some of the suggestions in this chapter will be hard to implement in some countries because of constitutional rules, and this is especially the case in the United States, which is why the influence of money is particularly strong in their elections. This does not mean nothing can be done, however. Constitutional amendments could make the president elected by popular national vote, so the candidates would have to court all voters instead of a few thousand swing voters in states such as Ohio and Florida. Independent committees should draw electoral boundaries to prevent the current wave of gerrymandering, and state and congressional elections should be on a proportional system. Smaller states should lose one senator, to be given to the more populous ones. And, of course, there needs to be a constitutional amendment to restrict the flow of corporate money to parties and candidates.

---

[242] corruption.net, 'Singapore: Lee Kuan Yew's fight against corruption', 31 March 2015. http://www.corruption.net/section/politics/singapore-lee-kuan-yew's-fight-against-corruption/154

5.20. Campaigning and Party Organisation

5.20.1. Campaigning

'They say I hate the party, and its traditions. I don't. I love this party. There's only one tradition I hated: losing'.

—Tony Blair, final Labour Party conference
speech, September 2006[243]

Conservatives on both sides of the Atlantic can barely contain their rage when the names Bill Clinton and Tony Blair are mentioned. This seems strange because, sexual indiscretions and the Iraq War aside, both pursued centrist policies and presided over booming economies in which the wealthiest did well. The reasons for this hatred are possibly that both displayed a degree of policy flexibility, which could be construed as ideological 'shiftiness', but mainly that they were, unusually for the centre left, fairly ruthless winners. They and their equally hated political advisors, James Carville and Alastair Campbell, took the traditional tools of political spin, media influence, and aggressive electioneering from the parties of the right and used it successfully against them.[244]

---

[243] Paul Owen and Jane Perrone, 'Key points from Tony Blair's speech', *The Guardian*, 26 September 2006. http://www.theguardian.com/politics/2006/sep/26/labourconference.labour1

[244] Alastair Campbell, The Blair Years: Extracts from the Alastair Campbell Diaries, edited by Richard Stott (London: Arrow, 2008).

Talk to conservatives about Ronald Reagan and Margaret Thatcher, and they will defend their most egregious policy errors, from the Iran Contra affair to arming the Taliban, and mass unemployment to the poll tax. Talk to many on the left about Tony Blair and Bill Clinton, and they will be much more equivocal, or even critical, the intellectual left especially. It has been suggested that this is because the liberal elite are more open-minded and evidence driven than those on the right, who are more ideological, but it could simply be that they are the more fickle and unreliable part of a political coalition. This is not to suggest that policy-making should not be open-minded and evidence based, or that the liberal elites should be shunned as a voting bloc, but that policy decisions should be directed at the economic and cultural interests of the poor and working classes. And at winning elections.

'He who controls the past controls the future'.

—George Orwell, *1984*[245]

It is also important to defend the past records of centre-left administrations because the political right are masters at re-writing history.[246] The Labour Party, in running away from the Blair–Brown economic record in 2010, allowed the Conservative Party to portray Labour as profligate when most economic experts agreed the financial crash caused the rise in government debt in 2008–10. This sowed the seeds of

---

[245] George Orwell, Nineteen Eighty-Four, Penguin Twentieth-Century Classics. (London: Penguin Books in association with Secker & Warburg, 1989), p.31.
[246] Paul Krugman, 'Fighting for History' *The New York Times*, May 13, 2015, http://krugman.blogs.nytimes.com/2015/05/13/fighting-for-history/

Labour's defeat in the 2015 election, as a large number of voters took the Tory accusations at face value.[247]

> **'He pulls a knife, you pull a gun. He sends one of yours to the hospital, you send one of his to the morgue! That's the Chicago way …'**
>
> —Jim Malone, *The Untouchables*[248]

After an election defeat, there is much wailing and gnashing of teeth on the left, who will blame the media, the electorate, their opponents, and anyone but themselves. However, they do not seem to be willing to do whatever is necessary to win, unlike those on the right, which is illogical if the stakes are as high as they believe. Take the environment as an example of the asymmetric campaigning styles of left and right. In February 2015, the chair of the US Senate Environment Committee, Jim Inhofe, threw a snowball on the Senate floor to 'disprove' climate change. Yet when extreme climate events present themselves, such as the record high 2015 winter temperatures, floods in northern England, and record wildfires in the United States and Australia, the intellectual left will make the case for climate change with the caveat 'of course we cannot link one event directly to climate change'. That caveat is unnecessary for those who understand climate change and confusing for those who don't. If we believe that climate

[247] Simon Wren-Lewis, 'Don't Ask What Lost, Ask What Won', Mainly Macro, 12 May 2015, http://mainlymacro.blogspot.sg/2015/05/dont-ask-what-lost-ask-what-won.html.

[248] *IMDb*, 'The Untouchables (1987), Quotes. http://www.imdb.com/title/tt0094226/quotes

change is a real and present danger, we should make the case as strongly as those seeking to refute it, and caveats should be left to the footnotes of scientific journals.

Handling of the media is another area where the left can push back more strongly, especially where the media tends to be majority-owned by right-wing oligarchs. In the 2015 UK general election, the campaign against Labour leader Ed Miliband in many newspapers was vitriolic and personal, and widely condemned. However, the two responses available to the Labour Party did not appeared to be used. First, there was plenty of material on UK Prime Minister David Cameron available on both a policy and personal level, as emerged soon after the election. [249]

Secondly, the media outlets can be influenced, with threats of boycotts, media ownership rule changes, and increased scrutiny of the proprietors and editors themselves. In 2001, the owners of the Express and Mail newspaper groups called a truce after a series of articles describing each other as 'pornographers' and 'Nazi supporters and adulterers'.[250]

[249] Rowena Mason, 'David Cameron Publicly Denies Lord Ashcroft Pig Allegation for First Time', The Guardian, 27 September 2015. http://www.theguardian.com/politics/2015/sep/27/david-cameron-denies-lord-ashcroft-allegations-call-me-dave-dead-pig

[250] Matt Wells, 'Mail and Express Back Off from Smear Campaigns', The Guardian, 26 February 2001, http://www.theguardian.com/media/2001/feb/26/dailymail.pressandpublishing.

5.20.2. Party Organisation

> 'Rule 1: Power is derived from 2 main sources—
> money and people. "Have-Nots" must build
> power from flesh and blood'.
>
> —Saul Alinsky's *12 Rules for Radicals*[251]

Parties of the centre left must be built on a large and committed membership. In the absence of this, they will come to rely on funding from trade unions, and be dragged politically to the left, or on money from corporations and wealthy individuals, and be pushed to the right. To attract large numbers of members, the party must be democratic and campaign across all constituencies. Members must be given a say on policy as well as fair and transparent candidate and leadership selection. Candidates must represent the area they are from and the membership of the local party. Recently, a divide has opened up between the representatives and membership of centre-left parties, as the leadership of the party imposes favoured candidates on local parties. Another of the advantages of a mixed member proportional electoral system is that local parties can select their favoured candidates for the regional elections, while the party leaders can select policy experts for the proportional slate of candidates.

The increased democratic power of the membership of the Labour Party led to the election in 2015 of the far-left Jeremy Corbyn as party leader. The membership of centre-left parties is often to the left of the party representatives and the electorate as a whole, and some fifth columnists try to use

---

[251] Saul David Alinsky, Rules for Radicals: A Practical Primer for Realistic Radicals, [ed. (New York: Random House, 1971).

the Trojan horse of an electable centre-left party to introduce an unelectable far-left agenda. For this reason, a party should have a clear constitution and explicit set of rules and policies that new members have to sign up for. If these rules and policies were explicitly centre left, then many of the far left would be unable to sign up for such a party and agenda or could be expelled once they had.

5.20.3. In Power

> **'I think Ronald Reagan changed the trajectory of America in a way that, you know, Richard Nixon did not and in a way that Bill Clinton did not'.**
>
> —Barack Obama, January 2008[252]

The most successful recent centre-left administrations, electorally, have tended to be those that built on the political consensus of the time and adopted, at least initially, moderate economic centrist policies, while successfully pushing more radical social policies. The Wilson and Blair administrations in the United Kingdom and the Kennedy-Johnson administration in the United States are typical examples of these. However, the leftist administrations that most changed their countries tended to be radical but short-lived administrations such as the 1945–1950 Attlee Government in the United Kingdom and the 1972-1975 Gough Whitlam premiership in Australia. The only administration that springs to mind that was economically

---

[252] The New York Times, 'In Their Own Words: Obama on Reagan',n.d. http://www.nytimes.com/ref/us/politics/21seelye-text.html

radical and politically long-lived was that of President Franklin D. Roosevelt in the United States from 1933 to 1945.

This book emphasises throughout the electability and practicality of policy measures, which is what sets it apart from the more utopian suggestions in other books about inequality. Once in power, however, does the centre left pursue a radical or safe agenda? They should start by enacting policies that would permanently change the direction of travel of the country and be difficult to reverse by any subsequent administrations. These may not be the first policies that spring to mind to reduce inequality, but their influence has the potential to be huge over the long term.

One of the first policies to pursue would be electoral reform. A more proportional electoral system coupled with campaign finance reform would begin to break the link between money and power. This would be coupled with reform of corporate governance, which would align the interests of big business more closely with that of society as a whole. These policies may take a few years to bear fruit, but their effects would be significant, and hopefully permanent.

Another priority should be reform of economic management, especially the replacing of GDP as the main measure of economic growth and social welfare. The reason for prioritising this change is that incorporating the negative effects of economic policies on inequality and the environment into measures of economic progress would force future governments away from policies that show a short-term improvement in GDP while damaging the environment and society over the long-term. It would also show certain 'savings' in government spending to actually be false economies and cost increasing over the longer term. If such reporting of the economy had been in place, the cuts by the UK government to flood defences after 2010 would have been shown for what it turned out to be—a massive deferred cost. The UK government cut about £1 billion from projected flood defence spending from 2010–15, while the latest cost estimate for the damage from the 2015 floods is £5 billion and rising.[253] [254]

Most other books on reducing inequality emphasise restoring trade union power and hiking the top rates of tax. This is like economic chemotherapy, unappealing to most, not guaranteed to work, and with many side effects. Note, also, how easy it is for future governments to reverse these policies. It is much better to make long-term holistic changes to economic and political life. Treating all income equally and abolishing most tax breaks will have a more permanent effect on inequality while seeming fair to the electorate. Weakening the power of large corporations and making boards of directors consider the interests of all stakeholders in a company will have a far greater effect and more popular support than re-empowering trade unions or nationalising swathes of industry. There will still be inequality, maybe more than we would like, but breaking the link between money and power, and between poverty and lack of opportunity, will mean this inequality need not translate into the spiritual malaise at the heart of modern society.

[253] Simon Wren-Lewis, 'UK flooding, austerity and the media', *mainly macro*, Monday, 7 December 2015. http://mainlymacro.blogspot.sg/2015/12/uk-flooding-austerity-and-media.html

[254] Matthew Taylor, Simon Goodley and Rajeev Syal, 'Cost of UK floods tops £5bn, with thousands facing financial ruin', *The Guardian*, 28 December 2015. http://www.theguardian.com/environment/2015/dec/28/uk-floods-costs-financial-ruin

6. Indexes

6.01. Index of Figures

6.02. Sources for Figures

Figure 1: E. P. Anthony, 2016. Data: Data: The World Wealth and Income Database,2016. Facundo Alvaredo, Tony Atkinson, Thomas Piketty, Emmanuel Saez and Gabriel Zucman. http://www.wid.world/#Database:

United Kingdom Income: Atkinson, Anthony B. (2007). The Distribution of Top Incomes in the United Kingdom 1908-2000; in Atkinson, A. B. and Piketty, T. (editors) Top Incomes over the Twentieth Century. A Contrast Between Continental European and English-Speaking Countries, Oxford University Press, chapter 4. Series updated by the same author (2012-2015, Methodological Notes). Wealth: Piketty T. and Zucman G. (2014), Capital is Back: Wealth-Income Ratios in Rich Countries 1700-2010, Quarterly Journal of Economics, 129(3): 1255-1310. Series updated by the same authors.

1913-1986 United Kingdom-Top 0.1% income share-married couples & single adults

1993-2007 United Kingdom-Top 0.1% income share-adults

United States Income: Piketty, Thomas and Saez, Emmanuel (2007). Income and Wage Inequality in the United States 1913-2002; in Atkinson, A. B. and Piketty, T. (editors) Top Incomes over the Twentieth Century. A Contrast Between Continental European and English-Speaking Countries, Oxford University Press, chapter 5. Series updated by the same authors. Wealth: Piketty T. and Zucman G. (2014), Capital is Back: Wealth-Income Ratios in Rich Countries 1700-2010, Quarterly Journal of Economics, 129(3): 1255-1310. Series updated by the same authors.

Figure 2: E. P. Anthony, 2016.

Figure 3: Christoph Lakner and Branko Milanovic. Global Income Distribution: From the Fall of the Berlin Wall to the Great Recession. Washington, D.C.: The World Bank, 2013. https://www.gc.cuny.edu/CUNY_GC/media/CUNY-Graduate-Center/PDF/Centers/LIS/Milanovic/papers/2013/WPS6719.pdf, p.31, Figure 1(a).

Figure 4: Richard G. Wilkinson and Kate Pickett, *The Spirit Level: Why Equality Is Better for Everyone* (London: Penguin Books, 2009), retrieved from https://www.equalitytrust.org.uk/sites/default/files/files/SpiritLevel%20slides.pptx, Slide 7.

Figure 5: E. P. Anthony, 2016. Data: OECD. An Overview of Growing Income Inequalities in OECD Countries: Main Findings.2011. http://www.oecd.org/els/soc/49499779.pdf.

Figure 6: HM Treasury, 'Statistical Bulletin: Public Spending Statistics', April 2013. https://www.gov.uk/government/uploads/system/uploads/attachment_data/file/193115/Public_spending_statistics_April_2013.pdf

Figure 7: E. P. Anthony, 2016. Data: Organisation for Economic Co-Operation and Development, 'Health Spending and Life Expectancy 2009', OECD, 2009. http://www.oecd.org/health/health-systems/44117530.pdf, p.7, Chart 1.

Figure 8: E. P. Anthony, 2016. Data: Dr. John Talberth, Clifford Cobb and Noah Slattery, 'The Genuine Progress Indicator 2006: A Tool for Sustainable Development', Redefining Progress, February 2007. http://rprogress.org/publications/2007/GPI%202006.pdf, p.21-22, Table 1.

Figure 9: : E. P. Anthony, 2016. Data: Office for Budget Responsibility. 'Economic and fiscal outlook', March 16, 2016. http://budgetresponsibility.org.uk/efo/economic-fiscal-outlook-march-2016/

Figure 10: E. P. Anthony, 2016. Data: Full Fact, 'Benefits and Tax Credits', Full Fact, last modified 10 July 2015. https://fullfact.org/economy/welfare-budget/.

6.03. Bibliography

AFL-CIO. 'CEO-to-Worker Pay Ratios Around the World', April 1, 2013. http://www.aflcio.org/Corporate-Watch/Paywatch-Archive/CEO-Pay-and-You/CEO-to-Worker-Pay-Gap-in-the-United-States/Pay-Gaps-in-the-World#_ftn1

Afonso, Alexandre. 'Agreement with "Government should redistribute incomes", British Election Study Wave 4'. *The London School of Economics and Political Science*. n.d. http://blogs.lse.ac.uk/politicsandpolicy/to-explain-voting-intentions-income-is-more-important-for-the-conservatives-than-for-labour/.

———. 'Voting Intentions by Household Income Quintile, British Election Study Wave 4'. *The London School of Economics and Political Science*. n.d. http://blogs.lse.ac.uk/politicsandpolicy/to-explain-voting-intentions-income-is-more-important-for-the-conservatives-than-for-labour/.

Alinsky, Saul David. Rules for Radicals: A Practical Primer for Realistic Radicals, [ed. (New York: Random House, 1971).

Alvaredo, Facundo, Tony Atkinson, Thomas Piketty, Emmanuel Saez and Gabriel Zucman. The World Wealth and Income Database, .2016. http://www.wid.world/#Database:

Angelova, Kamelia. 'Why CEOs are 4X more likely to be psychopaths', Business Insider (video interview with Jon Ronson), May 8, 2015. http://www.businessinsider.sg/psychopath-jon-ronson-ceo-traits-2015-5/#.VuKspZx96Uk

Anthony, E. P., 2016. Data: OECD. An Overview of Growing Income Inequalities in OECD Countries: Main Findings. 2011. http://www.oecd.org/els/soc/49499779.pdf.

Appleby, John, Ruth Robertson, and Eleanor Taylor. *British Social Attitudes 32: Health*. London: NatCen Social Research, 2015. http://www.bsa.natcen.ac.uk/media/38925/bsa32_health.pdf.

Atkinson, A. B. *Atkinson Review: Final Report: Measurement of Government Output and Productivity for the National Accounts*. Basingstoke: Palgrave Macmillan, 2005.

———. *Inequality: What Can Be Done?* Cambridge, Mass.: Harvard University Press, 2015.

BBC News. 'Former HMRC Boss Dave Hartnett Joins Tax Firm Deloitte'. *BBC News*. 28 May 2013. http://www.bbc.com/news/business-22686877.

Banks, J., M. Marmot, Z. Oldfield and J. P. Smith. 'Disease and disadvantage in the United States and in England', Journal of the American Medical Association (2006) 295 (17).

Bell, David, and David Blanchflower. 'Quarter 3 2013 Underemployment'. *Underemployment*. 10 February 2014. https://bellblanchflowerunderemployment. wordpress.com/2014/02/10/quarter-3-2014-data/.

Bertrand, Marianne, and Sendhil Mullainathan. 'Are Emily and Greg More Employable Than Lakisha and Jamal?' *American Economic Review* 94, no. 4 (2004): 991–1013.

Bessen James. 'How Technology Has Affected Wages for the Last 200 Years', Harvard Business Review, April 29, 2015. https://hbr.org/2015/04/how-technology-has-affected-wages-for-the-last-200-years

Blair, Tony. *A Journey*. London: Arrow, 2011.

Blastland, Michael, and D. J. Spiegelhalter. *The Norm Chronicles: Stories and Numbers About Danger*. London: Profile Books, 2013.

Bowers Simon. 'Osborne targets multinationals and tax evaders in budget crackdown', *The Guardian*, 18 March 2015, http://www.theguardian. com/politics/2015/mar/18/osborne-targets-multinationals-and-tax-evaders-in-budget-crackdown

Brynjolfsson, Erik, and Andrew McAfee. *Race Against the Machine: How the Digital Revolution Is Accelerating Innovation, Driving Productivity, and Irreversibly Transforming Employment and the Economy*. Lexington: Digital Frontier Press, 2011.

Buffet, Warren E. 'A Minimum Tax for the Wealthy', *The New York Times*, Nov 25, 2012. http://www.nytimes.com/2012/11/26/opinion/buffett-a-minimum-tax-for-the-wealthy.html

Campbell, Alastair. *The Blair Years: Extracts from the Alastair Campbell Diaries*. Edited by Richard Stott. London: Arrow, 2008.

Campbell Denis. 'Minimum alcohol pricing cuts serious crime, study reveals', The Guardian, 28 June 2015. http://www.theguardian.com/society/2015/jun/28/minimum-alcohol-pricing-cuts-serious-crime-canada.

Carroll, Aaron. 'Survival Rates Are Not the Same as Mortality Rates'. *The Incidental Economist*, 31 August 2010. http://theincidentaleconomist.com/wordpress/survival-rates-are-not-the-same-as-mortality-rates/.

Cass, Oren. 'The Wage Subsidy. A Better Way to Help the Poor'. *Manhattan Institute for Policy Research* 37 (August 2015).

CBC Radio. 'Medicine Hat Becomes the First City in Canada to Eliminate Homelessness'. *CBC Radio*. 14 May 2015. http://www.cbc.ca/radio/asithappens/as-it-happens-thursday-edition-1.3074402/medicine-hat-becomes-the-first-city-in-canada-to-eliminate-homelessness-1.3074742.

Cha, Mijin. 'What's Missing from GDP?' *Demos*. 29 January 2013. http://www.demos.org/publication/whats-missing-gdp.

Chu, Ben. 'Do the Latest GDP Revisions Vindicate Osborne's Austerity?' *The Independent*. 30 September 2015. http://www.independent.co.uk/.

———. 'Why Doesn't a Higher Minimum Wage Help the Poor More?' *The Independent*. 14 July 2015. blogs.independent.co.uk/2015/07/14/why-does-a-higher-minimum-wage-help-the-better-off-more.

Clarke, George R.G. 'Does over-regulation lead to corruption?', Texas A&M International University, 2014. http://www.aabri.com/LV2014Manuscripts/LV14025.pdf

Clark, Thomas G. The decline in political participation and the rise of the non-traditional parties, Another Angry Voice, September 27, 2014. http://anotherangryvoice.blogspot.sg/2014/09/decline-political-participation.html

Clotfelter, Charles T., and Philip J. Cook. 'On the Economics of State Lotteries'. *Journal of Economic Perspectives* 4, no. 4 (1990): 105–19.

corruption.net, 'Singapore: Lee Kuan Yew's fight against corruption', 31 March 2015. http://www.corruption.net/section/politics/singapore-lee-kuan-yew's-fight-against-corruption/154

Cowen Tyler. 'Why does Singapore have such a low birth rate?', MarginalRevolution, December 28, 2013. http://marginalrevolution.com/marginalrevolution/2013/12/why-does-singapore-have-such-a-low-birth-rate.html

Dalio, Ray. 'How the Economic Machine Works'. *Economic Principles* video, 30:59, 2015. http://www.economicprinciples.org/.

Daly, Lew and J.Mijin Cha, Dan Thompson, 'Does Growth Equal Progress? The Myth of GDP', Demos, January 26, 2012. http://www.demos.org/publication/does-growth-equal-progress-myth-gdp

Davis, Janel. 'Inperson voter fraud 'a very rare phenomenon', Politifact, September 19th, 2012, http://www.politifact.com/georgia/statements/2012/sep/19/naacp/-person-voter-fraud-very-rare-phenomenon/

Davis, Karen, Kristof Stremikis, David Squires, and Cathy Schoen. *Mirror, Mirror on the Wall: How the Performance of the U.S. Health Care System Compares Internationally*. New York: The Commonwealth Fund, 2014.

DeLong, Brad., 'Optimal Control, Fiscal Austerity, and Monetary Policy', The Washington Center for Equitable Growth, May 7, 2015. http://equitablegrowth.org/optimal-control-fiscal-austerity-monetary-policy/

———. 'Rethinking Macroeconomics'. *Bradford-delong.com*, 5 April 2015. http://www.bradford-delong.com/2015/04/draft-for-rethinking-macroeconomics-conference-fiscal-policy-panel.html.

Dillow, Chris. 'The Bosses' Pay Con-Trick'. *Stumbling and Mumbling.* 28 October 2011. http://stumblingandmumbling.typepad.com/stumbling_and_mumbling/2011/10/the-bosses-pay-con-trick.html.

Duncan, Greg J., and Aaron J. Sojourner. 'Can Intensive Early Childhood Intervention Programs Eliminate Income-Based Cognitive and Achievement Gaps?' *Journal of Human Resources* 48, no. 4 (Fall 2013): 945–68.

Durose, Matthew R., Alexia D. Cooper, Ph.D., and Howard N. Snyder, Ph.D, 'Recidivism of Prisoners Released in 30 States in 2005: Patterns from 2005 to 2010', Bureau of Justice Statistics, April 2014.

Dyson, Richard. The chart that shows there are 12 rates of income tax', *The Telegraph*, 07 jul 2015. http://www.telegraph.co.uk/finance/personalfinance/tax/11544301/The-chart-that-shows-there-are-12-rates-of-income-tax.html

Einstein, Albert. 'Why Socialism?' [New York?], 1949. *Monthly Review* 61 (2009). http://monthlyreview.org/2009/05/01/why-socialism/.

EWMI/PFS Program, 'Lectures on Corporate Governance - Three Models of Corporate Governance', December2005, http://www.emergingmarket-sesg.net/esg/wp-content/uploads/2011/01/Three-Models-of-Corporate-Governance-January-2009.pdf

Field, Christopher B. and Vicente R. Barros, eds., Climate Change 2014: Impacts, Adaptation, and Vulnerability (New York, NY: Cambridge University Press, 2014-)

Florio, Massimo. *The Great Divestiture: Evaluating the Welfare Impact of the British Privatizations, 1979–1997*. Cambridge, Mass.: MIT Press, 2004.

Frank, Thomas. *What's the Matter with Kansas? How Conservatives Won the Heart of America*. New York: Henry Holt and Co., 2007.

Freeland, Chrystia. *Plutocrats: The Rise of the New Global Super-Rich and the Fall of Everyone Else*. New York: Penguin Books, 2012.

Freeman, R. Edward, Jeffrey S. Harrison, Andrew C. Wicks, Bidhan L. Parmar, and Simone De Colle. *Stakeholder Theory: The State of the Art*. Leiden: Cambridge University Press, 2010.

Food, Inc. Directed by Robert Kenner. Los Angeles: Participant Media, 2008.

Fuchs, Erin. 'Why America Should Ditch The Jury Trial', Business Insider, July. 3, 2014, http://www.businessinsider.sg/america-should-get-rid-of-the-jury-trial-2014-7/#.VuKxRpx96Uk

Full Fact. 'Benefits and Tax Credits'. *Full Fact*. last modified 10 July 2015. https://fullfact.org/economy/welfare-budget/.

Future Spaces Foundation. 'Vital Cities not Garden Cities: The Answer to the Nation's Housing Shortage?' *Future Spaces Foundation*. 2015. http://www.futurespacesfoundation.org/our-work/garden-cities-report/.

Gallup. 'Confidence in Institutions', June 2-7, 2015. http://www.gallup.com/poll/1597/confidence-institutions.aspx

Galoozis, Caleb. 'It's the Economy, Stupid', Harvard IOP, 2016. http://www.iop.harvard.edu/it%E2%80%99s-economy-stupid-2

Garofalo Pat. 'Buffett On Why Romney Should Pay Higher Taxes: He's Just 'Shoving Around Money,' Not 'Straining His Back'', thinkprogress, JAN 23, 2012. http://thinkprogress.org/economy/2012/01/23/409332/buffett-romney-money-shoving/

Geffen Haley, 'The Napkin Doodle That Launched the Supply-Side Revolution', Bloomberg Businessweek, December 4, 2014. http://www.bloomberg.com/news/articles/2014-12-04/laffer-curve-napkin-doodle-launched-supply-side-economics

Goldenberg, Suzanne. 'Exxon Knew of Climate Change in 1981, Email Says—But It Funded Deniers for 27 More Years'. *The Guardian.* 8 July 2015. http://www.theguardian.com/environment/2015/jul/08/exxon-climate-change-1981-climate-denier-funding.

Greenslade, Roy. 'Labour is Falling Apart, But Don't Blame Jeremy Corbyn for Its Collapse'. *The Guardian.* 7 December 2015. http://www.theguardian.com/media/greenslade/2015/dec/07/labour-is-falling-apart-but-dont-blame-jeremy-corbyn-for-its-collapse.

Gregg, Paul, Sarah Jewell, and Ian Tonks. 'Executive Pay and Performance in the UK'. *London School of Economics and Political Science*, November 2010. http://www.lse.ac.uk/fmg/workingPapers/discussionPapers/DP657_2010_ExecutivePayandPerformanceintheUK.pdf.

Guild, Gerald. 'Happiness as Measured by GDP: Really?'.. Gerald Guild. 23 May 2012. http://geraldguild.com/blog/index.php?s=gdp+and+gpi+growth

Hanauer, Nick and Eric Beinhocker. 'Capatilism Redefined', Democracy, Winter 2014, http://democracyjournal.org/magazine/31/capitalism-redefined/

Harford, Tim. 'The Economists' Manifesto'. *Financial Times*, 17 April 2015. http://www.ft.com/intl/cms/s/2/7da2852c-e3af-11e4-9a82-00144feab7de.html.

Hart, Betty, and Todd R. Risley. 'The Early Catastrophe: The 30 Million Word Gap by Age 3'. *American Educator* Spring (2003): 4–9.

Hills, John. *Good Times, Bad Times: The Welfare Myth of Them and Us.* Bristol: Policy Press, 2015.

HM Treasury, 'Statistical Bulletin: Public Spending Statistics', April 2013. https://www.gov.uk/government/uploads/system/uploads/attachment_data/file/193115/Public_spending_statistics_April_2013.pdf

Holland, Ian and Sarah Miskin, Interpreting Election Results in Western Democracies, Politics and Public Administration Group, Parliament of Australia, 27 August 2002.

Hongo Jun. 'Tokyo Keeps Growing as Japan's Population Falls', The Wall Street Journal, Jun 26, 2014. http://blogs.wsj.com/japanrealtime/2014/06/26/to-kyo-keeps-growing-as-japans-population-falls/

IMDb, 'The Untouchables (1987), Quotes'. http://www.imdb.com/title/tt0094226/quotes

Inequality for All. Directed by Jacob Kornbluth. San Francisco: 72 Productions, 2013.

Ingram Chris. 'Portugal decriminalised drugs 14 years ago – and now hardly anyone dies from overdosing.',*The Independent*, 7 June 2015. http://www.independent.co.uk/news/world/europe/portugal-decriminalised-drugs-14-years-ago-and-now-hardly-anyone-dies-from-overdosing-10301780.html

Insley, Jill. 'NHS Hospitals Generating Millions from Parking Charges, Finds Which?' *The Guardian.* 9 June 2010. http://www.theguardian.com/money/2010/jun/09/nhs-generating-millions-parking-charges.

Ipsos MORI. 'How Britain Voted in 2015'. *Ipsos MORI.* 26 August 2015. https://www.ipsos-mori.com/researchpublications/researcharchive/3575/How-Britain-voted-in-2015.aspx?view=wide.

Ireland, Paddy W. 'Limited Liability, Shareholder Rights, and the Problem of Corporate Irresponsibility'. *Cambridge Journal of Economics* 34, no. 5 (2010): 837–56.

Jaimovich, Nir, and Henry E. Siu. 'The Trend is the Cycle: Job Polarization and Jobless Recoveries'. NBER Working Paper No. 18334. Cambridge, Mass: National Bureau of Economic Research, August 2012, revised March 2014.

Jake. 'Cost of Fraud (£billions) 2012-13'. *Ripped-Off Britons.* 28 December 2013. http://www.blog.rippedoffbritons.com/2013/12/graphs-at-glance-how-government-goes.html#.Vt7mBtBftf6.

James, Oliver. *Affluenza—How to Be Successful and Stay Sane.* London: Vermilion, 2007

———. *The Selfish Capitalist: Origins of Affluenza.* London: Vermilion, 2008.

Jaumotte, Florence, and Carolina Osorio Buitron. 'Power from the People'. *IMF, Finance & Development* 52 (March 2015). http://www.imf.org/external/pubs/ft/fandd/2015/03/jaumotte.htm.

Johnson, Michael. 'Costly and Ineffective: Why Pension Tax Reliefs Should be Reformed', Centre for Policy Studies, 03/03/2015, http://www.cps.org.uk/files/reports/original/121123104830-costlyandineffective.pdf

Jones Claire. 'Did QE only boost the price of Warhols?', *Financial Times*, October 18, 2013. http://www.ft.com/intl/cms/s/0/6f219ba8-327d-11e3-91d2-00144feab7de.html#axzz43tinrFJf

Jones, Owen. *Chavs: The Demonization of the Working Class*. London: Verso, 2012.

———. *The Establishment and How They Get Away with It*. London: Penguin Books, 2015.

Jones, Ros Wynne. 'Up to £20bn of benefits are UNCLAIMED every year', The Mirror, 15 JUL 2015. http://www.mirror.co.uk/news/uk-news/exposin g-figures-government-sweep-under-6067450

Jurist. 'Mexico Supreme Court Orders Wal-Mart to Stop Paying Workers in Store Vouchers'. *Jurist*. 5 September 2008. http://jurist.org/paperchase/2008/09/ mexico-supreme-court-orders-wal-mart-to.php.

Kahneman, Daniel. *Thinking, Fast and Slow*. London: Penguin Books, 2012.

Kasperkevic, Jana. 'How Do You Make Millions by Doing Good? Become a Whistleblower'. *The Guardian*. 14 May 2015. http://www.theguardian. com/business/2015/may/14/whistleblower-lawyers-corporations-us-government-awards.

Kalecki, Michal. 'Political Aspects of Full Employment'. *Political Quarterly*, 1943.

Keen, Steve. *Debunking Economics: The Naked Emperor Dethroned?* Revised and expanded edition. London: Zed Book, 2011.

Kellner, Peter. 'Welfare Reform: Who, Whom?' YouGov UK. 7 January 2013. https://yougov.co.uk/news/2013/01/07/welfare-reform-who-whom/.

Kerr Dara. 'Telecom monopoly overcharging Mexicans billions', CNET, January 31, 2012, http://www.cnet.com/news/telecom-monopoly-overchargin g-mexicans-billions/

Keynes, John Maynard. *The Great Slump of 1930*. (1930; Project Gutenberg, 2008). http://www.gutenberg.ca/ebooks/keynes-slump/keynes-slump-00-h.html

Klein, Matthew C. 'Aging, Real Rates, and Labour Bargaining Power: The Case of Japan'. *FT Alphaville*. 8 December 2015. http://ftalphaville. ft.com/2015/12/08/2147125/aging-real-rates-and-labour-bargaining-power-the-case-of-japan/.

Krugman, Paul. 'Inequality and Economic Performance'. Lecture presented at Columbia University, New York, NY, December 2014. https://webspace. princeton.edu/users/pkrugman/PK_Columbia.pdf.

———. 'Technology or Monopoly Power?' *The New York Times*. 9 December 2012. http://krugman.blogs.nytimes.com/2012/12/09/technology-or-monopoly-power/.

———.'Fighting for History' *The New York Times*, May 13, 2015, http://krugman.blogs.nytimes.com/2015/05/13/fighting-for-history/

———. 'Degrees and Dollars', *The New York Times*, March 6, 2011. http://www.nytimes.com/2011/03/07/opinion/07krugman.html?rref=collection%2Fcolumn%2Fpaul-

Kwak, James. 'Reducing Inequality with a Retrospective Tax on Capital'. *Cornell Journal of Law and Public Policy* (forthcoming). Published electronically 18 May 2015. http://papers.ssrn.com/sol3/papers.cfm?abstract_id=2607699.

Lakner, Christoph and Branko Milanovic. *Global Income Distribution: From the Fall of the Berlin Wall to the Great Recession*. Washington, D.C.: The World Bank, 2013.

Leunig Tim. 'The right to strike is an important one, but the public and private sectors should be treated equally', LSE, November 30th, 2011. http://blogs.lse.ac.uk/politicsandpolicy/public-private-sector-strike-equality/

Lewis, Michael. *The Big Short: Inside the Doomsday Machine*. New York: W.W. Norton, 2011.

———. *Liar's Poker* (London: Coronet, 1990, ©1989)

———. *Moneyball: The Art of Winning an Unfair Game,*. New York: W.W. Norton, 2004.

Lopez, German. 'Percent of Population Who Used a Drug in the Past Year'. *Vox*. Last modified 1 July 2014. http://www.vox.com/2014/7/1/5850830/war-on-drugs-racist-minorities.

———. 'US Drug Arrest Rates, per 100,000 Residents of Each Race'. *Vox*. Last modified 1 July 2014. http://www.vox.com/2014/7/1/5850830/war-on-drugs-racist-minorities.

Lynn, Barry C. 'Killing the Competition'. *Harper's Magazine*. February 2012.

MacKay, David J C. *Sustainable Energy—Without the Hot Air*. Cambridge, England: UIT, 2009.

Madrick, Jeff. *Age of Greed: The Triumph of Finance and the Decline of America, 1970 to the Present*. New York: Knopf Doubleday Publishing Group, 2011.

Mandelbrot, Benoit, and Richard L. Hudson. *The Misbehaviour of Markets: A Fractal View of Financial Turbulence*. Annotated ed. New York: Basic Books, 2007.

Mankiw, Greg. 'The Poverty Trap', Novemeber 11, 2009. http://gregmankiw. blogspot.sg/2009/11/poverty-trap.html

Manning, Alan. 'Why Increasing the Minimum Wage Does Not Necessarily Reduce Employment'. *LSE US Centre*. 27 January 2014. http://blogs.lse.ac.uk/ usappblog/2014/01/27/minimum-wage-employment/.

Manyika, James, Michael Chui, Jacques Buguin, Richard Dobbs, Peter Bisson, and Alex Marrs. *Disruptive Technologies: Advances that Will Transform Life, Business, and the Global Economy*. Washington: McKinsey Global Institute, 2013.

Mason, Rowena. 'David Cameron Publicly Denies Lord Ashcroft Pig Allegation for First Time', The Guardian, 27 September 2015. http://www.theguardian. com/politics/2015/sep/27/david-cameron-denies-lord-ashcroft-allegations-call-me-dave-dead-pig

Mayer, Colin. *Firm Commitment: Why the Corporation is Failing Us and How to Restore Trust in It*. Oxford: Oxford University Press, 2013.

Mazzucato, Mariana. *The Entrepreneurial State: Debunking Public vs. Private Sector Myths*. Revised ed. New York: Public Affairs, 2015.

McCoy Kevin. 'Walmart plunges on lower earnings forecast', *USA Today*, October 15, 2015. http://www.usatoday.com/story/money/2015/10/14/walmart-shares-plunge-lower-earnings-forecast/73921190/

Meade, James E. *Efficiency, Equality and the Ownership of Property*. London: Routledge/Taylor & Francis, 2012.

Mian, Atif and Amir Sufi. 'Who Spends Extra Cash?', House of Debt, April13, 2014. http://houseofdebt.org/2014/04/13/who-spends-extra-cash.html

Milesi-Ferretti, Gian Maria, Roberto Perotti, and Massimo Rostagno. 'Electoral Systems and Public Spending'. *The Quarterly Journal of Economics* 117, no. 2 (2002): 609–57.

Montier, James. 'Market Macro Myths: Debts, Deficits, and Delusions'. *GMO*. January 2016. GMOhttps://www.gmo.com/docs/default-source/research-and-commentary/strategies/asset-allocation/market-macro-myths-debts-deficits-and-delusions.pdf?sfvrsn=2.

———. 'The World's Dumbest Idea'. *GMO*. December 2014. https://www.gmo.com/docs/default-source/research-and-commentary/strategies/asset-allocation/the-world's-dumbest-idea.pdf.

Moore, Michael. 'The Price of Human Life, According To GM'. *Huffington Post*. 4 April 2014. http://www.huffingtonpost.com/michael-moore/gm-recall_b_5070492.html.

Morss, Elliott R. 'The Criminal Acts Of Large Banks: Are Substantial Fines/Penalties Enough?', *SeekingAlpha*, September 02, 2014. http://www.nasdaq.com/article/the-criminal-acts-of-large-banks-are-substantial-finespenalties-enough-cm386019.

Motesharrei, Safa, Jorge Rivas, and Eugenia Kalnay. 'Human and Nature Dynamics (HANDY): Modelling Inequality and Use of Resources in the Collapse or Sustainability of Societies'. *Ecological Economics* 101, no. 4 (2014): 90–102.

Murphy, Richard. 'The Tax Gap'. *Tax Research UK*. September 2014. http://www.taxresearch.org.uk/Documents/PCSTaxGap2014Full.pdf.

New Climate Economy. 'Estimates of Emissions Reduction. Seizing the Global Opportunity: Partnerships for Better Growth and a Better Climate'. *New Climate Economy*. 2015. http://newclimateeconomy.report/misc/working-papers.

North Atlantic Treaty Organisation. 'Wales Summit Declaration'. *NATO*. 5 September 2014. http://www.nato.int/cps/en/natohq/official_texts_112964.htm.

Nutt, David J. *Drugs—Without the Hot Air: Minimising the Harms of Legal and Illegal Drugs*. Cambridge, England: UIT, 2012.

Oborne, Peter. 'Why I Have Resigned from the Telegraph'. *Open Democracy UK*, 17 February 2015. https://www.opendemocracy.net/ourkingdom/peter-oborne/why-i-have-resigned-from-telegraph.

———. 'Europe is slowly strangling the life out of national democracy', The Telegraph, 26 March 2016. http://www.telegraph.co.uk/news/worldnews/europe/eu/10546394/Europe-is-slowly-strangling-the-life-out-of-national-democracy.html

O'Boyle Jr, E., and H. Aguinis. 'The Best and the Rest'. *Personnel Psychology* 65, no. 1 (2012): 79–119.

O'Brien, Neil, 'So what should the top rate of tax be? It all turns on the longterm effects of high taxes', *The Telegraph*, March 23rd, 2012, http://blogs.telegraph.

co.uk/news/neilobrien1/100146421/so-what-should-the-top-rate-of-tax-be-it-all-turns-on-the-long-term-effects-of-high-taxes/

OECD. An Overview of Growing Income Inequalities in OECD Countries: Main Findings. 2011. http://www.oecd.org/els/soc/49499779.pdf

Office for Budget Responsibility. 'Economic and fiscal outlook', March 16, 2016. http://budgetresponsibility.org.uk/efo/economic-fiscal-outloo k-march-2016/

Office for National Statistics, 'Components of household expenditure, 2013 United Kingdom', http://webarchive.nationalarchives.gov.uk/20160105160709/ http://www.ons.gov.uk/ons/dcp171766_383471.pdf

O'Keefe Daniel, 'Down on the farm: agricultural workers receive lower wages than other workers', Chicago Policy Review, February 13, 2015. http:// chicagopolicyreview.org/2015/02/13/down-on-the-farm-agricultural-workers-receive-lower-wages-than-other-workers/

Oreskes, Naomi, and Erik M. Conway. *Merchants of Doubt: How a Handful of Scientists Obscured the Truth on Issues from Tobacco Smoke to Global Warming*. New York: Bloomsbury Publishing, 2010.

Organisation for Economic Co-operation and Development. 'PISA 2012 Results in Focus: What 15-Year-Olds Know and What They Can Do with What They Know'. *OECD*. 2014. http://www.oecd.org/pisa/keyfind-ings/pisa-2012-results-overview.pdf.

———. 'The Distributional Effects of Consumption Taxes in OECD Countries'. *OECD Tax Policy Studies 22*. Paris: OECD/Korea Institute of Public Finance, 2014.

Organisation for Economic Co-Operation and Development Directorate for Employment, Labour, and Social Affairs. Focus on Inequality and Growth. [Paris?]: OECD, 2014.

Orwell, George, Nineteen Eighty-Four, Penguin Twentieth-Century Classics. (London: Penguin Books in association with Secker & Warburg, 1989),

Osborne, Hilary, 'Private landlords gain £26.7bn from UK taxpayer, says cam-paign group', *The Guardian*, 9 February 2015, http://www.theguardian. com/money/2015/feb/09/private-landlords-gain-26-7-billion-uk-taxpayer-generation-rent

Owen, Paul and Jane Perrone, 'Key points from Tony Blair's speech', *The Guardian*, 26 September 2006. http://www.theguardian.com/politics/2006/sep/26/labourconference.labour1

Peck Tom, "Sweetheart' deal between HMRC and Goldman Sachs was struck to save Government embarrassment, court hears', Independent, 3 May 2013. http://www.independent.co.uk/news/uk/home-news/sweetheart-deal-between-hmrc-and-goldman-sachs-was-struck-to-save-government-embarrassment-court-8601007.html

Penketh, Anne. 'France Forced to Drop 75 Percent Supertax after Meagre Returns'. *The Guardian*. 31 December 2014. http://www.theguardian.com/world/2014/dec/31/france-drops-75percent-supertax.

Pettinger, Tejvan. 'Chart 1: Real Terms Trends in Public Spending'. *Economics Help*. n.d. http://www.economicshelp.org/wp-content/uploads/blog-uploads/2013/01/Screen-Shot-2013-07-08-at-10.52.23-500x333.png.

———. 'Tax Revenue Sources'. *Economics Help*. 5 December 2014. http://www.economicshelp.org/blog/12272/economics/falling-uk-tax-revenue/.

Piketty, Thomas. *Capital in the Twenty-First Century*. Translated by Arthur Goldhammer. Cambridge, Mass.: The Belknap Press of Harvard University Press, 2014.

Pomeroy, James. 'An Age-Old Question: Massive Demographic Changes Help Emerging Markets—But Will Cut Global Growth'. *HSBC*. 30 November 2015. http://www.gbm.hsbc.com/insights/growth/an-age-old-question.

Porter Richard, Crap Cars (London: BBC Books, ©2004)

Pope Francis, Twitter post, 28 April 2014, 4:Source: 28 a.m., https://twitter.com/pontifex/status/460697074585980928

Pope, Thomas and Barra Roantree, 'A Survey of the UK Tax System', Institute for Fiscal Studies, November 2014, ch.3.9

Portes, J., and Simon Wren-Lewis. *Issues in the Design of Fiscal Policy Rules*. London: NIESR, 2014. http://www.niesr.ac.uk/sites/default/files/publications/dp429.pdf.

Poverty.org.uk, 'Working-age out-of-work benefit recipients',February 2009. http://www.poverty.org.uk/13/index.shtml

Prokop, Andrew. '40 Charts that Explain Money in Politics'. *Vox*. 30 July 2014. http://www.vox.com/2014/7/30/5949581/money-in-politics-charts-explain.

———. 'Study: Politicians Listen to Rich People, Not You'. *Vox*. 28 January 2015. http://www.vox.com/2014/4/18/5624310/martin-gilens-testing-theories-of-american-politics-explained.

Reinhart, Carmen M., and Kenneth Rogoff. *This Time Is Different: Eight Centuries of Financial Folly*. Reprint ed. Princeton: Princeton University Press, 2009.

Resnick, Brian, 'Chart: One Year of Prison Costs More Than One Year at Princeton', *The Atlantic*, NOV 1, 2011. http://www.theatlantic.com/national/archive/2011/11/chart-one-year-of-prison-costs-more-than-one-year-at-princeton/247629/

Roberts, Marcus. *Revolt on the Left*. (London: Fabian Society, October 2014). http://www.fabians.org.uk/wp-content/uploads/2014/10/RevoltOnTheLeft-Final4.pdf.

Roeder, Oliver, Lauren-Brooke Eisen, and Julia Bowling. *'What Caused the Crime Decline*?' New York: Brennan Centre for Justice. 12 February 2015. https://www.brennancenter.org/sites/default/files/publications/What_Caused_The_Crime_Decline.pdf.

Rosen Sherwen, 'The Economics of Superstars', The American Economic Review, Vol. 71, No. 5 (Dec., 1981), pp. 845-858, http://www.jstor.org/stable/1803469.

Sahin, Ayşegül, Joseph Song, and Bart Hobijn. 'The Unemployment Gender Gap during the 2007 Recession'. *Current Issues in Economics and Finance* 16, no. 2 (2010).

Sandel, Michael J. *What Money Can't Buy: The Moral Limits of Markets*. London: Penguin, 2013.

Sassen, Saskia. *The Global City: New York, London, Tokyo*. 2nd ed. Princeton, N.J.: Princeton University Press, 2001.

Shakespeare, Stephan. 'Voters Prefer Spending on Services to Cutting Borrowing'. *YouGov UK*. 14 January 2013. https://yougov.co.uk/news/2015/01/14/voters-prefer-spending-services-cutting-borrowing/.

Sheth, Jagdish, and Rajendra Sisodia. *The Rule of Three: Surviving and Thriving in Competitive Markets*. New York: Free Press, 2002.

Silver, Nate, *The Signal and the Noise: Why So Many Predictions Fail-but Some Don't* . Penguin Publishing Group, . (2012-09-27), Kindle Edition.

Skidelsky, Robert. *John Maynard Keynes, 1883–1946: Economist, Philosopher, Statesman*. New York: Penguin Books, 2005.

Smith, Adam, *An Inquiry into the Nature and Causes of the Wealth of Nations*,

Project Gutenberg EBook, https://www.gutenberg.org/files/3300/3300-h/3300-h.htm

Smithers, Andrew. 'Has Labour Lost Out to Capital?' *Financial Times*. 1 April 2015. http://blogs.ft.com/andrew-smithers/2015/04/has-labour-lost-out-to-capital/.

Smithers, Rebecca. 'UK Supermarkets Dupe Shoppers out of Hundreds of Millions, says Which?' *The Guardian*. 21 April 2015. http://www.the-guardian.com/business/2015/apr/21/uk-supermarkets-dupe-shoppers-out-of-hundreds-of-millions-says-which.

Social Mobility and Child Poverty Commission. *Elitist Britain?* London: Social Mobility and Child Poverty Commission, 2014.

Sorkin, Andrew Ross. *Too Big to Fail: The Inside Story of How Wall Street and Washington Fought to Save the Financial System—and Themselves*. New York: Penguin Books, 2010.

Stout, Lynn A. *The Shareholder Value Myth: How Putting Shareholders First Harms Investors, Corporations, and the Public*. San Francisco: Berrett-Koehler, 2012.

Stuart Wall, *Microeconomics*, Economics Express (Harlow, England: Pearson, 2013)

Talberth, Dr. John, Clifford Cobb and Noah Slattery, 'The Genuine Progress Indicator 2006: A Tool for Sustainable Development', Redefining Progress, February 2007. http://rprogress.org/publications/2007/GPI%202006.pdf

Taleb, Nassim Nicholas. *Fooled by Randomness: The Hidden Role of Chance in Life and in the Markets*. 2nd ed. London: Penguin, 2007.

———. *The Black Swan: The Impact of the Highly Improbable*. London: Penguin, 2008.

Tavernise, Sabrina, 'Life Spans Shrink for Least-Educated Whites in the U.S.', *The New York Times*, September 20, 2012. http://www.nytimes.com/2012/09/21/us/life-expectancy-for-less-educated-whites-in-us-is-shrinking.html?_r=0

Taylor, Matthew, Simon Goodley and Rajeev Syal, 'Cost of UK floods tops £5bn, with thousands facing financial ruin', The Guardian, 28 December 2015. http://www.theguardian.com/environment/2015/dec/28/uk-floods-costs-financial-ruin

Thames, Frank C., and Martin S. Edwards. 'Differentiating Mixed-Member Electoral Systems'. *Comparative Political Studies* 39, no. 7 (2006): 905–27.

The Economist. 'America's Elite: An Hereditary Meritocracy'. *The Economist*. 24 January 2015. http://www.economist.com/news/briefing/21640316-children-rich-and-powerful-are-increasingly-well-suited-earning-wealth-and-power.

———. 'Freeports: Überwarehouses for the ultrarich', Nov 23rd 2013, http://www.economist.com/news/briefing/21590353-ever-more-wealth-being-parked-fancy-storage-facilities-some-customers-they-are

———. 'Special Report: The Nordic Countries, February 2nd 2013'. *The Economist*. http://www.economist.com/sites/default/files/20130202_nordic_countries.pdf.

———. 'Tax havens: The missing $20 trillion', Feb 16th 2013, http://www.economist.com/news/leaders/21571873-how-stop-companies-and-people-dodging-tax-delaware-well-grand-cayman-missing-20

———. 'More or less', Sep 1st 2012. http://www.economist.com/node/21561112

The Guardian. 'Liverpool's Mario Balotelli Could Be Forced to pay €10,000 in Speeding Fines'. *The Guardian*. 8 January 2015. http://www.theguardian.com/football/2015/jan/08/mario-balotelli-speeding-fines-italy.

———. 'George Osborne: low taxes, high pay – and high charges', 18 November 2015, http://www.theguardian.com/commentisfree/2015/nov/18/the-guardian-view-on-george-osborne-low-taxes-high-pay-and-high-charges

The New York Times, 'In Their Own Words: Obama on Reagan', n.d. http://www.nytimes.com/ref/us/politics/21seelye-text.html

The Straits Times, 'Saudi millionaire cleared of rape after claiming he fell and accidentally penetrated teenager', DEC 16, 2015. http://www.straitstimes.com/world/europe/saudi-millionaire-cleared-of-rape-after-claiming-he-fell-and-accidentally-penetrated.

The Urban Child Institute. 'Barriers to Educational Achievement Emerge at a Very Young Age'. *The Urban Child Institute*. n.d. http://www.urbanchildinstitute. org/brainscience/.

Thomson-DeVeaux, Amelia, 'Should States Spend Billions To Reduce Class Sizes?', *FiveThirtyEight*, Dec 11, 2014, http://fivethirtyeight.com/features/shoul d-states-spend-billions-to-reduce-class-sizes/.

Trabandt, Mathias and Harald Uhlig. 'The Laffer Curve Revisited'. *Journal of Monetary Economics* 58, no. 4 (May 2011): 305–27.

United Nations. *Human Development Report 2009: Overcoming Barriers*. New York: United Nations, 2009.

UK Ministry of Justice and National Offender Management Service. 'Transforming Rehabilitation—Policy Papers and Publications about the Transforming Rehabilitation Programme'. *GOV.UK*. 19 December 2014. https://www.gov. uk/government/collections/transforming-rehabilitation.

UK Ministry of Justice. 'Revision to Attitudes to Sentencing and Trust in Justice: Exploring Trends from the Crime Survey for England and Wales'. *GOV.UK*. 16 August 2013. https://www.gov.uk/government/uploads/system/uploads/ attachment_data/file/230186/Attitudes_to_Sentencing_and_Trust_in_ Justice_web_.pdf.

US Department of Defense. 'Climate Change Adaptation Roadmap'. *US Department of Defense*. 2014. http://tn.gov/assets/entities/health/attachments/CCA_ Report_Pentagon_Climate_Change.pdf.

Valero, Anna, and Isabelle Roland. *Productivity and Business Policies*. London: LSE Centre for Economic Performance, 2015.

Van Reenen, John, 'Profiting from Productivity: Ensuring investment and produc-tivity growth feed through to wages', 30/03/2015, Resolution Foundation, http://immersive.sh/resolutionfoundation/3CNr4MvOb

Waldman, Steve Randy. 'Bernanke on Monetary Policy and Inequality'. *Interfluidity*. 2 June 2015. http://www.interfluidity.com/v2/5918.html.

Wells, Matt. 'Mail and Express Back Off from Smear Campaigns'. *The Guardian*. 26 February 2001. http://www.theguardian.com/media/2001/feb/26/ dailymail.pressandpublishing.

Welsh, Irvine, *Trainspotting* (London: Vintage, 2004)

Wherry Fredercik, 'Payday Loans Cost the Poor Billions, and There's an Easy Fix', *The New York Times*, OCT. 29, 2015 http://www.nytimes.com/2015/10/29/opinion/payday-loans-cost-the-poor-billions-and-theres-an-easy-fix.html?_r=0

Whitney, Lance. 'Apple, Google, Others Settle Anti-Poaching Lawsuit for $415 million'. *CNET*. 3 September 2015. http://www.cnet.com/news/apple-google-others-settle-anti-poaching-lawsuit-for-415-million/.

Wilkinson, Richard G., and Kate Pickett. *The Spirit Level: Why Equality Is Better for Everyone*. London: Penguin Books, 2009.

———. *The Spirit Level: Why Equality Is Better for Everyone*. Revised ed. London: Penguin Books, 2010.

Willetts, David. 'Pensioners Prosper, the Young Suffer. Britain's Social Contract Is Breaking'. *The Guardian*. 24 October 2015. http://www.theguardian.com/commentisfree/2015/oct/24/young-bear-burden-of-pensioner-prosperity.

Wintour, Patrick, 'Tristram Hunt warns private schools to help state pupils or lose £700m in tax breaks', *The Guardian*, 25 November 2014. http://www.theguardian.com/education/2014/nov/24/private-schools-labour-warning-tax-breaks-tristram-hunt

Wolf, Martin. *The Shifts and the Shocks: What We've Learned—and Still Have to Learn—from the Financial Crisis*. London: Penguin Books, 2015.

———.'Corporate surpluses are contributing to the savings glut', *Financial Times*, November 17, 2015, http://www.ft.com/intl/cms/s/0/b2df748e-8a3f-11e5-90de-f44762bf9896.html#axzz42ao8q8ko

Woolf, Steven H., and Laudan Y. Aron. *U.S. Health in International Perspective*. Washington, D.C.: The National Academies Press, 2013.

Wren-Lewis, Simon. 'Don't Ask What Lost, Ask What Won'. *Mainly Macro*. 12 May 2015. http://mainlymacro.blogspot.sg/2015/05/dont-ask-what-lost-ask-what-won.html.

———. 'Privatisation and Government Debt'. *Mainly Macro*. 5 June 2014. http://mainlymacro.blogspot.sg/2014/06/privatisation-and-government-debt.html.

———. 'The Austerity Con'. *London Review of Books* 37 (4): 9–11.

———. 'The Last 7 Years are an Argument against Inflation Targeting'. *Mainly Macro*. 22 October 2015. http://mainlymacro.blogspot.sg/2015/10/the-last-7-years-are-argument-against.html.

———. 'The State, Corporations, and Markets'. *Mainly Macro*. 26 May 2014. http://mainlymacro.blogspot.sg/2014/05/the-state-corporations-and-markets.html.

———. 'The UK as a test case for NGDP targets', Mainly Macro, 7 September 2015, http://mainlymacro.blogspot.sg/2015/09/the-uk-as-test-case-for-ngdp-targets.html

———. 'UK flooding, austerity and the media', mainly macro, Monday, 7 December 2015. http://mainlymacro.blogspot.sg/2015/12/uk-flooding-austerity-and-media.html

Years of Living Dangerously, season 1. Showtime Networks. 2014. USA: Showtime. TV.

Zumbrun, Josh, 'How to Save Like the Rich and the Upper Middle Class (Hint: It's Not With Your House)', The Wall Street Journal, Dec 26, 2014. http://blogs.wsj.com/economics/2014/12/26/how-to-save-like-the-rich-and-the-upper-middle-class-hint-its-not-with-your-house/

6.04. Index

infrastructure strategy board, ISB
160, 167, 170
inheritance 85, 177, 181, 182,
183, 266
inheritance tax 85, 182, 183, 266
Inhofe, Jim 278
innovation 43, 50, 69, 70, 159, 205,
217, 233, 289
interest rates 9, 12, 13, 14, 18, 42,
64, 65, 66, 72, 73, 74, 75, 76,
163, 164, 165, 166, 167, 168,
169, 241
internship 97, 211, 266
Iraq War 150, 276
Ireland 50, 70, 74, 102, 294
Ireland, Paddy 50, 294
Italy 21, 107, 115, 116, 118, 256,
272, 303

J

James, Oliver 1, 89, 123, 217, 294
Japan 44, 75, 119, 120, 142, 144, 165,
209, 213, 215, 217, 239, 244,
293, 295
Japan Post Bank 239
joint stock companies, JSC 49, 50
Jones, Owen 96, 97, 295
jury 258, 292

K

Kahneman, Daniel 37, 295
Kalecki, Michal 165, 295
Keen, Steve 16, 295
Keynesian economics 10
Keynes, J. M. 10, 135
Krugman, Paul 2, 42, 100, 101, 209,
277, 295

L

labour market 37, 60, 63, 93, 101,
103, 108, 197, 210, 265
Labour party 131, 173, 174, 264, 276,
277, 279, 280
Laffer, Art 26, 77
Laffer curve 26, 28, 29, 30, 178, 304
Lamont, Norman 65
land value tax, LVT 178, 179
large corporations 18, 37, 38, 79, 99,
110, 113, 225, 226, 283
leisure time 40, 152, 153, 155
leverage 69, 70
Lewis, Michael 1, 70, 296
liberal elites 131, 262, 263, 264, 265,
266, 277
LIBOR 256
life expectancy 138, 142, 143, 147,
148, 244, 245, 287
limited liability 49, 50, 51, 54, 227,
228, 230, 231, 294
liquidity trap 12
living wage 179, 202, 203, 204
local government 81, 137, 138
long-term unemployed 162, 197, 202
lotteries 80, 81, 85, 267, 290
Low Pay Commission 199
Luddite 40, 94
luxury tax 185

M

MacKay, David 213, 214, 296
macroprudential regulation 167
Magna Carta 258
management board 231, 232
Mandelbrot, Benoit 16, 297
Mandelson, Peter 86
manufacturing 41, 43, 65, 103,
111, 131

university 20, 57, 68, 72, 96, 97, 98,
        101, 124, 126, 151, 159, 160,
        170, 205, 206, 208, 209, 210,
        217, 221, 222, 230, 247, 248,
        260, 265, 266, 286, 288, 290,
        292, 295, 297, 300, 301
urban garden cities 218
US presidential election 174, 272
utilitarian 83, 84, 131
utilities 5, 10, 18, 32, 49, 51, 83, 86,
        126, 136, 185, 215, 232, 233

V

value-added tax 8, 175, 184.
        See goods and services tax
Volcker, Paul 65, 69
voter fraud 272, 273, 291
voting franchise 272
voting public 2, 76, 170, 191,
        226, 246

W

wage compression 198, 199
wage subsidy 171, 200, 201, 202,
        203, 204, 290
welfare budget 76, 193, 216
welfare cliff 192. *See* poverty trap
welfare policy 191
welfare spending 167, 195
Wherry, Frederick 241
whistle-blower 188, 235, 256, 257
white-collar crime 256, 257, 269
Wilkinson and Pickett 2, 89, 95, 195.
        See The Spirit Level
Wilson, Harold 281
Winter of Discontent 61
Wolf, Martin 164, 165, 235, 236,
        239, 305

working-class communities 128, 129,
        150, 155, 247, 261, 263, 264,
        265, 267
working-class voters 112, 128, 131,
        262, 263, 265
working tax credits, WTC 194,
        200, 201
Wren-Lewis, Simon 2, 33, 34, 66, 76,
        166, 169, 278, 283, 300, 305

Y

Years of Living Dangerously 57, 58,
        105, 212, 306
youth unemployment 108, 118